Tragedies of Spirit

SUNY Series in Contemporary Continental Philosophy
Dennis J. Schmidt, Editor

Tragedies of Spirit
Tracing Finitude in Hegel's *Phenomenology*

Theodore D. George

State University of New York Press

Published by
State University of New York Press, Albany

© 2006 State University of New York

All rights reserved

Printed in the United States of America

No part of this book may be used or reproduced in any manner whatsoever without written permission. No part of this book may be stored in a retrieval system or transmitted in any form or by any means including electronic, electrostatic, magnetic tape, mechanical, photocopying, recording, or otherwise without the prior permission in writing of the publisher.

For information, address State University of New York Press, 194 Washington Avenue, Suite 305, Albany, NY 12210-2384

Production by Kelli Williams
Marketing by Anne M. Valentine

Library of Congress Cataloging-in-Publication Data

George, Theodore D., 1971–
 Tragedies of spirit: tracing finitude in Hegel's phenomenology/ Theodore D. George.
  p. cm.—(SUNY series in contemporary continental philosophy)
 Includes bibliographical references and index.
 ISBN-13: 978-0-7914-6865-4 (hardcover: alk. paper)—ISBN-10: 0-7914-6865-8 (hardcover: alk. paper) 1. Hegel, Georg Wilhelm Friedrich, 1770–1831. Phänomenologie des Geistes. 2. Finite, The.
 3. Tragic, The. I. Title. II. Series.
   B2929.G46 2006
   193—dc22
                            2005036233
   ISBN-13: 978-0-7914-6866-1 (pbk. : alk. paper)

Contents

Preface — vii
Acknowledgments — xi

Introduction: Spirit and Its Tragedies — 1

Chapter 1. The Tragedy of Experience — 27

Chapter 2. The Tragedy of Freedom — 49

Chapter 3. The Tragedy of Ethical Life — 73

Chapter 4. Tragic Wisdom — 97

Postscript. "Life Hangs in the Balance" — 121

Notes — 135
Bibliography — 163
Index — 171

Preface

The present study has emerged in part as a response to questions that confronted me from certain heritages of post-Kantian German philosophy, which have come, for a number of theoretical and historical reasons, to address some of the time-honored problems and concerns of philosophers to Greek tragic drama. Scholars familiar with this trajectory of continental thought will recognize that I am by no means the first to be taken with it, and, indeed, will know that inquiries into the philosophical significance of tragic art play an important role in the thought of galactic figures, such as Gadamer, Heidegger, Nietzsche, Hegel, Schelling, and Hölderlin. They will also be aware that scholarship on the intersection of philosophy and tragedy forms an important and growing line of inquiry in contemporary continental philosophy. For those unacquainted with the landscape, perhaps its most characteristic feature turns on the provocation that tragic drama, and the notion of the tragic, need not be seen only as objects of interest in the field of aesthetics, but may also be interpreted as resources that illuminate a number of core issues often approached under the signs of metaphysics, ontology, social and political philosophy, and ethics. In these post-Kantian heritages, the concern is not simply to develop aesthetic or poetic theories of tragic drama (though of course figures, such as Hegel and Schelling also do this), but, rather, to use tragedy as a guidepost for inquiries into fundamental problems in philosophy.

My own scholarly interest in this broader vein of thought has led me to focus my attention on some of the implications of Hegel's concern for tragedy in his *Phenomenology of Spirit*. Of course, my orientation toward this project, too, has already been traced out by a larger body of scholarship. Perhaps not unlike others before me, I have been drawn to the *Phenomenology* in part because of the peculiar, and, indeed, highly ambiguous place it holds in the post-Kantian heritage of philosophical interest in tragedy. For many of the figures in this heritage, such as Heidegger and Nietzsche, may be said to enlist resources of tragedy in response to their dissatisfaction with traditional philosophical categories, and to their efforts to stretch beyond customary modes of philosophical discourse. Figures in this same heritage of thought elicit us to remain wary of those of Hegel's claims which suggest that he, by contrast, sees his *Phenomenology* as part of a philosophical system that would form the apotheosis of this tradition that many after him will wish to question. Yet, it might equally be said that many of the most important philosophical engagements with tragedy after Hegel would not have been possible without the questions, concerns, and context developed by figures in German Idealism and Romanticism in general, and in Hegel in particular.

Of the contributions and interpretive sensibilities I have tried to bring to this project, perhaps two things in particular might be mentioned in preface of my study. First, I have attempted to introduce a wider frame of textual reference than is sometimes taken. My reading of the *Phenomenology* has convinced me that Hegel's concern for tragedy in this text is pervasive and deep, and I have thus developed my approach not on the basis of just one or two of his more celebrated references to tragedy, such as the one found in his discussion of ethical life. Rather, I have considered the implications of a number of his uses of tragedy, some subtle, and have tried to show that his multiple turns to tragedy combine to form a consistent concern for issues of human finitude. Second, I have tried to bring a spirit of philosophical openness to the project. The influences that organize my approach come from continental philosophy, and perhaps especially from quarters influenced by Heidegger, philosophical hermeneutics, and deconstruction. But, I have endeavored to let the richness and power of these discourses break open new interpretive possibilities in Hegel and forge ties with problems and issues that emerge from outside of continental thought, not to foreclose or forestall connections with other research in Hegel studies.

Tragedies of Spirit is intended to be not a commentary on Hegel's *Phenomenology*, but rather a thematic study of insights into human finitude that arise from his engagements with tragedy in the text. Due to this, and since the questions that guide the project arise from a larger milieu of post-Kantian philosophers, it is not the principal aim of this book to reconstruct Hegel's thematic purpose, his intention, or even to reconstruct what he thought his main arguments were. Rather, the project is to address questions of human finitude to Hegel's interest in tragedy as he presents it in the *Phenomenology*. Although it has not been my explicit plan to develop a 'Gadamerian' approach to Hegel, some of his larger claims about text interpretation capture the spirit of my own. As it has been posed in the "Introduction" to a recent collection of essays on Hegel's *Phenomenology*,

> The reception of an old text into a new context of thought is, as Hans-Georg Gadamer reminded us, the delicate (and fallible) attempt to get at

the questions it conceived and answered through the questions that we put to it.[1]

Although some may see approaches of this sort prejudicial or impure, it might be suggested that, on the contrary, they are guided by the deepest belief that philosophical texts of the past remain relevant and have much to say. Indeed, they suggest that texts from the past are not to be left buried behind us, but rather continue to demand our scrutiny and thus lie always still in front of us.

Besides, despite important innovations in text interpretation achieved by philosophical hermeneutics and other discourses in recent continental philosophy, the idea that the meaning of a philosophical text might exceed the intentions of its author is not new. After all, Hegel, too, recognized that there is always more at stake in a philosophical work from the past than its author was able to see. Of course, whereas scholarship in contemporary continental philosophy characteristically takes this 'more' to indicate the irreducibility of the text to any hegemonic, complete, and settled interpretation, Hegel might be seen to place it in the service of his efforts to establish a systematic view of the coherent development and unity of the history of philosophy as such.[2] Even so, Hegel recognized that genuinely philosophical inquiries into texts from the history of philosophy requires us to approach them in light of their living relation to the present.

In the *Differenzschrift*, for example, Hegel admonishes scholars who would fail to bring pertinent philosophical questions to bear on their approaches to philosophers of the past, comparing them to mere 'collectors,' whose purported objectivity actually serves to conceal a deeper fear of the transformative power of philosophical texts. He writes,

> The collector stands firm in his neutral attitude towards truth; he preserves his independence whether he accepts opinions, rejects them, or abstains from decision. He can give philosophical systems [of the past] only one relation to himself: they are opinions—and such incidental things as opinions can do him no harm.[3]

Hegel recommends, by contrast, that a more philosophical approach to the history of philosophy would make it possible to discern essential and lasting insights. "The living spirit that dwells in a philosophy," he tells us, "demands to be born of a kindred spirit if it is to unveil itself."[4] From such a standpoint, the philosopher of one age finds in the philosophy of another "spirit of its spirit, flesh of its flesh. . . . "[5] Certainly, critical questions about the extent of Hegel's belief in the coherence and unity of the history of philosophy require serious attention. To the extent his position cautions us not to approach philosophical views of the past simply as disinterested parties, however, it might be applied at the present historical juncture to Hegel himself.

A brief word on texts and translations. Throughout this study, I have relied upon the Suhrkamp edition of Hegel's works: Hegel, *Werke in zwanzig Bände* (Frankfurt am Main: Suhrkamp, 1986). The translations of Hegel's texts, as well as some other German texts, are generally my own, though I have mentioned in my notes those occasions on which my translation is either borrowed or derived from another translator. For quotations cited from the *Phenomenology of Spirit*, I have provided cross-references to Miller's translations, which I often consulted and invariably found extremely helpful.

Acknowledgments

There are a number of colleagues and friends without whom I would not have been able to bring this project to term. The scope of my gratitude to Dennis Schmidt exceeds my facilities of expression, certainly for the influence of his scholarship on my research, but also for the years of extraordinary and abiding mentorship, friendship, and caring he has offered me. I am deeply appreciative of his generosity of spirit and his concern for my intellectual and personal growth. Of colleagues in Europe, I am especially indebted to Günter Figal, as well as to Lore Hühn, to other faculty members and students now at the University of Freiburg, and to Violette Waibel at the University of Tübingen, each of whom has played an important role in the inception and development of this project. I would like to extend thanks to the faculty members and participants of the *Collegium Phänomenologicum*, conversations with a number of whom have, directly and indirectly, helped to give shape to many of the ideas that appear in this book. It has been my exceptionally good fortune to have received thoughtful, thorough, and extremely helpful reader reports on my work, which provided me with much guidance in my efforts to revise and improve my manuscript. Of colleagues in Texas, I would like to thank Jim Rosenheim and the Melbern G. Glasscock Center for Humanities Research, the support of which helped me to complete the book. Conversations with Steve Daniel, the Junior Faculty Group, and others in the Philosophy Department at Texas A&M University helped me to develop and clarify many of my ideas. I also appreciate the insights Mary Lynn Dixon gave me into the world of academic publishing. John McDermott's concern not only for my project, but also my intellectual and spiritual health, his infectious insistence upon authenticity, his uncanny ability to advise without paternalism, as well as our many, many philosophical conversations—in short, his friendship—has left a profound mark on this book and on me as a person.

Introduction

Spirit and Its Tragedies

What is the philosophical significance of tragedy? What does a philosophical investigation of the tragic aspects of our lives teach us about the human condition? What philosophical questions draw our attention to Hegel's insistence that there is an intimate tie between the aspirations of his *Phenomenology of Spirit* and the insights of tragic drama? Over the course of his project, Hegel repeatedly turns to the resources of tragedy—sometimes explicitly, but often indirectly, even tacitly—in order to capture the essence of crucial junctures in the life of spirit. Hegel makes multiple references to specific Greek tragedies, especially to Sophoclean tragedies, though he also alludes to modern tragedians such as Shakespeare, and he conscripts for his own presentation of spirit important concepts from theoretical works on tragic poetry such as Aristotle's *Poetics*. What is at stake in Hegel's invocation of these things in his presentation of spirit? Of course, we say far too little if we only say that Hegel's interest in tragedy rests on some personal idiosyncrasy, a special predilection for things tragic. The *Phenomenology* is crafted with too much rigor and care, and his references to tragedy are too methodical and prevalent. But, then what are we to make of Hegel's coupling of speculative philosophy and the notion of tragedy in this text? What does Hegel's speculative interest in the notion of tragedy teach us about the life of spirit, about our world and ourselves?

Hegel maintains that the purpose of speculative philosophy turns on nothing less than the demonstration of the absolute.[1] Hegel's conceptions of speculative philosophy and absolute knowledge are no doubt as difficult to grasp as they are foreign to current sensibilities. For some years, a number of important Hegel commentators have started to reconsider whether his claims about speculation and the absolute are as grandiose in scale and scope as has been previously thought. Moreover, this trend has led to a revival of interest in the relevance of Hegel's thought for current debates in fields such as epistemology, the philosophy of language, and the philosophy of science.[2] However, much scholarship in continental philosophy emphasizes that Hegel's more ambitious claims about speculation and the absolute demand continued suspicion and scrutiny, and many question whether philosophy in our time has adequately come to terms with what they worry are highly ambiguous and even dangerous assumptions that inform Hegel's thought.[3] As Stuart Barnett observes, something of a "general critical consensus" has emerged about Hegel in continental approaches that he exemplifies "the modernity that our postmodern era seeks to escape."[4] For on Hegel's view, it is plausible for us to be concerned, speculation is supposed to culminate in a knowledge that may be achieved only by a deathless subject, the ultimate unification of experience in thought, and, thereby, to accomplish a certain philosophical resolution to our confrontations with discontinuity, disunity, incompleteness, and limit.[5]

Yet, although it would be as irresponsible as naïve to relinquish the suspicion that Hegel's conception of speculative philosophy is directed by something at least analogous to what Nietzsche might have called a reactive will, it would also be a misrepresentation to allege that Hegel is a philosopher of empty identity. For there can be no doubt that Hegel intends, at least, for his speculative approach to be much more rich and open than many of us remember. On Hegel's view, speculative philosophy is supposed to achieve a form of knowledge directed not by the aspiration to discharge or deny difference, but rather to embrace, respect, and include all of our confrontations with incommensurability, otherness, discontinuity, strife, and crisis, or, as we might discuss it today, our encounters with finitude. Indeed, it is too often forgotten that Hegel is among the great critics of the penchant in philosophy to trade on overgeneralizations and impoverished, abstract identities.[6] Hegel poses speculation as a corrective against the tendency in philosophy to fabricate cut-to-fit concepts and commonsense categories that blind out the multiplicity of things; he opposes the tendency to produce a unity that reduces everything, as Hegel famously (if somewhat unfairly) charges of Schelling, to "a night in which all cows are black."[7]

From this standpoint, we see that it is precisely the scope of Hegel's commitment to the richness of the speculative unity that compels him to remain vigilant to questions of finitude. The standard that Hegel sets for the speculative unity requires him to pay much more than lip service to disunity, strife, and difference. Rather, it demands that Hegel give full voice to our experiences of finitude in its multiple dimensions and that they be preserved and protected in the life of spirit.

The hypothesis guiding this book is that Hegel turns to the idiom of tragedy to elucidate some of the most pressing of these claims of finitude. Hegel's *Phenomenology* unfolds preeminently as the presentation of the triumph of the speculative unity as it emerges in historical spirit. But, in Hegel's efforts to grant to finitude its due, his presentation of this triumph is punctuated by tragedy. In a form of philosophy dedicated to the absolute, it is tragedy that comes to speak for the forms of discontinuity and limit that spirit encounters in the course of its development. Hegel's speculative interest in the tragic demands our attention because his references to tragedy offer crucial insights into human finitude as it appears in some of its most important aspects: in our experience as historical beings, in our prospects for freedom, in ethical life, and in our desire to achieve self-knowledge. Indeed, even though the purpose of the *Phenomenology* is to present the achievement of the speculative unity as it unfolds in the development of spirit, from our current standpoint, it is not difficult to see how some might be led to wonder whether Hegel's depiction of the tragic character of finitude is so powerful that it threatens to undermine our faith in the power of spirit to achieve ultimate unity.

It should come no more as a surprise to us than it did to Hegel's contemporaries that he would associate tragedy with disunion, strife, incommensurability, and difference. Not only Hegel but others on the German intellectual scene of his day connected artistic genre such as that of tragic drama, especially in its Greek form, with the presentation of vehement forms of irresolvable conflicts and the experiences of limit they expose.[8] If Hegel is dedicated to the achievement of a speculative unity that contains even extreme forms of disunion within it, then, we might argue, the confrontation of spirit with tragedy forms an ordeal or crucible that tests the resilience of spirit's capacity for integration. Hegel characterizes spirit as an agile learner that has the power to overcome many forms of disunity and strife it faces in the course of its education. Yet, we may question whether Hegel's introduction of tragic resources to capture the character of disunity, strife, and difference might be seen to strain the synthetic powers of spirit to the breaking point.

But, even if scholarship in current continental philosophy compels us to remain vigilant of Hegel's speculative ambition, perhaps hubris, to achieve knowledge in its absolute form, we might nonetheless investigate whether the interplay of speculation and tragedy in his text draws out a sense of finitude. As we shall see, one question that we must ask in this book is whether Hegel's conception of the speculative unity in the *Phenomenology* is not simply preoccupied and enriched by his uses of tragedy, but instead comes to be predominated, perhaps even transformed by them. If this is the case, Hegel's vision of the human spirit may be guided not simply by his confidence in our capacity to unify experience but also by a humble recognition of limits. No doubt some might worry that this more tragic view emphasizes the negative side of things too much. But, one of the deepest motivations for this book turns on the claim that Hegel's uses of tragedy result in an affirmative vision of the human condition that helps us to reclaim a more balanced view of our possibilities and limits. In his more tragic moments, it is one of my intentions to suggest, Hegel enables us to catch sight of a view that allows us to identify our dignity as human beings not so much with the scope of our powers, but instead with our resolve to accept, even apprize, and cherish the terms of our finitude. Before we turn to the *Phenomenology* in order to consider this possibility in more detail, however, it may help us further to illuminate what is at issue in Hegel's uses of tragedy if we contextualize Hegel's *Phenomenology* within a broader range of questions about the relationship between philosophical inquiry and tragedy.

PHILOSOPHY AND TRAGEDY

One of the most important, and familiar, motifs of post-Kantian continental philosophy is the view that the current historical juncture is called to confront problems and questions that the intellectual heritage of the West is unable to address. It is this view that comes to expression, for example, in Philippe Lacoue-Labarthe's recent claim, which itself in part hearkens back to Friedrich Hölderlin's use of the term two centuries ago, that the present age is disjoined from its heritage in the manner of a caesura.[9] Certainly, many philosophers of the present age have concluded from this not only that we are cut off from the heritage of Western philosophy, but, moreover, that this end of philosophy calls for us simply to abandon traditional forms of philosophy altogether. It has been argued of Richard Rorty's peculiarly American and bourgeois blend of postmodernism, for example, that he supposes our current dedication to the preservation of many presuppositions of Western philosophical heritage should be treated as something of a bad habit to be broken.[10] But, in contrast to this idea, some movements in continental thought recommend, if often in very different idioms, that philosophical inquiry in the current age is significantly informed by pre-thematic, inchoate presuppositions that have been unquestioningly and involuntarily taken over from the past.[11] From these standpoints, the achievement of genuinely novel philosophical insights is predicated on sustained and critical engagement with the traditions of thought that continue to permeate present sensibilities.

It is true that in this regard Hegel deserves our attention because, as figures in postmodernity have taught us, his philosophical system forms a certain summit of the tradition we are now called to scrutinize. One of the convictions Hegel holds about speculative philosophy is that it forms the culmination, and, thus, completion, of all historical developments in the discipline of philosophy. So in a sense, Hegel himself casts the speculative unity as the end of philosophy. Yet, in contrast with figures who follow after him, however, Hegel conceives of this end not as an extinction, but, instead, as a kind of final summit of the tradition that brings it to its fruition.[12] He asserts, for example, that his own speculative system, itself "latest in time," forms "the result of all previous philosophies and thus must contain the principles of all of them."[13] Yet, from our current vantage point we see that even if Hegel's speculative thought can be cast as the culmination of certain traditional forms of philosophy, it also enables a new direction within philosophy that wishes to break from the tradition. In retrospect we see that Hegel's speculative interest in tragedy not only serves his own system of philosophy, but also opens the door for a new movement of philosophers who believe that in order to overturn philosophy in its traditional forms, it is necessary to enlist the help of resources they find at the dawn of the West, in Greek tragedy.

From among the figures of the nineteenth century, it is perhaps the Nietzsche of the *Birth of Tragedy* who does the most to cast the post-Kantian philosophical interest in Greek tragedy as a subversive moment directed toward the overcoming of mainstream tenets of philosophy in its traditional forms. Already in this early phase of his philosophical life, Nietzsche offers a diagnosis of the exhaustion and "homeless wandering" that has resulted from the "Socratic" impulse in the Western tradition.[14] Yet, despite what he sees as the decadence of his age, Nietzsche holds out hope that the future may bring about new possibilities for human thought and experience due to what he calls the "abiding love-bond" between modern German intellectual culture and the culture of pre-Socratic Greek tragedy.[15] Of course, we know that in this early book Nietzsche is still enamored of the idea that the German affinity for ancient tragedy reaches its height in Wagnerian opera, an idea that he will later reject.[16] But, even in this early stage of his life, Nietzsche observes that the love-bond between modern Germany and the age of Attic tragedy subtends not only German music but also what he refers to as "the bourgeoning spirit of German philosophy," and he specifies Kant and Schopenhauer as representatives of the potential for the birth of a tragic age in modern times.[17] To Nietzsche's mind, the philosophical prospects of the future lie largely in the hands of the intellectual and artistic avant-garde; but in the *Birth of Tragedy* he seems to suggest that those who do the most to twist free from the tradition are precisely those who owe the greatest debts to the vision of human affairs expressed in Greek tragedy.

From our current vantage point, it is clear that the liaison between post-Kantian philosophy and Greek tragic poetry remains strong throughout the twentieth century and in our day. In the *Birth of Tragedy*, Nietzsche elaborates primarily on a lineage of philosophers that extends to Schopenhauer from its latent origins in Kant's characterization of reason as a realm of transcendental illusion.[18] In hindsight, it is clear that the progeny of this family of philosophers who associate our hopes to overcome philosophy with the resources of tragedy are strewn across the twentieth century. No doubt Heidegger, especially in his treatment of Greek tragedy in the *Introduction to Metaphysics* and in other works from the 1930s and 1940s, is among the most celebrated. In postwar France, Sartre, Camus, and de Beauvoir explicitly align the existentialist movement with themes of ancient tragedy. Today figures such as Philippe Lacoue-Labarthe, Jean-Luc Nancy, Christoph Menke, François Dastur, Veronique Foti and Dennis Schmidt continue to develop questions about the need to overturn traditional forms of philosophy in reference to the resources of Greek tragedy. Across disciplinary lines, in French psychoanalysis and in feminism, for example, figures such as Jacques Lacan and Luce Irigaray, and, recently, Judith Butler also continue to rely on the resources of tragedy to further their research.[19]

Even if the contemporary project of overcoming traditional forms of philosophy is still coupled with the issue of tragedy, this love-bond nevertheless has its origins in Hegel's day. It is only from an exceedingly de-historicized vantage point that we might believe in the novelty of our attempts to overcome the presuppositions inherited from the past; and it is not only in the academic debates found at the dawn of the current century, but in intellectual circles at the turn of the nineteenth century, that some of the most radical and original challenges to traditional forms of philosophy are posed. In the period that unfolds in the aftermath of Kant's critical project, figures such as Goethe, Schelling, Hölderlin, and the early German, or, as they are also called, Jena Romantics all begin to dispute the traditional assumption, characteristic of mainstream assumptions in the discipline of philosophy, at least, that our knowledge of things reaches its highest expression only in the idioms of conceptual language and mathematical formulation. Some figures on the intellectual landscape of the time even begin to entertain the idea that it is preeminently in the work of art, especially in genre of poetry such as tragic drama, and not in philosophy, science, or mathematics, where we win our deepest insights into the issues of freedom, politics, history, nature, and ethical life. It is an intellectual atmosphere also captured by Friedrich Schlegel's belief that philosophy should become more like poetry, or again, by Schelling's final claim from the *System of Transcendental Idealism*, that if philosophical inquiry is to succeed it must give itself over to the "universal sea of poesy."[20]

Many of the figures in the Age of Goethe to set poetic art off against philosophy felt a profound admiration and affinity for ancient Greek culture, language, and intellectual life, and important aspects of their claims about poetic art may almost be read as an extension of what Plato has Socrates refer to in the *Republic* as the "ancient quarrel between philosophy and poetry."[21] From this standpoint, crucial lines of the late eighteenth- and early nineteenth-century German case for the primacy of poetic art unfold as if in rejoinder, presented on behalf of sensibilities about art associated with the Attic period, we might suggest, against the objections to poetry found in the *Republic*, Books II and III. In other words, important strands of the German intellectual scene at the dawn of the nineteenth century may be seen to anticipate, in a provocative respect, the call later fleshed out and made famous by Nietzsche, namely, to overturn Platonism.[22] Of course, not only the German response to the Platonist charge against poetic art, but also Plato's presentation of these criticisms of poetry is itself difficult to interpret properly, not least of all because Plato elucidates them in a dialogue form that employs a number of poetic devices. In the course of the recriminations, two broader concerns come to stand out: first, that poetic forms of speech may be deceptive; and, second, that these forms are dangerous, politically and ethically, because they involve the power to corrupt the soul, especially those of the youth.[23] Thus, it should not come as a surprise if we find out that German figures who wish to uphold the worth of art underscore its significance for questions pertaining to the presentation of truth, and to the fulfillment of our deepest political and ethical concerns.

It is true that the heightened attention to antiquity that emerges in eighteenth-century Germany stems in no small part from the influence of figures such as Winkelmann and Lessing, and, more generally, may be associated with the adoption of French classicism that began to arise in

Germany already in the seventeenth and early eighteenth century.[24] Yet, by the outset of the nineteenth century, the widespread attention given to the Greeks in Germany was driven not just by the interest in the French model, but also by what has aptly been called an avant-garde concern for a number of issues, including the relevance of poetic forms of expression for philosophical inquiry.[25]

It is precisely in this intellectual milieu that Hegel comes of philosophical age. Indeed, much of Hegel's own philosophical development is profoundly impacted by those who claimed that new directions in philosophy might be opened up by the revivification of interest in ancient Greek culture, art, and tragic drama. Hegel's overall interest in ancient tragedy may be measured by the attention he devotes to the theme in every stage of his philosophical life, from its appearance in some of his earliest writings, such as the 1802 Natural Law Essay, to his much later discussion of tragic drama and specific tragic dramas in the *Lectures on Aesthetics*. However, Hegel's assessment of the importance of tragedy for his philosophical system changes over the course of his development, and, I would submit, shifts from playing a central role in his thought to a more marginal position. For in some of the earliest phases of his philosophical life, for example, in Tübingen, in Frankfurt, and, perhaps, to a certain extent still in Jena, Hegel at times goes so far as to entertain the possibility that poetic art in general, and tragic drama in particular, forms a template or model for the speculative unity itself. But, by the time Hegel reaches the final phase of his career, in the Berlin period, he appears largely to have abrogated the prospect that tragedy might comprise a fundamental issue for his conception of the speculative unity, and largely restricts his considerations of tragic drama to his inquiries into aesthetics.[26] Contextualized within this broader trajectory of Hegel's evolving approach to the issue of tragedy, the *Phenomenology* unfolds as a transitional, and, thus, in important respects, conflicted text, in regard to Hegel's position on the relationship between philosophical inquiry and the idiom of tragedy.

Earlier and Later Hegel

The extensive and rich heritage of scholarship on Hegel's early life presents a thorough and diverse array of insights into the character of his thought prior to the publication of the *Phenomenology of Spirit*, and there is a range of perspectives on the young Hegel's approach to ancient Greek culture, art, and tragedy. Any historiographical survey of approaches to the young

Hegel would have to consider, as important nineteenth-century contributions, Karl Rosenkranz's *Life of Hegel* and Rudolph Haym's *Hegel and his Time*. The history would also have to include, as decisive early twentieth-century sources, Wilhelm Dilthey's *Jugendgeschichte Hegels*, and the appearance of Herman Nohl's compilation of some of Hegel's oldest surviving texts, under the title *Hegel's Early Theological Writings*. Of course, a complete survey would also need to attend to further interpretive approaches to some of Hegel's early writings, such as those found in Herbert Marcuse's *Hegel's Ontology of Life* and Gyorgy Lukács' *Young Hegel, Studies in the Relations Between Dialectics and Economics*. In T. M. Knox's 1946 "Prefatory Note" to his expanded, English translation of Nohl's collection, he claims that while a substantial body of scholarship on the young Hegel had emerged in continental Europe, little work had appeared in the English-speaking world.[27] But certainly, if such a lacuna did once exist, it has not for some decades; and thus the history of studies on the young Hegel also embraces a large body of post-war era Anglophone contributions, which is punctuated by major scholarly accomplishments, perhaps none greater in sweep than H. S. Harris' two volume study, *Hegel's Development*.[28]

Even though the magnitude and depth of this heritage makes it impossible to provide a unified summary account of Hegel's early thought, it may nonetheless be said that the mainstreams of research on the young Hegel coalesce around several distinct but, for him, interrelated themes. Some of the most celebrated among them are: first, the ambiguous influence of the French revolution, the aspirations and ideals of which inspired him at the same time its destructiveness and violence terrified him, and, second, the bequest of Kant's critical project. Much scholarship has familiarized us with the impression made on Hegel by the fervor caused by the recent events in France that he and his companions Schelling and Hölderlin encountered and embraced while at the *Tübinger Stift*, as well as with stories, mythic in stature, of their dedication of a 'freedom tree' to the revolution, and of Hegel's life-long celebration of Bastille Day.[29] But, to the young Hegel's mind, the accomplishment of the political freedom promised by the French Revolution required that we pay heed to the results of another revolution, not in the social order of European life, but in philosophy, achieved by Kant's critical project. Of course, Hegel's relation to Kantian thought, even at this early stage, is already sophisticated and nuanced, but much of Hegel's concern turns on the construction of a speculative system of philosophy that alleviates problems in Kant's critique of theoretical reason, and that outlines a path to the creation of a rational political, and social world in Germany embodying Kantian principles of practical reason.[30]

Hegel's dedication to the formation of a modern, rational, and free German state comprises an important motivation for a third theme that runs through many of his early writings, namely, his interest in the establishment of Christianity as a national, or, people's religion (*Volksreligion*).[31] Although Hegel's view grows and shifts over the course of his early life, his general idea is that the establishment of a rational, free nation-state founded on (Kantian) ideals depends on the support of a national religion, whose charge it is to foster these ideals and to instill in the people a range of values, habits, and affects that accord with reason. Indeed, Hegel appears to charge that the collapse of the French Revolution into the Terror itself is due in no small part to the absence of a genuine people's religion in France able to sustain a society founded on the aspirations embodied by the storming of the Bastille and the principles of liberty, equality, and fraternity.[32] Thus, he reasons, the successfulness of the revolution, if not after all in France, but perhaps in the Germanic world, is contingent on the establishment of a genuine and robust form of popular religion.

Hegel develops his conception of speculative philosophy and its relation to the establishment of a people's religion in a number of his early discussions of Christianity. However, numerous scholars recognize that Hegel's speculative approach to Christianity in this period of his life is deeply informed by a fourth theme, of special import for the present project, namely, the 'Hellenic Ideal' he brings to bear on his overall vision of speculation, religion, and political and social life.[33] Numerous scholars have taught us that the young Hegel holds up his notion of the Hellenic society, which he derives as much from his contemporaries, especially Schiller, as he does from his studies of antiquity, as an organic, dynamic, and happy people, that integrates intellectual, spiritual, and political needs into a beautiful harmonious whole.[34] From this vantage point, Hegel associates the prospect for Christianity to comprise a people's religion with its potential to revive, in a modern form, the organic unity formed by religious and political life in the ancient *polis*. Thus, Hegel arrives at the view, by a thought process that might strike us today as somewhat circuitous, that the establishment of a modern nation state, which both fulfills the promise of the French Revolution and realizes Kantian principles, requires the establishment of a people's religion mirroring the religious life of ancient Greece. But more broadly, he further holds up the Hellenic ideals of organicity, modeled on the sense of harmony found in beauty, to capture the character of his speculative philosophy, the nature of its systematicity, and its incorporation of spiritual, religious, and political concerns and needs. From this standpoint, speculative philosophy itself, in addition to the worlds of religion and politics, aspire to his image of the Hellenic ideal of beauty and art.

Yet, important developments in continental philosophy, perhaps especially Heidegger's research on German Idealism, and on ancient philosophy and art, have summoned numerous scholars of the young Hegel to emphasize that this Hellenic ideal might have led him to conceive of the sense of unity found in beauty and in art as an archetype or template for the speculative unity itself. Indeed, cognizant of the importance of tragic art to influential figures such as Hölderlin and Schelling for the young Hegel, and of Hegel's awareness of the significance of tragic drama in the Hellenic world, many scholars suggest that Hegel holds up not only the work of art in general, but the work of tragedy in particular, as the highest model of speculation. Although this idea perhaps currently plays a less prominent role in recent Anglo-American studies of Hegel, on the continent it has, in Lacoue-Labarthe's turn of phrase, become "scarcely a thesis, so evident is the point," that "tragedy, or a certain interpretation of tragedy . . . is the origin or matrix of . . . speculative thought."[35] In his work on the relationship between Heidegger's thought and German Idealism, Jacques Taminiaux notes that in the first years in Jena, Hegel employs an "aesthetic schema" that associates the character of the speculative unity with concepts usually reserved to describe art, such as "*production, figure, work.*"[36] Although it is no stretch to claim that Hegel enlists such a schema earlier, in Frankfurt, it is no surprise that some point to an even earlier text, the "Oldest System-Programme of German Idealism," as evidence of his reliance on the work of art as a model for speculation. Of course, as is well-known, the authorship of this fragmentary piece found in a bundle of Hegel's papers in 1917 is disputed, and although it is usually attributed to him, it is sometimes attributed to Schelling, or Hölderlin, or even Friedrich Schlegel.[37] But, in this piece, Hegel (if it was Hegel) offers some of his most radical claims about his speculative project, and asserts, for example, that "I am now convinced that the highest act of reason, in that it embraces all ideas, is an aesthetic act," and claims, further, not only that "the philosophy of spirit is an aesthetic philosophy," but also that "the philosopher must possess as much aesthetic power as the poet."[38]

By now it should be clear that Hegel's uses of the work of art, and in particular his uses of tragedy, range beyond questions in the field of aesthetics. What Peter Szondi notably says of Schelling's thought we may also say of Hegel's earliest conception of the speculative unity: that it forms a "philosophy of the tragic," not a "poetics of tragedy."[39] Some of Hegel's early writings suggest that he turns to tragic poetry as the highest model for the speculative unity itself, not just as one subject matter among others for research in the field of poetics. The result, we might propose, is a vision of philosophical inquiry that far exceeds conventional views. For the most part, philosophers have believed that our power to unify things in thought (and also to distinguish among them) reaches its highest form in the languages of the concept and of number. By contrast, some of Hegel's early views in Tübingen, Frankfurt, and perhaps in the early Jena years appear to tarry with the idea that our power to unify things reaches one of its summits in artistic expression. Hegel's notion of the speculative philosopher as a figure who must possess as much aesthetic power as the poet is a profound departure from traditional presumptions about philosophical practice that might be seen to adumbrate controversial and original views, such as those indicated, for example, by the early Nietzsche's notion of the music-playing Socrates, or some of Heidegger's claims about the thinker.[40]

The promise of Hegel's early philosophy of the tragic, in fact, not entirely unlike Nietzsche's and Heidegger's views of philosophy that follow it, turns at least in part on the creation of a form of inquiry that exceeds conceptual frameworks and propositional language in its ability to attend to incommensurability, strife, difference, and otherness. In a deep *rapprochement* with important current figures, not to mention with his contemporaries such as Schelling and Hölderlin, the young Hegel recognizes that it is among the chief perfections of art to represent the things that most resist combination. Hegel's earliest conception of the speculative unity is aligned with a view of art that Taminiaux, at least, believes to have been around "from time immemorial," namely, that the "resource" of art is

> its bursting forth from the power of the earth, its connectedness with the unnamable, its relationship to the surprising, to the enigmatic, and to what, always, remains on the outside.[41]

From this vantage point, Hegel's reliance on the sense of unity found in artistic expression as a model for the speculative unity might suggest to us that it serves not to reduce or exclude forms of otherness and difference, but to embrace and remain open to them, even to bear within it their resistance to integration itself.

In this light, we see that Hegel chooses to use tragic poetry from among all of the arts as a model for the speculative unity because of its special power to present even the most antithetical forms of difference. For on Hegel's view, tragic poetry stands out as the form of art in which the power of art to offer a unified presentation that remains connected to otherness and difference is most pronounced. From our current perspective today it may be difficult to accept the hierarchical conception of the arts that Hegel's view here implies.[42] It nonetheless makes sense that Hegel might single out tragic poetry, especially in its Greek form, as a variety of art that is especially keyed to the presentation of forms of conflict that turn on otherness, difference, incommensurability, and strife. In Schelling's *Letters on Dogmatism and Criticism*, written while he was still at the seminary together in Tübingen, Schelling notes, for example, that the Greeks turned to tragedy precisely because of its power to gather together and express even the most monstrous contradictions.[43] For Hegel too, it would seem, it is in tragic poetry that the potential of all art to present otherness and difference is the most highly developed. Owing to its capacity, tragedy is, from among all the arts, an especially well-suited model for the speculative unity, as speculation must encompass, preserve, and protect even the most tenacious forms of conflict and difference.

Yet, by the end of his career Hegel appears to have lost much of the revolutionary fervor of his youth. During his time in Berlin in the 1820s and until his death in 1831, Hegel continues to associate his thought with German Idealism and to associate the project of idealism with speculation. But, Hegel himself no longer associates speculation with the philosophical vanguard of his day. Of course, Hegel's more muted tone during this period might be in part due to the magnificent rise of his stature in the world of professional philosophy. In the height of his career, Hegel had not only become something of a state philosopher in Prussia, but his speculative system had come to dominate the landscape of German philosophy. By the time Hegel had become settled in Berlin, he could no longer count himself a philosopher of the avant-garde because by then he was the establishment.[44] Even if we put these factors aside, by the 1820s Hegel's vision of the speculative unity had undergone a number of transformations that, one might wonder, appear to have worn down its revolutionary edge. In his political philosophy, for example, Hegel remained an advocate of universal freedom and a staunch critic of the failures of the political vision of liberalism, especially in its British forms. But in the end, Hegel's fervor for the ideals of the French Revolution appears to have faded, and he became an advocate of a form of constitutional monarchy that might translate into moderate reform for the existing government of Prussia.[45]

Perhaps one of the most illuminating measures of Hegel's transformation, however, turns on his reassessment of the philosophical significance of poetic art. By the 1820s, Hegel identifies the model of the speculative unity with the traditional philosophical idiom of the idea, and no longer with the resources of art, though, of course, he continues to understand the idea speculatively as a complex identity of identity and difference.[46] This is not to say that late in his career Hegel comes to deny the speculative significance of art completely. Hegel continues to admit that there is an intimate tie between knowledge and art. However, by this later phase of his life, Hegel has come to hold that the form of knowledge we win in the philosophical idea is more complete, robust, and clear than the more intuitive insight presented in art. From the standpoint of this commitment to conceptual thought, Hegel now maintains that in the modern period, there is no longer any speculative need for art at all; from the standpoint of philosophy, art "no longer counts," and is thus "a thing of the past."[47] Ironically, in the Berlin period Hegel dedicated more of his time and effort to the consideration of actual, specific works of art than at any other point in his life. Not only does the sheer volume of his *Lectures on Fine Art* attest to this, but also his travels to the Low Countries to experience the works of Dutch masters, as well as his support of Hinkel's efforts to establish a national museum in Berlin.[48] Despite these things, Hegel not only abandoned his earlier desire to overturn the Platonic verdict on poetry, but also allowed his interest in tragic poetry as a model for the speculative unity to recede into the background.

The larger course of post-Kantian continental philosophy, then, forms a stark contrast to the transformation in Hegel's appraisal of the philosophical status of tragic poetry. Whereas the broader history of post-Hegelian continental European philosophy has seen a proliferation and intensification of the love-bond between philosophy and tragedy, Hegel's initial affair with the tragic ultimately turns cold. Yet, within the larger scheme of this double movement, we may nonetheless find some of the most important contributions to the philosophy of the tragic not only in later figures such as Nietzsche and Heidegger, nor only in Hegel's contemporaries, nor even only in Hegel's earliest thought. Interestingly, some of the most profound insights into the philosophical significance of tragedy lie in Hegel's *Phenomenology*, itself from the initial phase of Hegel's career in which he *relinquishes* tragedy and art as models for his speculative approach. On the one hand, the *Phenomenology* should be counted as one of Hegel's first mature works, not simply because of its systematicity and completeness, but because in it, he associates the fulfillment of the speculative unity with the powers of the concept. While Hegel's conception of his philosophical system will undergo important changes over the years, by the appearance of the *Phenomenology* he has already undergone a decisive shift away from his allegiances to his earliest programme for German Idealism and the exemplary status it affords to poetic art.

Yet, on the other hand, Hegel's *Phenomenology* also forms the culmination of his first projects, and thus it remains deeply informed by the questions and issues that animated his earliest thought. Indeed, it may be that Hegel's *Phenomenology* offers some of his most profound insights into the philosophical significance of tragedy precisely because it is the most conflicted of his texts. Even though Hegel's explicit intention in the *Phenomenology* is to present the speculative unity in the concept as it emerges in experience, Hegel's earlier dedication to tragic poetry continues to play an important role in his account. In the Berlin period, much of Hegel's thought appears to uphold the supremacy of conceptual thought and the idea over poetic art and tragedy as a tacit assumption, and, thus, we might conclude, a foregone conclusion. But, in the *Phenomenology*, by contrast, the claims of tragedy remain fresh in Hegel's mind. Even though Hegel identifies the achievement of the speculative unity with the capabilities of conceptuality, Hegel nevertheless continues to rely on the notion of tragedy in order to capture some of the most crucial moments and most difficult challenges in the development of spirit. The work of figures such as Heidegger and Nietzsche after Hegel, as well as of Hegel's contemporaries such as Schelling, and even some of the first works of Hegel's life are all informed by a certain love-bond between philosophy and tragedy. While Hegel's thematic view of the purpose of the *Phenomenology* may be aligned with a Platonic antagonism toward tragic poetry, we might wonder if it forms more of a lovers' quarrel than anything else. If so, then perhaps the tensions between philosophy and tragedy in the *Phenomenology* might tell us more about their reciprocal affinity than their mutual repulsion.

THEMATIC AND OPERATIVE

Hegel's presentation in the *Phenomenology* remains extraordinarily sensitive to the variety and diversity of phenomena that spirit encounters and the forms of incommensurability, strife, and difference that emerge because of this diversity. Yet, Hegel's own characterization of the purpose of the *Phenomenology*, as well as aspects of his own rhetoric about the project often conceal his genuine concern to attend to the most varied nuances in the life of spirit. If we consider the multitude of phenomena that Hegel entertains in the *Phenomenology*, it becomes clear that few philosophers before or after him have devoted themselves to as much of the variety in human experience with as much care. Hegel not only considers the spiritual significance of more global issues still on the forefront of philosophical inquiry today, such as the diversity of nations and peoples, of natural languages, of historical epochs, and of the difference of the sexes; Hegel's commitment to pay heed to the varieties and differences of phenomena we encounter also lead him to find significance even in things that appear in the most unexceptional and offbeat nooks and crannies of spirit. In the course of his presentation, for example, Hegel attends to the spiritual significance of phenomena such as the pseudo-science of phrenology, and, at one point, he even pauses to wonder at the twofold function of the male member.[49]

Hegel is not however always his own best spokesman for his careful attention to the variety and difference in things. This is perhaps especially true of some of his best remembered assertions from the celebrated 'Preface' to the *Phenomenology*. For although the 'Preface' is one of Hegel's most widely read texts, we might worry that some of its more grandiose claims about his project overshadow his sensitivity to the variegated and difficult contours of spiritual life. But, Hegel's 'Preface' in fact uses the dramatic language of violence, anxiety, pain and death to remind his readers that the development of spirit is punctuated by multiple and difficult confrontations with incommensurability and otherness.[50] Even so, perhaps too many readers of the *Phenomenology* continue to focus on those passages from the 'Preface' guided by Hegel's desire to assert the superiority of his speculative philosophy in comparison with other forms of thought and the merits of his speculative unity and the power of the concept. Unfortunately, some of Hegel's own rhetoric in these remarks not only appears to gainsay his more dramatic language about spirit's confrontation with difference, but also to preclude what is really the mainstay of his later presentation: his highly differentiated and careful presentation of the difficulties and challenges spirit faces in the course of its development.

If it is possible to sense an arrogance in certain of Hegel's thematic claims in the *Phenomenology*, then perhaps it comes out most plainly in his claim that his own speculative philosophy forms the summit of philosophy in general, and of the philosophical aspirations of modernity in particular. Hegel aligns the thematic purpose of the *Phenomenology* with the completion of the philosophical projects inaugurated by early modern figures such as Descartes and Galileo on the continent, and, also, Hobbes in the British Isles.[51] Although Hegel's aspirations to complete the projects of his predecessors in modernity unfolds along a number of fronts, one of the crucial lines of his approach may be summed up as a wish to fulfill the promise of his predecessors' interest in the *mathesis universalis*.[52] Hegel, not unlike his predecessors in modernity, maintains a marked faith in our prospect to determine absolutely certain foundations of knowledge, and holds that the human subject stands at the center point of a universe that it is able entirely to comprehend, a power that, in earlier times, might have been reserved only for God.

Certainly, it is a credit to the present age that many now cast a distrustful eye on such aspirations, if only because after three centuries of philosophical and scientific research, the promises of modernity remain largely unfulfilled. Perhaps we have come to see what Dostoevsky, one of the earliest and most prescient critics of modernity, saw more than a century and a half ago: that the modern vision of things, to include the *mathesis universalis*, forms something of an ethereal 'crystal palace,' as little desirable as it is possible.[53]

Yet, one of Hegel's most important intentions in the *Phenomenology* is to align his philosophy with the achievement of the *mathesis universalis*. Hegel inherits the projects of pioneers of the earlier modern period who focused on the belief that the proper purpose of philosophy is to achieve an indubitable, and, if possible, even exhaustive system of knowledge.[54] However, Hegel contends that his predecessors fail because they relied on inadequate notions of systematicity and method. Hegel's broadest criticism of his modern forerunners is that they misconstrue our cognitive powers as an instrument.[55] The critique is supposed to capture not only the rationalist camp in its widespread, but to Hegel's mind unfounded, use of the mathematical model, but also the empiricist camp in its representational theories of knowledge. But, perhaps most important for us now is Hegel's characterization of the speculative unity as a corrective that overcomes the failings of the philosophical views predominating early modernity and that yields the exhaustive, indubitable science for the first time in its absolute form. Hegel maintains that his speculative philosophy is guided by the early modern vision of the *mathesis universalis*, but he believes that his own philosophy is the first and only to make the vision a reality.

Strangely, it is precisely Hegel's thematic commitment to fill out and shore up the modern *mathesis universalis* that draws him to explore questions of finitude as they emerge in our encounters with incommensurability, strife, confusion, and difference. This is because Hegel's quest to bring universal knowledge to its completion forces him to extend the purview of rigorous philosophical inquiry to, for example (though it is more than an example) the issue of history. In contrast with some moderns before him, Hegel maintains that the ultimate foundation of our knowledge is derived neither from the abstractions of mathematical reason, nor from nature, but instead may be discerned in the dynamics of historical life. Hegel believes that the unconditioned conditions of our knowledge may be divined in historical circumstances, the prejudices and beliefs we inherit from the past, as well as their embodiment in our institutions and customary practices. Owing to this, the *mathesis universalis* must incorporate the establishment of an exhaustive and indubitable theory of the life of history itself, its structure, operations, and development. In order to fulfill the promise of the *mathesis universalis* as a complete science (*Wissenschaft*), we must begin with a science of what today we might almost call historical existence. Hegel calls it the science of experience.[56]

Hegel's wish to extend the *mathesis universalis* to the domain of history forces him to confront and to clarify the difficulties, confusions, and overall messiness of human affairs. Indeed, Hegel suggests that philosophers before him (and, we may add, after him) failed to afford to history its proper "dignity" precisely because of its apparent lack of structure and sense. Hegel writes, "The eye of spirit had to be turned and held firmly toward earthly matters with force; and it has required a long time to achieve the same clarity had in celestial matters in the haziness and confusion in which the sense of this world lies. . . ."[57] Hegel's dedication to the *mathesis universalis* means that he cannot simply be satisfied to abstract eternal verities from the logic of mathematics or from cyclical movements of the heavens and the blind mechanisms of nature. It also requires him to discern the indispensable structures and dynamics of history. This is not only precariously difficult because we are ourselves, in our own powers of cognition, in our preconceptions, and even in the language we use to formulate our thoughts, nothing other than the result of the very history we wish to investigate. It also seems unworkable to achieve a rigorous account of the rational patterns in history because history itself does not seem to exhibit them: for above all history appears to us as the domain of the incalculable, of unpredictable, often violent change, of unprecedented and unforeseen events, of irreconcilable purposes, and, in the end, of sheer fortuitousness.

Hegel evokes the resources of tragedy to capture and clarify what he understands to be the most monstrous of these crises of spirit. Whereas Hegel's rather ambitious and very modern aspiration to achieve an absolute, exhaustive, and indubitable knowledge of things comprises the thematic purpose of the *Phenomenology*, Hegel's reliance on the resources of tragic poetry, especially ancient tragedy, serves as an operative voice of the incommensurabilities, incongruities, and vicissitudes of historical existence within the pages of the text. Like Hegel's later works, the *Phenomenology* is dedicated to the aspirations of modernity and the logic of conceptuality, not poetry. But in this text, there appears to remain an important place for his earliest conviction that tragic poetry is a genre of difference *par excellence*. Even if the notion of tragic poetry no longer forms a model for the speculative unity itself, Hegel now uses tragedy to put the speculative unity of the concept to the test. Due to this, the accomplishment of the speculative unity in the emergence of the concept finds its most profound trials in the dynamics of history that are the most tragic.

Many of the most important and original twentieth-century commentators on the *Phenomenology* came to believe that Hegel's thematic dedication to the speculative unity of the concept was tested to the breaking point, and even beyond it, by the operations of the tragic within his text. Of course, there are some commentators who disagree, and, in fact, claim that Hegel's dedication to the speculative unity of the concept lead him to adopt a rather benign view of the disruptive powers of tragedy. This may be said, for example, of a figure such as Martha Nussbaum, who, though not primarily focused on Hegel, nonetheless recognizes the need to address Hegel's view in her research on Greek tragedy. In her *Fragility of Goodness*, Nussbaum may be seen to hold that the tragic poetry of classical Greece provides a powerful expression of our encounter with finitude in our ethical affairs. On this background, Nussbaum criticizes Hegel's interpretation of tragedy in the *Phenomenology* as it is embodied in his use of Sophocles' *Antigone* in his discussion of ethical life (*Sittlichkeit*). Nussbaum charges that Hegel's view fails because he believes that the ultimate lesson of tragedy is that it is within our power to overcome incommensurability and conflict.[58] Nussbaum's interpretation of Hegel's notion of tragedy is perhaps less a characterization of his view, however, than it is a picture of Hegel in broad strokes that fails to capture the subtle contours of his concern for the experiences of limits. For while Hegel is certainly dedicated to the belief that the speculative unity encompasses all differences, he enlists the resources of tragedy not so much to confirm the unifying power of the concept as to scrutinize it.

In contrast with figures such as Nussbaum, who might not adequately admit the extent to which Hegel uses tragedy to put the claims of the speculative unity to the test, others wonder whether Hegel's reliance on the resources of tragedy emphasize incommensurability and difference to such an extent that it transforms and stretches the scope of his dedication to the speculative unity itself. Perhaps one of the most seminal of these commentators is Jean Hyppolite. While Hyppolite recognizes that Hegel's *Phenomenology* struggles to achieve the speculative unity of the concept, his approach suggests that there may nevertheless be times when this "panlogism" of Hegel's thought in 1807 may not be too distant from the "pantragedism" of Hegel's youth.[59] Figures such as Peter Szondi go even farther. In his landmark *Versuch Über das Tragische*, Szondi maintains that despite Hegel's thematic dedication to the logic of the concept, his reliance on tragedy comes to form a "global law" of Hegel's dialectic. Szondi writes,

> The *Phenomenology* places the tragic, admittedly without characterizing it in this way, as the center point of Hegelian philosophy and indicates it as the dialectic under which [it] is subjugated.[60]

For some of the most provocative commentators of the past century, Hegel's *Phenomenology* characterization of the speculative unity of the concept, despite its claims to encompass, preserve, and protect difference in all of its forms, is ultimately overwhelmed by the notion of tragedy and its ties to incommensurability, strife, confusion, and even to insuperable conflict and irreconcilable difference.

If interpretations such as Nussbaum's surely downplay Hegel's persistent drive to test the elasticity of the concept by means of tragedy, I believe it remains an open question whether figures such as Szondi overplay the impact of Hegel's uses of tragedy on his intentions for the speculative unity. It is true that claims such as Szondi's show a certain distance from Hegel's apparent thematic intentions as he announces them in the *Phenomenology*. But, it does not follow from this that Szondi and those who make similar claims fail to understand the inner significance of Hegel's thought, perhaps better than Hegel himself was able. Of course, in the end there may no final answer to the question at all. Yet, Hegel's strange intermarriage of his aspirations for a speculative unity of the concept with the resources of tragedy—at bottom, a coupling of his unsurpassed modern faith in an exhaustive, indubitable, and thus infinite science with the most ancient wisdom of what Dennis Schmidt refers to as "the infinity and inexhaustibility of our limits"[61]—yields important insights into the structures and dynamics of our encounters with finitude. Of course, in order to win these insights, it is necessary to turn to Hegel's specific uses of the resources of tragedy within the *Phenomenology* itself and to measure his thematic interests against the force of their operations.

Scope and Purpose

The scope and purpose of this book are guided by a number of closely related questions. What do Hegel's uses of tragedy in the *Phenomenology* have to say about the life of spirit, about the lessons it learns from its encounter with tragic incommensurability, conflict, and catastrophe?

What insights does Hegel's reliance on the resources of tragedy yield about the confrontation between the deepest aspirations of spirit and its tragic limits? What does the more tragic aspect of Hegel's vision of the human condition teach us about ourselves, our lives, and our relation to the world? To address these matters it will certainly be necessary to develop a more thoroughgoing and precise interpretation of Hegel's concept of tragedy. One of the important tasks of this book is to clarify precisely what notion of tragedy emerges from Hegel's text, and just how it informs his presentation of spirit. Yet, Hegel's *Phenomenology* never offers an explicit definition of tragedy, and he never overtly explains the *raison d'etre* behind any of his specific uses of tragedy within course of the text. Even though his reliance on the notion of tragedy forms one of the most important aspects of his presentation of historically developing spirit, he neither sees fit to acknowledge it as such, nor, perhaps, even recognizes the scale of its consequences for his view. Thus it will be necessary to piece together a full picture of the concept of tragedy in his text, its place in the life of spirit, and its implications for human finitude, as a kind of collage of interpretations of Hegel's specific references to tragedy in the course of his presentation.

It is precisely in those moments of Hegel's presentation directed most by his thematic intentions to fulfill the promises of modernity that his most important uses of tragedy come into focus. Some of Hegel's highest and most modern aspirations are his assertion of the omnipresence of reason in historical experience, his claims about independence, his confidence in our powers to surmount the persistent aporias of ethical life, and his belief in our ability to attain absolute knowledge as the result of the historical developments of spirit. But, his discussions of these themes of experience, freedom, ethical life, and absolute knowledge all set the stage for some of Hegel's most profound questions about the tragic character of our lives. So the plan for this book is to develop a more comprehensive view of Hegel's uses of tragedy, its place within his larger presentation of spirit, and its implications for the dimensions of finitude that we encounter in our lives, by means of a careful interpretation that focuses on each of these important uses of tragedy in turn. Each of the chapters in this book stands on its own as a self-contained interpretation of one aspect of Hegel's use of tragedy. Yet, the book also forms a coherent whole because Hegel's uses of tragedy ultimately coalesce to form a rather extensive view of the dimensions of finitude that run through Hegel's presentation of spirit, and also through our own lives.

The questions that will guide chapter 1 concern the tragic dimension of Hegel's doctrine of experience. Hegel's speculative approach leads him to argue that although the achievement of absolute knowledge is within the reach of human cognitive powers, our consciousness achieves the absolute not through formalism or empiricism, but rather only as a result of experience. While it will prove helpful to situate Hegel's notion of consciousness on the backdrop of central themes in Husserlian phenomenology and of current debates within the philosophy of mind, the tragic aspect of Hegel's theory that first came to prominence in the French reception of Hegel in the 1930s and 1940s comes into focus if we see his view as a speculative corrective against Kant. Hegel will reject Kant's claim that reason is subject to a 'peculiar fate,' namely, that despite the faculty's ineluctable affinity for the unconditioned, the domain of reason remains separate from the realm of experience, and thus that reason is ultimately powerless to unify our knowledge. Instead, Hegel maintains that reason forms a fundamental structure of reality that guides all of our experiences. Yet, Hegel argues that consciousness only recognizes the rational structure of reality once it becomes fully educated, and that in the course of its development it is nevertheless fated time and again to experience the limits of its awareness and to lose certainty in its knowledge of itself and its world.

As we shall see, Hegel speculatively appropriates a resource of tragedy, the Aristotelian notion of reversal, to characterize this loss of certainty, and thereby to emphasize the tenuousness of human knowledge, as well as to remind us that our cognitive powers remain crucially dependent on conditions hidden from us. Indeed, Hegel's invocation of the notion of reversal to capture the character of this blindness may even raise questions about the justification for his confidence in our powers to attain absolute knowledge.

In chapter 2 I shall turn to certain post-Hegelian engagements with Hegel's discussion of self-consciousness, recognition, and the master/servant relation to develop some tragic aspects of human freedom. Much of Hegel's account places him squarely within the main streams of modernity, and his thematic position involves the idea that self-consciousness is indexed to the achievement of independence. Hegel recognizes that the achievement of independence comes only at a price, and is born of an extensive struggle in which self-consciousness in the condition of servitude overcomes its dependence on a master through a reversal in the terms of their relation. Now, Hegel's invocation of the notion of reversal in this context appears to refer more to a triumph than a tragedy of spirit, insofar as it refers to a significant step in the liberation of self-consciousness from its bondage. But, in chapter 2, I plan to examine important strands of continental approaches that expose tragic aspects of human freedom that subtend Hegel's narrative. First, I wish to consider the efflorescence of a certain

Nietzschean vein of approaches to Hegel in the early Derrida, who identifies the reversal in mastery and servitude not foremost as the success of the servant, but, rather as a sort of tragedy of the sovereign, and as a singular loss of self-assertive, affirmative, free play of life, and of meaning.

My discussion will then turn to another approach, developed in part from issues broached by Gadamer that provides insights into the finitude of human freedom by focusing on tragic elements of the experience of servitude. Hegel will hold that in mastery and servitude, masters retain power over their servants through the constant threat of death, the 'absolute master.' As we shall see, Hegel's view of the relationship between the absolute master and death suggests a restricted and narrow notion of freedom understood as a finite power or ability to transform the conditions of our existence.

Chapter 3 concerns Hegel's use of tragedy to elaborate on questions raised in his treatment of ethical life. In this celebrated portion of the *Phenomenology* Hegel enlists the storyline, plot, and characters of Sophocles' *Antigone* as a sort of matrix for his presentation of consciousness' experience of the ethical world. Hegel's discussion of ethical life has received much attention from scholars in recent times, and it ranges over questions about antiquity, cultural heritage, state power, the force of law, gender and sex, war, and death. But, one of the central concerns of Hegel's treatment is consciousness' aspiration to reconcile its awareness that it has larger political, social, and ethical commitments with its sense of itself as a rational individual that lays down its own principles of action. As we shall see, Hegel holds what Charles Taylor has called a 'qualitative' theory of action, and, on this view, Hegel argues that an agent's intentions or purposes form not an antecedent cause of action, but rather inform and inhabit actions as their guiding principles.

Hegel's reliance on the *Antigone* as a script for his presentation of ethical life will result in the insight that even consciousness' most principled intentions and actions may turn out to be criminal, and, ultimately, that all of a rational agent's actions are inextricably bound up with guilt. Hegel will characterize an agent's guilt not as the result of her bad character, weak will, or bad luck, but neither will he argue that human beings' actions lead to guilt as a consequence of some original sin. Instead, Hegel believes that rational agency leads us to guilt as an unavoidable and inherent predisposition for waywardness or errancy (ἁμαρτία) that inhabits all of our actions. In light of this, it will be possible to see instructive connections between Hegel's views and later themes in existentialism.

My project culminates in chapter 4 with a discussion of Hegel's conception of speculative knowledge and his claim that the tragic drama is a form of art that results in certain wisdom about human limits. Hegel characterizes philosophy, religion, and art primarily as forms of consciousness dedicated to contemplation and self-reflection. Although Hegel maintains that speculative knowledge reaches its highest form in philosophy, he nonetheless believes that tragedy, especially in its classical Greek form, not only provides profound insights into the human condition but also answers to the multiple forms of tragic disunity, strife, and limitation it encountered over the course of its education. Hegel thus casts our experience of tragic drama primarily as a medium that allows us to reflect on the tragic character of life itself. Although it would certainly be natural to suppose that tragic drama evokes a negative view of life, Hegel actually believes that it points to a profoundly affirmative and beautiful image of the human condition. Whereas the speculative knowledge attained in philosophy takes conceptual form, the kind of wisdom achieved in tragedy is primarily affective, and thus may not be conceived, but rather only suffered. Hegel argues that as consciousness' experience of a tragic drama reaches its completion, the performance produces in us a complex of emotions. He holds that a tragic drama results in a positive, pleasurable affect only in relation to a set of negative, painful feelings, namely, the emotions that have always, since Aristotle at least, been associated with tragic drama: fear and pity. But, on Hegel's view, these painful emotions transport the viewer and induce a certain positive response. Hegel does not, as one might expect, directly identify this positive pleasure with catharsis, but, instead, characterizes it as a sense of simple acceptance and even affirmation of the tragic performance and the tragic difficulties it reflects.

Taken together, Hegel's tragedies of spirit draw a beautiful, richly human, and even affirmative picture of our affairs. In contrast with Hegel's more thematic, modern, and triumphant vision of the human spirit, his more subterranean, tragic view forces us to acknowledge multiple forms of difficulty, disunity, strife, and irreconcilability. However, the larger view that emerges from Hegel's uses of tragedy provide an important reminder that our humanity and dignity is found not primarily in our prideful powers to master ourselves and our world, but rather in our more humble ability to come to terms with and even embrace the insuperability of our limitations. Although this more propitious side of Hegel's tragic vision forms an important motivation for all of his uses of tragedy, it reaches a certain highpoint in his final reference to tragedy. For on the Hegelian account, tragic drama is a form of art that cultivates our sense for human experience, and encourages us to see the beauty of, and even in a sense to love, our fate as monstrous beings animated by aspirations we cannot fulfill, and confronted with obstacles we cannot pass.

In something of a postscript to my study, I shall turn to Hegel's discussion of Sophocles' *Oedipus at Colonus* in the *Lectures on Aesthetics* to provide further context for and to shed further light on Hegel's concern for the tragic in his *Phenomenology*. Taking as my point of departure a line from the drama in which Sophocles has Oedipus say, 'life hangs in the balance,' I suggest that together, the *Phenomenology*'s tragedies of spirit urge that the fullest and most intense life is the one that remains most keenly aware of the fractured character of spirit and of the interconnectedness of death, limit, and life. As I will also suggest, the tragic side of his view in the *Phenomenology* also enriches further avenues of inquiry into other philosophers, critics, and poets indebted to tragedy, not only those who come after Hegel, but also many of his contemporaries, such as F. W. J. Schelling, Friedrich Schlegel, and Friedrich Hölderlin.

1

The Tragedy of Experience

Hegel underscores his thematic intention to complete and thus reach the end of philosophy in a remarkable passage from the 'Preface' to the *Phenomenology*. He writes, "to bring it about that philosophy may become closer to the form of science [*Wissenschaft*]—toward the goal of being able to lay aside its name as the *love* of *knowledge*, and be *actual knowledge*—this is what I have set out to do."[1] Hegel tells us that his speculative philosophy is supposed to consummate our knowledge of the world, our past, and ourselves, and so alleviate any need for further philosophy understood in the sense of the ancient Greek φῐλοσοφία, the loving pursuit of wisdom. Yet, it is precisely the compass of Hegel's ambitions that compel him to explore the issue of finitude as it appears in human affairs under its multiple guises of incommensurability, strife, confusion, and difference. For Hegel's desire to achieve knowledge in its absolute form leads him to turn his speculative eye toward history and to develop a systematic, unified knowledge of a phenomenon that appears, perhaps more than any other, to be guided not by rules, but by incalculable and often violent transformations, catastrophe, innumerable collisions, and interminable change.

While Hegel's thematic purpose is to show that our powers of synthesis ultimately prevail even in the face of such apparent disjointedness, Hegel's references to tragedies and theoretical works on tragedy are decisive for his project because he turns to tragedy as the supreme type of expression to capture and clarify the most terrible and aporetic of such dynamics of historical life. If Hegel dedicates the *Phenomenology* to one of the grandest of unities imaginable—the speculative unity of the concept—he nevertheless recommends tragedy as an indispensable voice of incommensurable differences, disunity, confusion, and strife.

Perhaps none of Hegel's uses of tragedy has broader application, or deeper consequences, than his reliance on a resource of tragedy to characterize the phenomenon of experience. One of Hegel's most overarching purposes in the *Phenomenology* is to present absolute knowledge as it emerges in the life of spirit. Hegel rejects the idea that the absolute arises either through formalism or empiricism, and he argues instead that it ultimately comes about only thanks to the education we receive through concrete experience.[2] In this light, the *Phenomenology* unfolds primarily as an effort to depict not only the final accomplishment of knowing in its absolute form, but also the progression of spirit toward this end through each of the essential moments in its experiential growth. Hegel's presentation of spirit thus affords a central position to the notion of experience as the fundamental principle of spiritual transformation, and Hegel's association of experience with tragedy has implications not only for the concept of spirit in general, but also for every moment of its development. Moreover, the connection Hegel sees between experience and tragedy also supplies something of a prototype for all of his further references, insofar as he uses each of them to shed light on the tragic dimension of specific forms of experience.

It is true that much of Hegel's thematic, and triumphant, vision of spirit is sustained by the claims he makes about experience. After all, on his view the attainment of absolute knowledge is ultimately contingent on and enabled by the expansion of our awareness that is precipitated by experience. But, Hegel believes that it is only from the speculative standpoint of his celebrated 'we,' the philosophers for whom this expansion of our awareness is already complete enough to recognize the internal necessity in the progression of experience, that we see absolute knowledge as the final destination of the lessons learned from experience. From the more natural, or naïve, standpoint of consciousness that remains on the path of its education, by contrast, it is impossible yet to see any necessity in absolute knowledge as the end result of our edification, and our encounters with experience unfold primarily as a series of difficult and unanticipated trials that force us not only to confront, but also to overcome the hitherto latent oppositions and limitations in our preconceived awareness of things.[3] Yet, even from the vantage point of Hegel's 'we,' our awareness continues to include the memory of the difficulties faced along the way. Despite Hegel's belief in the positive outcome of experience, he acknowledges that it is a Janus-faced phenomenon. In fact, Hegel delivers strong words to convey the consequences of the negative aspect of experience for his conception of spirit. He writes, "the life of spirit is not the life that shrinks from death and keeps itself undefiled by devastation, but the life that endures and lingers upon death. . . ."[4]

Hegel's use of such language appears to place his concept of experience well within the vicinity of the tragic. But, Hegel scholarship has seen much debate about the importance of Hegel's rhetoric for his larger view. On one end of the discussion, we expect some commentators may maintain that Hegel's more tragic remarks on experience anticipate important post-Hegelian (and even anti-Hegelian) movements in philosophy. In some figures to approach Hegel in this vein, such as Jean Hyppolite, for example, we hear the suggestion that Hegel's tragic depiction of experience as it appears for naïve consciousness points to something of a theory of existentialism *in nuce*.[5] On the opposite extreme, it would probably not be hard to find philosophers today who would simply write off Hegel's use of notions, such as death, ruination, destruction (and, as we shall see), anxiety, doubt, and despair, as so many overwrought metaphors and rhetorical flourishes without substantial bearing. Yet, still others maintain that while we must proceed with caution, Hegel's use of concepts such as these to describe experience cannot be ignored. Merold Westphal poses the sentiment as a genuine question:

> When Jean Wahl tells us that Hegelian doubt is more like that of Pascal or Nietzsche than that of Descartes, and when Jean Hyppolite suggests that we have to do here with *une angoisse existentielle*, is it Hegel or the intellectual atmosphere of France in the forties which is speaking to us?[6]

Indeed, we are tempted to say that Westphal's question is perhaps really an *Urfrage* for Hegel studies—a provocation that is as unavoidable as it is undecidable—and thus continues to pose a challenge for commentators today as it did for those a half-century ago.

But what, precisely, is Hegel's conception of experience? Before it is possible to measure the larger significance of Hegel's association of experience with tragedy, we must consider Hegel's view in some detail. What is Hegel's concept of absolute knowledge, and how does he believe experience will lead us to it? And what, precisely, makes experience so tragic?

Important scholars of Hegel in recent decades, perhaps, especially those interested in the epistemological dimensions of Hegel's notion of the absolute, have fruitfully approached his conception of absolute knowledge as a response to Kant's critique of reason.[7] In what follows, I also wish to interpret Hegel's notion of absolute knowledge in terms of his relation to Kant, with an eye to illuminating Hegel's notion of experience. However, by focusing on some of what might be called the more ontologically-motivated concerns that inform Hegel's response to Kant, I hope to emphasize that Hegel's conception of experience involves important, and even tragic, consequences for the character of life of spirit. As we shall see, Hegel points to the tragic side of his view in his contention that the education we receive through experience unfolds as a path not only of 'doubt,' but also of 'despair.'[8]

Hegel believes that the expansion of our awareness through experience is predicated on doubt, as experience compels us to recognize and relinquish our certainty in things as we have hitherto conceived of them.[9] Hegel claims that this form of doubt is also, and more crucially, a form of despair, for our doubt in the reality of things unfolds as much more than a mere, Cartesian-style epistemological and methodological exercise. Instead, as genuinely conscious and concerned beings, our loss of certainty crucially upsets our sense of ourselves and our place in the world because it forces us to recognize that in the flow of experience our knowledge remains importantly finite, not simply incomplete or partial, in the sense that our store of knowledge is less than comprehensive, but finite, as our knowledge remains dependent on conditions that we can neither control, nor even survey. While Hegel uses a number of ideas and images to point out the tragic aspect of this dynamic, none is more important than the concept of reversal, a notion that Hegel might be seen to borrow, albeit somewhat obliquely and with important qualifications and innovations, from Aristotle's *Poetics* and its effective history. Hegel's use of this notion emphasizes that for naïve consciousness, at least, experience brings us face to face with a form of finitude that bespeaks the tenuousness of even our deepest beliefs about ourselves and our world, and that thus exposes the precariousness and vulnerability of human affairs.

Absolute Knowledge as Speculative Self-Knowledge

Scholarship on Hegel's conception of absolute knowledge is as expansive and rich as it is varied, and, as John Burbridge recently points out, the interpretation of Hegel's complete view is made all the more difficult by the fact that he himself appears to employ the notion of the absolute in a number of contexts and senses.[10] But in the *Phenomenology*, at least, one of Hegel's chief claims about absolute knowledge suggests that it may properly be viewed as a speculative form of self-knowledge accomplished in the expansion of our awareness that results from experience. By 'absolute knowledge,' Hegel refers neither to a form of romantic insight, of the sort we might find exemplified in, say, J. G. Hamann, nor to, say, an exhaustive catalog of the fruits of human learning, as might have been envisioned by some of the eighteenth-century encyclopedists.[11] Rather, Hegel identifies absolute knowledge primarily as a special type of self-reflection, a manner or way of knowing the self that is distinguished from other forms of cognition by its self-sufficiency, or sovereignty. On Hegel's view, absolute knowledge is constituted as that form of self-conscious reflection that is complete and sound because it is completely free of qualifications and constraints. Hans-Georg Gadamer points out, "the word means nothing other than 'the absolved,' and in classical Latin stands as the antonym of 'the relative.' It indicates the independence from all restrictive conditions."[12] For Hegel, the absoluteness of knowledge turns not foremost on the breadth of its substantial content (though, certainly, he believes that it covers an expansive range of phenomena), but, rather, on its independence from those conditions that threaten the completeness of its veracity.

But, Hegel identifies the accomplishment of speculative self-knowledge, this absolutely self-conscious awareness, principally, as the culmination of a dynamic process, and not simply as a static, cognitive content. The achievement of absolute knowledge comprises the final stage in a development, an education (*Bildung*), that we receive from experience.[13] In the *Phenomenology*, Hegel maintains that consciousness develops dialectically in stages, and he argues that with each of its advances, it relinquishes its former convictions because it comes to appreciate that they resulted from a merely relative, or limited, perspective. Indeed, Hegel's account of this process is grand in sweep, and, as we know from the overall itinerary of his narrative, it encompasses experiences not only of more basic cognitive functions such as sensation, perception, and understanding, but also of history, multiple forms of practical relations, theoretical and practical rationality, ethical life, culture, and religion. From this standpoint, speculative self-knowledge requires us not to abstract ourselves from all conditions that restrict our perspective, nor to meditate on ourselves as unsituated subjects in order to discern our essential features. Rather, speculative self-knowledge demands that we come to see ourselves as nothing short of the end result of the lessons we learn from experience, and, thereby, as the totality of all of the merely relative certainties held in the course of our development.[14]

But this tells us perhaps too little, and in order to determine Hegel's conception of absolute self-knowledge in adequate detail, we might consider the issue, as Hegel did, in light of larger philosophical questions of his times. It is too often forgotten today that the topic of absolute knowledge forms not only a vital issue in Hegelian philosophy, but also the centerpiece of a broad range of intellectual debates in German Idealism and Romanticism. Hegel's conception of absolute knowledge is deeply informed by the concerns that drive these debates, and though there are important differences among Hegel and figures such as Johann Gottlieb Fichte, F. W. J. Schelling, Friedrich Schlegel, and Friedrich Hölderlin, it may safely be said that important aspects of their approaches are galvanized by an extremely rich, and ambivalent, relation to Kant.[15] Indeed, much of Hegel's project in the *Phenomenology* (and, of course, elsewhere), as well as his conception of absolute knowledge and his view of its connection with experience, can be seen as part of a larger effort in German Idealism and Romanticism to resolve decisive tensions in Kant's philosophical project. The intellectual atmosphere of German Idealism and Romanticism was alive with the enthusiasm that Kant's critical philosophy marked a brilliant and decisive break with both the rationalist and empiricist traditions of modern philosophy. Yet, many believed that even though Kant's breakthrough made it impossible to return to earlier schools of thought, his critical project, nevertheless, demanded further attention and emendation because it was imbued with internal inconsistencies that threatened its overall coherence.

The influence of Kant's radical departure from the tradition on German philosophy took hold so rapidly and was so extensive that it led Schelling, in a notice penned on the occasion of Kant's death in 1804, to say that the Kantian critical project formed nothing less than "the boundary of two epochs of philosophy, of one, which he puts to an end forever, of another, which he prepared negatively. . . ."[16] A survey of Kant scholarship might bear out that a greater share of recent Anglo-American approaches focus on the aspects of his thought that are relevant for questions in fields such as epistemology and the philosophy of science, and, perhaps, on themes that Kant develops in the portions of the *Critique of Pure Reason* devoted to the first part of his 'Transcendental Doctrine of Elements,' the 'Transcendental Analytic' of our cognitive faculties of the intellect (*Verstand*) and of sensibility. In German Idealism and Romanticism there is also extensive interest in these parts of the first *Critique*, and no doubt much of the widespread enthusiasm for Kant's critical project at the time stems from the implications of it. Of the numerous lines of Hegel's corrective of Kant, for example, Hegel's critique of Kant's views of the unity of apperception and of the categories stand out.[17] However, some lines of debate about the absolute in this period, including Hegel's contributions to them, can be seen as centering not on the first part of Kant's Doctrine of Elements, but on the second, his 'Transcendental Dialectic' of reason (*Vernunft*).

Even though the German Idealist and Romantic reception of Kant is animated by the desire to scrutinize and improve on the critical project, the period after Kant may, nonetheless, be said largely to embrace Kant's identification of the purpose of reason with the unconditioned. In the first *Critique*, Kant identifies reason as our "highest" cognitive faculty because its predilection for synthesis outmatches those of our other important theoretical faculty, the intellect. It is true he believes our power of reason to be bound up in "transcendental illusion" because it bears no intrinsic relation to intuition, but nevertheless, reason retains its paramount status because its proper function, the *telos* that defines it and directs its activity, is the accomplishment of universality. Indeed, the proper vocation of reason is to represent universal ideas with an unrestricted extension and not simply ideas that cover only a limited, specific domain of particulars. At this highest level, the universal is "explained by the concept of the unconditioned, insofar as it entails a basis for the synthesis of everything that is conditioned."[18] Reason is our greatest synthetic faculty, and its purpose is to represent unconditioned, universal ideas, in contrast with the faculty of the intellect, a lower-order power; all knowledge derived from which remains dependent on and bounded by our reception of the phenomena through the sensibility.

If much of German Idealism and Romanticism is animated by the wish to fulfill the promise of reason as Kant describes it, then it might also be said that some of the concerns for absolute knowledge in this period unfold in attempts to elaborate further on and to determine in more detail Kant's vision of an unconditioned, universal idea. Evidence of this is found, we might suggest, in the widespread circulation of the term 'absolute' itself among Hegel and his contemporaries, as the term may be traced back to an important, though sometimes overlooked, passage from the first *Critique*. Indeed, in the course of his discussion of the concept of unconditioned knowledge, Kant pauses to observe:

> Because the loss of a concept . . . can never be a matter of indifference to philosophers, thus I hope that the determination and careful protection of the expression, on which the concept depends, will also be no matter of indifference to them. . . .

"Then," he says, properly to express the concept of the unconditioned, "I . . . will use the word: *absolute*. . . ."[19] If the enthusiasm that figures such as

Hegel, Schelling, Fichte, and Hölderlin have for Kant's account of the purpose of reason permeates their thought, then, perhaps, one important dimension of their approach turns on a certain deference to Kant's judgment in their use of the term 'absolute' to capture the form of knowledge that reason seeks.

Yet, figures in German Idealism and Romanticism, perhaps especially Fichte, Schelling, and Hegel, owe still more to Kant, for in their attempts to determine absolute knowledge in deeper detail they follow Kant's further claim: that reason reaches the highest form of universal, unconditioned knowledge in the idea of the unity of *subject* and *world*.[20]

Certainly, Kant's account of the absolute synthesis of subject and world in reason is quite intricate, and he envisions this unity as a third and final form in a hierarchy; the first synthesis turns on the unity of the subject in its own right and the second turns on the unity of the world. But while figures such as Schelling and Hegel retain a critical distance from many aspects of Kant's view, their research unfolds in no small part under the sign of the Kantian conclusion that the purpose of reason, namely, to represent absolutely unconditioned knowledge, attains its height in the idea of a unity of the human subject, identified by its rationality and autonomy, with the material world of phenomena, known, through the powers of the intellect at least, to be governed by the mechanical laws of nature. Important streams of intellectual debates in Germany at the dawn of the nineteenth century were animated by the conviction that Kant not only properly discerned the purpose of reason, and found the suitable expression for it, but also discovered the specific form that the absolutely unconditioned universal idea would take, the unity of subject and world, reason and matter.

Despite their debts to Kant's discussion of reason in the first *Critique*, Hegel and some of his contemporaries may nevertheless be seen to argue that Kant's conception of reason is laden with decisive problems and is thus unacceptable as it stands. One of the troubles lies in Kant's contention that it is impossible for reason completely to fulfill its own purpose. While Kant believes that the ambitions of our highest cognitive faculty know no limits, his view of reason is nevertheless tempered by his further claim that our power of reason effaces itself in its very efforts to attain the absolute—that reason's demands exceed its grasp. It is this vision of reason that Kant wishes to express, in distilled form, in the very first lines of the first edition of the *Critique of Pure Reason*. The passage reads,

> Human reason has the peculiar fate in one species of its knowledge: it is troubled by questions that it cannot dismiss, for they are given to it

through the nature of reason itself, but that it also cannot answer, for they overstep all of the powers of human reason. It finds itself in this embarrassment through no fault of its own.[21]

Our greatest cognitive gift, reason, is guided by its intrinsic inclination to represent the absolutely unconditioned, in the end, the unity of subject and world. Yet, despite this native proclivity, reason is ill equipped to make good on its *telos*. What is worse, this impotence of reason is unavoidable, for it results not from some corrigible failure, but, rather, from the operations of reason as such. This conviction ultimately leads Kant in the *Critique of Pure Reason* to conclude that the only legitimate use of reason is regulative, and not constitutive, in nature.[22] Yet, Hegel is convinced that this conclusion, along with others in Kant, comprises an embarrassment to philosophy that must be addressed and corrected.[23]

One focal point of Hegel's approach to Kant turns on Kant's elaboration of this 'peculiar fate' in his discussion of how reason, in virtue of its very efforts to attain its end, necessarily falls into multiple and irresolvable dialectics. The architectonic structure of Kant's text suggests that his discussion of the third and final dialectic, 'the ideal of pure reason,' should treat the difficulty that plagues our power of reason in its attempt to represent its highest synthesis of subject and world. But, Hegel and others in German Idealism and Romanticism do not always attend to the letter of Kant's account, and influential here is the view first developed by Schelling in the 1790s that the focal point of Kant's treatment of the unity of subject and world is found in the 'Third Antinomy of Pure Reason.'[24] Kant actually indicates that his purpose in this particular section of the first *Critique* is to show that reason succumbs to a formidable dialectic in its endeavor to discern an unconditioned, universal principle of causation that directs the universe, which would thus represent a unified idea not of the subject and world, but simply of the world on its own terms. The German Idealists' concern for Kant's elucidation of this dialectic has decisive implications for their take on Kant's idea of the unity of subject and world, and of equal importance, some idealists suggest the dialectic exposes inconsistencies in the Kantian conception of reason.

Although numerous approaches to Hegel's conception of reason may be found in the literature, it may be asserted, minimally, that central to his reception of Kant is the objection that important difficulties in Kant emerges from his confusion about the ontological status of reason, and the unity of being and thought.[25] While Kant's critical project constitutes a revolutionary and original movement in philosophy that resists being pigeonholed as a representative of any one school of thought, it may be said that Kant's critical philosophy is a form of transcendental idealism, at least insofar as he maintains, for example, that the ideas of reason have no basis in, and indeed bear no intrinsic relation to, the phenomenal order of spatiotemporal entities. However, the emphasis in Kant's critical project is preeminently on epistemological issues, as one of the overarching purposes of Kant's project is to use reason as the basis to critique our theoretical and cognitive faculties; and for Kant the critique of a faculty does not require that we determine its ontological status, but, instead, only that we determine all of the possibilities and limits, or, as Henry Allison puts it, the 'epistemic conditions,' that direct it.[26]

Yet to Hegel's mind, Kant's critical philosophy fails on its own terms, or, as Paul Guyer puts it, Hegel argues that "Kant's conclusions fall short of his own philosophical expectations."[27] In this vein, one of Hegel's chief concerns is that despite the broadly epistemological focus of the *Critique of Pure Reason*, Kant's discussion points to the need for a more fully ontological conception of reason than Kant explicitly provides. Although Hegel does not organize his treatment of reason in the *Phenomenology* expressly as such a response to Kant, the central lines of his argument might be stated as follows. Kant tells us that the highest idea of reason seeks to represent the unity of subject and world. But he conceives the subject as the organic unity formed by its cognitive faculties, and he defines the world in regard to the phenomenal order. Thus, on the Hegelian approach, Kant's discussion implies that the true vocation of reason is really to represent itself, not merely from an epistemological standpoint as a cognitive faculty, but rather from an ontological standpoint as something that underlies and gives determinacy to reality. Indeed, to the extent that the principal directive of reason is to represent itself as real, all epistemologically oriented, merely regulative employments of reason, such as those endorsed by Kant, are really only incomplete and limited uses, inadequate to the demands of speculation.

From this standpoint, Hegel's speculative philosophy may be characterized as a fully ontological determination of transcendental idealism that would promise to show more fidelity to Kant's conception of reason than Kant himself shows. Moreover, Hegel's *Phenomenology* may, then also, at least in part, be viewed as a corrective against Kant that works to represent the being of reason.

One of the most important foci of Hegel's rejoinder is his concept of experience. Hegel recognizes that for Kant, our cognitive powers enable us to conceive of, or think [*denken*] any number of things. But Kant believes that genuine knowledge—what we may genuinely know [*erkennen*] in the strict sense—is circumscribed by and therefore limited to the domain of things we can experience.[28] In the first *Critique*, this leads Kant to the conviction that the faculty of the intellect forms the seat of all our true knowledge, as its concepts result from the cooperation of its categories with sensible intuitions, the ineluctable source of experience. Kant concludes that by contrast, our highest synthetic faculty, reason, provides no actual knowledge at all, since its ideas bear no essential relation to intuition.

Yet Hegel, in direct contradistinction to Kant, maintains that the ideas of reason, even the highest, unconditioned ideas, *do* provide true knowledge—though, Hegel does not arrive at this view because he disregards Kant's association of knowledge with experience. On the contrary, Hegel actually concurs with Kant that all of our genuine knowledge must have a basis in experience. While it can be argued that both Hegel and Kant subscribe to versions of transcendental idealism, neither of them gainsays the importance of concrete life, and each believes that philosophical research is spurious and empty unless it maintains a firm foundation in aesthesis. Instead, Hegel develops his belief in the consanguinity of reason and knowledge based on his rejection of Kant's claim that rational ideas bear no intrinsic relation to sensible intuition. Hegel believes that the domain of experience entails much more than Kant had thought, and one of Hegel's most important labors in the *Phenomenology* is to elaborate on the conditions that allow us to achieve genuine knowledge of reason through experience, and, ultimately, absolute knowledge of the unconditioned, universal synthesis of subject and world, reason and reality.

The purpose of speculative philosophy is to achieve absolute knowledge, but since in its highest form, this knowledge takes shape as an unconditioned idea of the being of our power of reason, absolute knowledge may be understood as a certain form of self-knowledge. In the speculative sense, however, self-knowledge requires us to see ourselves not simply from an epistemological standpoint as rational subjects defined by their cognitive powers, but rather to discover through experience that we ourselves, at least insofar as we participate in reason, form the constitutive basis of reality.[29] On Hegel's thematic view, speculative philosophy culminates in the form of absolute self-knowledge that not only fulfills the promise of reason, but thereby offers a corrective against the Kantian belief in a peculiar fate of reason that would leave us unable to find our place in the world.

Scholars have commented that the explosion of interest in tragedy after Kant unfolds in no small part as a response to his characterization of human reason, as a power guided by aspirations it cannot realize, and we may wonder if the peculiar fate of reason leads less to embarrassment, as he says, than to humility.[30] But if this is the case, then Hegel's thematic vision of absolute knowledge can be seen as a triumphant conception of reason that counters the Kantian, tragic view, and that places experience in the crux of their difference from one another. Can absolute self-knowledge be won through experience? Do we really come to know reason in the course of our concrete affairs, and, if so, does reason really overcome its peculiar fate through experience? Does reason ever encounter its own limits in experience? Although in the end Hegel contends that our power of reason fulfills its purpose to attain speculative self-knowledge though experience, he does not think that this happens all at once, nor does he think that it is easy. On the contrary, the attainment of absolute knowledge is contingent on education in the experience of spirit that incorporates the speculative whole of history. Hegel calls this educational itinerary "a long path," and, though it results in the absolute, the way is punctuated at each step by difficulty and confusion.[31] Even if Hegel believes his view of absolute knowledge forms a sort of corrective against the Kantian view of reason's peculiar destiny, Hegel nevertheless appears, at least, to think that the course of experience itself has something peculiarly tragic about it.

The Long Path of Experience

Hegel's *Phenomenology* presents absolute knowledge as it emerges through experience in the course of the history of spirit. Insofar as the attainment of absolute knowledge turns on the unity of the rational subject and reality, the absolute can be understood as a form of self-knowledge, and the lessons we learn from experience thus teach us primarily to understand ourselves. Hegel's conception of the course of experience may be characterized as a process by which the rational subject becomes aware of itself more and more fully as the constitutive basis of the world. Hegel's view of this process is complicated and intricate enough that in our efforts to understand him, we should be wary of oversimplification. However, in his 'Preface' he associates his view with a classical notion of purposive activity, and at one point compares the expansion of our philosophical awareness, and our understanding of truth, with the process of natural growth.[32] But although Hegel calls the path of experience the "royal road of science [*Wissenschaft*]" because it results in the majesty of absolute knowledge, he also believes that it must "be seen as the way of doubt, or, more to the point, despair."[33] For absolute knowledge results not in an infinite increase in the positive content of our comprehension of things, but instead in an expansion of our awareness that results from our total divestiture of certainty in the legitimacy of our preconceived ideas, values, and customary practices.

Hegel structures his explanation of the emergence of absolute knowledge through experience in a narrative about the education of conscious beings, and thus Hegel's approach requires us to consider at least the broader strokes of his conception of consciousness itself. In general terms, Hegel's interpretation may be seen as an intentional theory of consciousness, and one that is distinguished by his insistence that the cognitive subject forms a synthetic unity with its world. Hegel's conception of conscious life differs in a number of respects from many of those found in the mainstreams of the philosophy of mind today, though, of course, this is not to say that his approach has nothing to say to scholars in the field. On the contrary, Hegel's overall view of consciousness may be seen to offer a critical perspective on what Daniel Dennett has referred to as the "the orthodox choice today in the English-speaking world,"[34] broadly, those interpretations of consciousness that seek a description of mental life in physical terms. Hegel's view could also be seen as a fecund resource for scholars who, led by figures such as Thomas Nagel and John Searle, "have in different ways insisted upon the irreducibility of the subjective point of view and the intrinsic or original intentionality of consciousness."[35] But for purposes of the present study, it might not make sense to develop the relation between Hegel's view and those in the philosophy of mind at length.

Still, if the concerns that guide recent Anglo-American approaches to mind remain somewhat foreign to Hegel's approach, important discourses in continental heritages of thought illuminate his view. For example, important aspects of Husserlian phenomenology resonate with, and thus help to shed light on, Hegel's view. Certainly, differences between Husserl and Hegel, both in sensibility and in substance, abound, not least of which is their divergent views of the relationship between the philosophical enterprise and phenomenological research.[36] For whereas Husserl identifies phenomenology as the foundational philosophical science (*Wissenschaft*), the Hegel of the *Phenomenology* maintains that philosophical science involves two parts—not only phenomenology, the science of experience, but moreover the science of logic, for which phenomenology prepares us.[37] But both Husserl and Hegel envision phenomenology principally as the scientific study of consciousness as an exclusive province of what appears to us as given. Moreover, both figures, if in somewhat different idioms, identify consciousness as a purposive, organic locus of intentional activity, which, in Hegel, unfolds "simultaneously in the diremption and correlation of knowing and being, of the for-itself and the in-itself."[38] As Hegel states it in the 'Preface' to the *Phenomenology*, consciousness, in its characteristic intentional activity "*differentiates* something from itself, to which it at the same time relates itself; or, as this is expressed: consciousness is for this something; and the determinate side of this *relation*, or of *being* for a consciousness, is *knowledge*."[39] For Husserl and Hegel, consciousness should not be cast reductively as a substantial, static entity, a 'thinking thing' (*res cogitans*), but must instead be grasped as a dynamic complex of activities.

Yet, despite their similar notions of consciousness, a venerable heritage of post-Husserlian continental philosophy, which includes figures as diverse as Heidegger and Derrida, and a number of current scholars associated with them, points to a criticism of Husserl's conception of phenomenological research that emphasizes an instructive difference between Husserl and Hegel.[40] Though criticisms of this type unfold along a number of lines, one of the most general worries turns on Husserl's view that phenomenological research is predicated on the achievement of the phenomenological step back, the *epoché*. The concern, we might assert, is that Husserl's notion of the epoché uncritically presupposes the possibility of a theoretical attitude that abstains from all involvement with and engagement in the world. From this standpoint, critics often charge that Husserl's notion of phenomenological method retains a residual trace of Cartesianism, not, of course, because Husserl engages in the methodological doubt of the existence of the external world, but, rather, because the epoché, perhaps not unlike Descartes' methodological doubt, appears to rest on the assumption of a disengaged, even disembodied, cognitive subject. As Donn Welton argues, for continental philosophers critical of the purported Cartesian deposit in Husserlian phenomenology such as John Caputo, Husserl's approach to phenomenological description here fails to put enough weight on the hermeneutic elements that inform our conscious life.[41] From such a standpoint, Welton cites Caputo, we may worry that Husserl even "asks us to believe in two selves: one situated in the world and the other, its transcendental double."[42]

Criticisms of this sort sometimes are pressed into the service of scholarly research on figures, such as Heidegger and Derrida, and are used to separate their views from what are cast as (Cartesian) assumptions informing Husserl's approach. Yet, some commentators recognize that it is possible to differentiate Hegel, too, from the alleged difficulties in Husserl.[43] For, we might assert, not entirely unlike figures such as Heidegger and Derrida, Hegel, too, maintains that phenomenological research remains deeply interested in and involved with the world. It is true that like Husserl's phenomenologist, Hegel associates his 'we,' that is, those philosophers, or, perhaps again, those phenomenological observers, who have already achieved the standpoint of absolute knowing, with a reflective stance toward the experiences of consciousness.[44] But in contrast with Husserl, Hegel conceives of our reflection on our experience not as a disengaged and detached investigation, but, rather, as the very culmination of our experience itself, and, indeed, a form of reflection that is directed by our desire for self-knowledge, which, thus, is characterized not by *disinterest*, but, rather, by *interest in the most intense and robust sense*.[45] Moreover, Hegel maintains that his philosophical 'we' achieves its reflective stance by means not of a methodological invocation of an *epoché*, but, quite to the contrary, of its observation of consciousness' dialectical struggles in the course of its concernful participation in the world through experience.

Recent scholarship on Husserl has challenged many of the assumptions held by his critics in continental heritages of philosophy, and some commentators argue that Husserl offers a much more robust picture of the interplay of phenomenological research and our involvement in the world.[46] Indeed, one commentator suggests that Husserl's thought includes a "generative phenomenology" that provides an account of the interplay of the phenomenologist and history, culture, and other complex aspects of the world that rivals, if not exceeds, Hegel's phenomenology of spirit in richness.[47]

But for Hegel, the interrelationship between the phenomenological observer's standpoint of absolute knowledge and our involvement in the world is predicated on the long path of experience, which he characterizes as the developmental process that leads consciousness to gain an ever-deeper awareness of the intrinsic unity of the rational subject and the material world. Hegel is able to claim that for conscious beings, at least, this unity is essential and in principle always obtained, as the consciousness of the rational subject grants being to the world and its objects in the first place. But Hegel also believes that from the standpoint of naïve consciousness, at least, we fail to see this unity and fall into the common sense, but false, belief that the being of things is independent of us, insofar as we exhibit the tendency to disregard or forget the essential role of our own conscious activity in the constitution of the world and its objects.[48] We attain absolute knowledge of the genuine unity of subject and world as the result of a course of experience that increases the sophistication of our awareness and, finally, that overcomes the deceptive clarity of our naïve, commonsense beliefs. Absolute knowledge turns on the insight that we ourselves, as rational conscious beings, ensure our unity with reality, and this knowledge results from an itinerary of experiences that lead us to self-discovery through a certain abnegation of the self's commonsense commitments.

But if absolute knowledge—the triumphant awareness of the unity of subject and world, of reason and reality—is the destination of the long path of experience, why is it also a path of doubt and despair? The primary answer turns on Hegel's view that in experience, we only progress to more sophisticated, highly differentiated forms (*Gestalten*) of consciousness on the basis of—indeed, in a sort of speculative exchange for—difficult confrontations with phenomena that force us to lose faith in and, thus, to sacrifice the forms of awareness that have hitherto guided our conscious lives. Hegel elaborates on the attainment of higher forms of consciousness through self-sacrifice in his claim that each of our experiences occurs as a movement in consciousness from 'certainty' to 'truth.'

Hegel maintains that even though our consciousness is malleable and dynamic, it always appears at each stage of its development in a definite form, and in each case, this form is granted to it by its specific composite of intentional structures. For every form of consciousness, it is this composite that dictates the possibilities and limits of consciousness' powers to constitute its objects, and, by the same token, to determine the character of their being. Hegel's developmental model of conscious life suggests, for example, that at one of its more rudimentary levels, our consciousness is formed by an unsophisticated nexus of intentional structures that allow it only to constitute objects as mere perceptual objects, or things. This form of consciousness might be said, in a somewhat Husserlian idiom, to lack the sophisticated network of noetic structures that it would need in order to constitute more complex objects; and it is thus powerless properly to understand the phenomena that consciousness becomes able to cognize later in its development, such as desire, other human beings, rationality, ethical life, culture, religion, and absolute knowing. But such a rudimentary form of consciousness nevertheless becomes complacent in the certainty that its composite of intentional structures is adequate and that all of its objects really are nothing more than mere things. Hegel maintains that all forms of consciousness tend to fall into this certainty insofar as their intentional activity is not self-consciously directed back on themselves, but is rather directed outwardly. We become certain of the form that our constitution of objects takes, but really only because we tend to forget that it is nothing other than our own conscious activity that gives the world we are in its profile.

But on Hegel's view, our consciousness is led to transform and expand itself through a course of experiences. Experience wrests us from our complacent certainty in the independent being of the objects we encounter, and experience not only reminds us of our essential role in the determination of reality, but also compels us to acquiesce to the truth that our consciousness' intentional structures are simply inadequate to the objects they seek to constitute. In the *Phenomenology*, Hegel identifies each experience as an "*investigation*" and a "*test*" in which a form of consciousness is confronted by the overly complex and intense phenomena that are too robust and rich for its composite of intentional structures and thus overwhelm its powers of cognition.[49] The excessiveness of such phenomena constitutes a shock for consciousness that not only rouses us from our naïve belief in the independent being of the world, but also forces us to reflect on the fact that we ourselves, as conscious beings, form the final ontological condition of reality. Moreover, this reflection reveals, in turn, that the phenomena have outmatched consciousness' powers because of insufficiencies and limitations that had been latent in its own composite of intentional structures. For Hegel, experience unfolds as a test that reveals a disjunction between our cognitive powers and the phenomena we encounter. The exposure of this disjunction leads to the supercession (*Aufhebung*) of the form our consciousness has taken up until now, and establishes a new form endowed with cognitive powers that can accommodate the phenomena that had previously overwhelmed it.[50] In the end, this process leads to the highest form of consciousness, absolute knowledge, and the unrestricted awareness of the synthetic unity of the rational subject and reality.

Hegel believes that the path of experience is punctuated by doubt and despair because, even though all experiences lead to an expansion of our consciousness, this expansion is contingent on our recognition of the limits of our power to understand ourselves, our world, and its objects. Speculative self-knowledge forms the end result of the long path of experience, but at each juncture of this path our progress is measured not by an increase in the things we know, but rather by an expansion of our awareness that results from a recognition of truth and the relinquishment of our certainty in the independent being of the world and its objects. This abdication of our certainty is a form of doubt because it requires us to deny our naïve, commonsense belief in reality. But for Hegel, our doubt in the independent being of reality is identified more properly as a form of despair, for our doubt is not merely epistemological or methodological in nature. In his 'Introduction' to the *Phenomenology*, Hegel rejects all Cartesian-style methodological doubt on the grounds that it reduces the problem of doubt to a mere abstraction and conceals its true import.[51]

In actual experience, by contrast, our doubt in the independent being of reality genuinely matters to us, for it emerges in the course of our very real efforts to comprehend ourselves, our world, and its phenomena. This doubt is thus also a form of despair because in experience our renunciation of certainty requires us not simply to concede that our knowledge is limited, in the sense that there are gaps in its positive content, but, rather, finite. In the strict, Hegelian sense, experience is always much more than the mere encounter with phenomena that remain within the grasp of our cognitive powers, even if they are phenomena that are unfamiliar to us. From this standpoint, our consciousness is not forced to undergo a true experience so long as the phenomena we encounter fall into some class of things that our consciousness' composite of intentional structures is already able to constitute. Instead, Hegelian experience emerges in our encounters with phenomena that actually overwhelm our intentional structures. Hegel thinks that this leads us to doubt in the independent being of reality, as it throws us back on ourselves and compels us to see that it has been consciousness itself, and not the external world, that forms the ultimate condition of our knowledge. But experience also leads us to despair of ourselves, for we must also come to terms with the fact that the form our consciousness has taken up until now is sorely inadequate, and that its constitution of objects has been dependent on intentional structures imbued with forms of negativity to which we have been blind.

The Tragedy of Experience

How are we to understand this finitude of our knowledge more fully? What is this doubt and despair? Hegel believes even though absolute knowledge is the destination of the long path of experience, the path itself nevertheless forms an inalienable and integral aspect of the human condition that forces us time and again to doubt our certainty in things. Hegel associates doubt with despair to remind us that our abdication of certainty in the independent being of reality is much more than a merely methodological exercise, but also to underscore that in experience, we are forced to recognize that our powers of cognition are imbued with negativity we ourselves had not seen. But what does this mean? What does our consciousness of doubt and despair tell us about ourselves and our lives, insofar as we are concerned, conscious beings who undergo experience? While, as I mentioned earlier, Hegel offers a number of general images allied with tragedy to characterize experience, he also elucidates the doubt and despair that result from experience by means of the more determinate idea of reversal.

Hegel's use of this notion suggests that in experience the collapse of our certainty forms a kind of crisis in the life of spirit that exposes the instability and precariousness of human affairs.

In the larger scheme of Hegel's presentation of spirit in the *Phenomenology*, his discussions of tragedy become ever-more extensive and intricate as spirit reaches later and later stages of its development. This may be at least in part because Hegel thinks that as our conscious awareness of ourselves, our world, and our past expands, we become more and more explicitly present to the tragic dimension of our affairs. However, in his general elaboration of experience in the 'Introduction' to his larger presentation of spirit, Hegel's use of the notion of tragic reversal is quite dense and extremely brief. He claims that in experience, the emergence of higher forms of consciousness is predicated on a transition in consciousness to doubt and despair from certainty, and that this movement is caused not by an external force, but "through *the reversal of consciousness itself.*"[52] Despite its brevity, Hegel's claim here is decisive, and he returns to the notion of reversal a number of times over the course of his presentation of spirit, perhaps most famously in his discussion of mastery and servitude. But to unpack Hegel's conception of reversal, it may help to see it in the light of its relation to Aristotle's treatment of a similar notion in the *Poetics*.

Now, the relationship between Hegel's discussion here and the *Poetics* has different stakes than the relation between his *Lectures on Aesthetics* and Aristotle's text. In the *Aesthetics*, Hegel's official view of the *Poetics* is that his own speculative aesthetics supercedes all other historical theories of art, to include the *Poetics*, though Hegel admits that the *Poetics* "is still of interest now," and, indeed, important aspects of the structure of Hegel's account of the genre of ancient drama appear to be borrowed from Aristotle's analysis.[53] But even so, in the *Aesthetics* Hegel's uses of the *Poetics* are in the service of his efforts to understand issues that surround the work of art. By contrast, at this juncture of the *Phenomenology*, Hegel may be seen as using the (Aristotelian) notion of reversal as a deep ontological and epistemic structure of conscious life, and thereby introduces an interest in tragedy that extends beyond the confines of those typically found in traditional forms of the discipline of aesthetics. From this angle, it would be possible to claim that the deepest meanings of Aristotle's *Poetics* might have remained unnoticed by its author, insofar as he failed to approach tragic drama as an exemplification of crucial facets of human being and knowing. But properly grasped, the Aristotelian analytic of the elements of tragic poetry is nonetheless valuable, as it provides, if in a transmogrified form, decisive aspects of conscious life itself.

But even if Hegel's larger interest in the *Poetics* here diverges from that of his *Aesthetics*, and, indeed, even contravenes Aristotle's original intention, Hegel's use still closely follows some of the basic terms of Aristotle's analysis. As Hegel recognizes in the *Aesthetics*, the purpose of Aristotle's *Poetics* is to inquire into poetic practice, focusing on the epic, tragic, and comic genre of poetry (though, as we know, Aristotle's treatment of comedy is among the casualties of history, if it indeed existed in the first place). Aristotle defines tragedy as a form of representation focused on *praxis* "that is serious and also, as having magnitude, complete in itself."[54] He goes on to maintain that the special perfection of this genre of art is its ability to produce a peculiar form of pleasure in its audience, catharsis, through the production of two other, painful emotions: fear and pity. We will encounter these Aristotelian concepts once again later in our work on Hegel in this book. But for now we turn our attention to Aristotle's subsequent discussion of what he understands to be the essential elements of any work of tragic art capable of achieving these effects—six basic parts—"plot, characters, diction, thought, spectacle, and melody."[55] Aristotle raises the issue of reversal in his treatment of that element of tragedy that he takes to be more important of these, the "incidents of the story," or "plot."[56] For Aristotle, the plot of a tragic drama consists of the sequence of events by which the action of the drama unfolds. On his view, the crucial feature of a tragic plot is that it contains "reversals;" in turn, Aristotle defines the reversal as "a change . . . from one state of things . . . into its opposite."[57] In tragic drama, the reversal is the crucial moment in the plot in which the fortunes of the protagonist are transformed.

Hegel's more thematic, modern, and triumphant vision of the human spirit is to a large extent sustained by his claim that absolute knowledge forms the positive outcome of the long path of experience. Yet, Hegel, nevertheless, suggests a tragic view of life, at least for naïve consciousness, in his association of experience with his speculative appropriation of this Aristotelian notion of reversal. As Dennis Schmidt asserts, Aristotelian reversals "disclose a situation that is rent by contradictions and ambiguities that easily—and without warning—convert into their opposite. They thus expose the fragility, the vulnerability of human affairs."[58] Hegel's reliance on Aristotle's notion suggests that Hegel, too, believes our lives to be bound up with forms of ambiguity and uncertainty that indicate the precariousness of our condition. But on Hegel's speculative appropriation of the notion of reversal, we do not learn the lesson that human beings are susceptible to unpredictable and sudden changes in fortune from the relative safety of the theater and the imaginary world of a dramatic performance.

Instead, Hegel believes we encounter this vulnerability as a fundamental dynamic that results from our concrete efforts to understand ourselves and our world. Prior to the attainment of absolute knowledge, the long path of experience is a volatile and perilous one, and Hegel's association of each of naïve consciousness' experiences with Aristotelian reversal suggests a form of life that, in our very efforts to understand ourselves, necessarily leads to difficulty, failure, pain, and suffering.

Hegel ultimately associates the attainment of absolute knowledge with the figure of the philosopher, or, perhaps better, with the final philosopher that completes philosophy and thus brings it to an end. But, perhaps, the figure that best represents the forms our consciousness takes prior to our attainment of absolute knowledge, while we remain as it were only part way along the path of experience, is not the triumphant, even heroic philosopher, but, instead, the tragic hero. In contrast with the Hegelian figure of the final philosopher, this tragic hero of experience enjoys no complete speculative self-knowledge, but is instead subject time and again to encounters with phenomena that overthrow her sense of self and of the world, and reveal the finitude of her cognitive powers. If Hegel believes that it is ultimately our destiny to attain absolute knowledge and thus overcome what Kant called the peculiar fate of human reason, then Hegel nevertheless acknowledges that for naïve consciousness, at least, our cognitive powers are destined repeatedly to encounter their own failure to grasp things. We are almost tempted to say that the long path of experience is one traversed by a kind of tragic consciousness, and that each of its experiences unfolds as a new drama with its culmination in yet another reversal. Hegel's presentation of spirit as it unfolds in experience is, whatever else it is, a presentation of spirit's tragedies.

In the *Phenomenology*, Hegel identifies properly speculative self-knowledge with the attainment of the absolute at the end of the long path of experience. Yet, we might nevertheless conclude that there is another, albeit quite different, tragic sense of self-knowledge exhibited in naïve consciousness in the aftermath of each of its experiences. To be sure, this is not the speculative self-knowledge of the final philosopher that knows herself to be the culmination of history and the constitutive basis of reality. Instead, it is perhaps the insight of one who, for a moment at least, recognizes her inadequacies and limitations. Prior to the completion of our speculative education, the form of self-knowledge yielded by experience is not so much triumphant and modern, as it is Delphic and ancient, and it teaches us not of our infinite powers of comprehension, but rather of a certain humility that results when we see our former certainty in things for a form of false pride. It is hardly a great leap to entertain the question, what conception of experience would emerge if Hegel's insistence on the absolute could somehow be disentangled from his claims about experience? What would the Hegelian discourse on experience look like, stripped of its absolutist pretenses, leaving its tragic aspects in tact?

Yet, of course, Hegel *does* maintain that the human spirit ultimately attains absolute knowledge, and so the question that confronts us most immediately is, what place does he ascribe to this more tragic form of self-knowledge in his larger view? Hegel maintains that absolute knowledge forms the final 'station' on the long path of experience, and he thereby appears to imply that the attainment of the absolute thus means the cessation of further new encounters with the tragic dynamics of our affairs.[59] But Hegel does not believe that in our achievement of absolute knowledge we simply forget about or ignore the tragic aspect of experience. On the contrary, Hegel maintains that absolute knowledge, as a fully speculative form of self-knowledge, focuses not simply on the knowledge of our consciousness as it appears in its final form, but, moreover, contains within it the memory of consciousness' development over the course of its long path of experience,[60] as well as, we might add, the tragic dynamics that underpin this path. Even on his more triumphant, modern vision of speculative self-knowledge, Hegel acknowledges that the tragic aspect of human affairs forms an integral part of what and who we are. For Hegel, the attainment of unrestricted self-knowledge is only genuinely unrestricted to the extent that it entails an awareness of the long path of experience and its many tragic reversals.

In this light, if we are to achieve a more comprehensive and robust conception of the tragic aspect of our lives, then it is necessary to turn to Hegel's presentation of the long path of experience itself, and to focus on the multiple forms that the tragic dynamics of human affairs take for specific forms of consciousness. So far, our consideration of Hegel has been guided by his reliance on tragedy to illuminate the broadest structural dynamics of experience. But in order to comprehend the full scope of Hegel's association of experience and tragedy in the *Phenomenology*, we must see how the tragic dynamics of experience appear concretely for naïve consciousness in the actual course of its development. Of course, Hegel would insist that this task requires us to focus on every moment in his presentation, given that for naïve consciousness, every experience unfolds as a kind of tragic reversal. While this is certainly true, it is also true that Hegel believes the tragic aspect of our affairs to be more pronounced and tenacious at some junctures on the long path of experience than at others. So if our project is to develop a fuller account of Hegel's vision of the tragic aspect of our condition, then these especially tragic experiences are a natural place to start.

2

The Tragedy of Freedom

Hegel's more thematic, modern vision leads him to the conviction that spirit is destined to arrive at a speculative form of self-knowledge in the culmination of its long (and decidedly tragic) path of experience. However, Hegel is a tenaciously synthetic philosopher, and he believes that the accomplishment of this sovereign form of self-knowing through experience is ineluctably bound up with the development of our consciousness of practical concerns, and, above all, our awareness of ourselves as free beings. Hegel contributes to his explanation of the intricacies of the ties between our interests in self-knowledge and in freedom at a number of junctures in the *Phenomenology*, and his approach compels him to range over multiple and different determinations of freedom in the course of his presentation. He considers, for example, not only the speculative sense of sovereignty that informs absolute knowing, but, also, the appearance of universal freedom in the enlightenment, and the horrendous consequences of its 'absolute' form, found in the Reign of Terror, as well as the dialectical unfolding of other, more rudimentary and self-effacing expressions of freedom, such as those found in stoicism, skepticism, and the unhappy consciousness.[1] But Hegel offers some of his deepest insights into the character and relation of our interests in self-knowledge and practical concerns in his elucidation of the central themes of his initial discussion of self-consciousness in chapter 4: independence (*Selbstständigkeit*), recognition, and the relation of mastery and servitude.

Hegel's approach to these issues comprise one of the richest aspects of his thought as a whole, and it has, to say the very least, given rise to much productive and highly original scholarship in diverse fields.[2] Some relatively recent trends in Hegel studies, perhaps especially those influenced by Robert Pippen's groundbreaking research, have focused on the theoretical concerns that inform Hegel's account of self-consciousness. This direction of research has already begun to result in new insights into the epistemological and hermeneutical implications of Hegel's account, and to show that Hegel understands his doctrine of self-consciousness to address difficulties he sees in Kant's deduction of the unity of apperception.[3] But, there are other important discourses on Hegel, perhaps especially those in continental heritages of thought, that underscore the practical dimensions of his account, and serve to break open original questions about and meanings of freedom by means of critical approaches that break apart the presumptions of modernity that animate his discussion. From this standpoint, it might be said, the project of discerning post-modern possibilities for freedom itself elicits a return to the bequest of modernity, and, perhaps in particular, to the summits it reached in Hegel, in order to interrogate the fundamental assumptions that our age is called to scrutinize, and, thereby, to release current thought for new prospects and insights.[4]

For scholars who take such a tact, Hegel's thematic account of the independence of self-consciousness in chapter 4 of the *Phenomenology* certainly might be seen to offer a host of claims that demand careful, critical examination. Although Hegel's speculative approach compels him to consider not only the character of independence in general, but also the conditions under which it could emerge in intersubjective, historical life, his overall discussion of the independence of self-consciousness appears, at least, to comprise a paradigmatically modern, triumphant narrative of our potential to achieve self-sufficiency, and even ultimately to overcome subjugation in practical relations. Of course, it would be not only orthodox Hegelians who might embrace this picture. Although scholars interested in the Marxian implications of Hegel's account might wish to maintain critical distance from many tenets of Hegelian philosophy, important aspects of Hegel's discussion of the independence of self-consciousness anticipate a number of Marxian themes. We shall have to develop Hegel's claims here, as well as some of its Marxist overtones, at greater length, but the well-known centerpiece of his view will be the conviction that the human spirit's struggle to achieve independence begins in a 'reversal' in the relation of mastery and servitude. Hegel's basic idea is that while self-conscious life is destined to become independent, the fulfillment of this destiny hinges on a decisive transformation, a turnaround of terms, in what he believes to be the most oppressive, one-sided, and originary self-conscious relation, namely, of mastery and servitude, by which the life of mastery reveals itself to be unfree, and the life of servitude proves to contain within it the seeds of independence.

It is possible to question the extent to which Hegel's conception of this reversal may be counted as a tragedy of spirit, given that it appears to speak more to our potential for independence than to our limits. In chapter 1 we saw that for Hegel the long path of experience is punctuated at each step by consciousness' tragic loss of certainty in favor of truth. Even if Hegel believes that each experience is in some sense tragic, the reversals in the fortunes of master and servant point to a triumphant result.

Yet in what follows, I wish to explore and examine original insights into the relationship between freedom and finitude that emerge from what I understand to be two important and distinct strands of continental Hegel studies that center on Hegel's silence, or, at least, his relative silence about certain tragic aspects of his reversal in mastery and servitude. In the first strand, the emphasis is on Hegel's relative silence about what might be called the tragic fate of the master, in which Hegel's triumphant narrative of the independence inaugurated in the reversal in the life of servitude is seen to point to an unspoken, tragic demise of the sovereign freedom of mastery, and, in turn, to the rise of repression, mediocrity, and docility. This more patrician perspective on Hegel forms an important subtext for much scholarship in twentieth-century France, and, in this chapter, I will focus my attention on the Jacques Derrida of the celebrated, early essay, "From Restricted to General Economy: Toward a Hegelianism without Reserve." Though important in numerous twentieth-century continental approaches to Hegel, this strand might nonetheless be named 'Nietzschean,' insofar as it finds some of its origins (if at times tacitly) in Nietzsche's conviction in texts such as the *Genealogy of Morals* that the highest potentials for human freedom lie not in the life of submissiveness and timidity, but, rather, in the self-assertive, aristocratic, and warrior-like life of the sovereign.[5]

In a second strand, which might be said to reach one of its flourishes in Gadamer's discussion of Hegel's dialectic of self-consciousness, the focus is not on Hegel's relative silence about a tragedy of mastery, but, rather, on the tragic aspects of servitude that, we might submit, the overall tenor of his narrative serve to downplay. Although of course Gadamer may be identified as a hermeneutical philosopher, his account draws on a number of phenomenological and existential themes, and, his account focuses especially on Hegel's insights into the relationship between our prospects for freedom and our encounters with the possibility of our own death. Hegel believes that in her bondage, the servant is actually beholden not to one, but two masters: the human master who has put her in chains, and the "absolute master," death, since human masters, he tells us, maintain their control over servants through intimidation and the constant threat of murder.[6] From this vantage point, it will turn out that the releasement of our potentials to undertake projects and appropriate the conditions of our existence—in Gadamer's idiom, the freedom of ability (*Können*)—is contingent on our experience of our own mortality and also of the ultimate futility of our endeavors.[7]

One of the things I wish to urge in this chapter is that important insights into the relationship between finitude and freedom emerge from both of these strands of approaches to Hegel's discussion of the independence of self-consciousness. However, although what I have referred to as a Nietzschean strand of approaches to Hegel has perhaps gained more currency in the larger streams of twentieth-century continental thought, I wish to conclude my discussion with a brief *cri de coeur* for the second. Whereas representatives of both strands will associate the finitude of freedom with the specter of death, it is perhaps above all in this second strand the scope and weight of the tragic implications of the relation between freedom and death make themselves felt. But, before it is possible to consider either of these post-Hegelian interpretive engagements with Hegel's discussion, it is first necessary to outline some of the central concepts that govern the more practical side of Hegel's thematic view of self-consciousness in Chapter 4 of the *Phenomenology*.

HEGEL'S TRIUMPHANT PATH TO INDEPENDENCE

In Hegel's thematic narrative, the hopes of the human spirit to attain freedom lie not in the hands of those with dominion and power, but, rather, with the humble servant and the education she receives through her perseverance and hard work. It is not difficult to see why there are deep resonances between philosophical movements indebted to Marx and to Hegel's view.[8] It has become a commonplace, both in the English- and French-speaking worlds, to treat the Hegelian conception of servitude as if it were simply a form of slavery; and Hegel's discussion of mastery and servitude is often simply referred to as his 'master and slave dialectic.' But, Hegel is a precise thinker who chooses his terms with great care, and for him the relation is between master (*Herr*) and servant (*Knecht*), not slave (*Sklave*).[9] In contrast both with the views of philosophers such as Nietzsche and with many prejudices of Aristocratic Europe at the dawn of the nineteenth century, Hegel completely rejects the idea that the life of servitude forms a merely slavish existence. On the contrary, Hegel believes that all of spirit's highest achievements—indeed, *all* of its achievements—are ultimately born of the experience of servitude, and he believes it is the archetype of the servant, not the master, that embodies our highest nobility as humans and our greatest capacity to affirm life. Later in the chapter we shall see that the dignity of the servant is bound up not simply with the scope of her successes but also with the tragic aspect of her experience. However, in order to see Hegel's larger view, we must first consider the claim that the path to complete freedom originates in the reversal of the relation between lordship and bondage.

Independence and Recognition

In one of his most concise statements of his early view of communism, Marx writes in the *German Ideology* that "only in the community is . . . freedom possible. In community . . . individuals obtain their freedom in and through their association."[10] While the vast differences between Marx and Hegel surely outweigh their similarities, Hegel, too, believes that our aspirations for independence require us to enter into a larger social arena and form bonds with others that empower us and open up possibilities for free actions. Scholars unfamiliar with Hegel might be tempted to suppose that, because he identifies his speculative idealism as a philosophy of the subject, he must also associate independence with individualism, or even egoism. Yet, Hegel defines the subject not as an unsituated individual but, instead, as spirit. Due to this, Hegel's speculative thought may be seen as a philosophy of a sort of social subject, as well as a philosophy of the social conditions that determine the specific shape of each individual's particular consciousness, and a philosophy of the form of social relation that first grants to us our independence. Hegel believes that spirit attains a figure of conscious life that engenders independence only after Herculean labor and much experience, but, as Allen Wood argues, "the full actualization of spirit is possible only through the relation between selves that recognize each other."[11] Indeed, in the *Phenomenology*, Hegel contends that establishing relations of mutual recognition (*Anerkennung*) is the chief condition of our attainment of independence.

Hegel maintains that questions about the achievement of speculative self-knowledge cannot be separated from the issues of independence and recognition, and he addresses important aspects of the grounds of each in his discussion of the structure and the dynamics of self-consciousness. Hegel, first and foremost, identifies independence as the sense of self-certainty that guides us in our self-conscious relations with others. In the last chapter we saw that Hegel subscribes to a certain intentional theory of consciousness, and we saw that he believes that each form of consciousness is comprised by a composite of what Husserl would have called noetic and noematic structures. Hegel's conception of the self-certainty of self-consciousness can be fruitfully understood as what Peter Dews calls a "post-Cartesian theory of the self," wherein "selfhood, which means self-consciousness, consists in a relation in which the subject turns back on itself and grasps its own identity with itself, in which the object is the reflection of the subject, rather than something *other than* the subject."[12] Hegel argues that in contrast with self-consciousness, mere consciousness, or consciousness in its common-sense form, remains restricted, dependent and relative, as it erroneously clings to the naïve certainty that the external world, and not consciousness itself, is the ultimate basis of reality and our knowledge of it. By contrast, self-consciousness is a fully independent form of awareness, as in its reflection on itself, self-consciousness attains the certainty that consciousness itself forms the constitutive basis of what is.

Yet, Hegel believes that the independence we attain through the certainty of self-consciousness is contingent on a relation with objects in the world that negates our initial belief in their self-standing existence. Hegel rejects the idea that self-consciousness constitutes an immediate and simple form of awareness.[13] Instead, self-consciousness unfolds as a process that results in self-awareness only through the negation of its objects. He writes, "certain of the nothingness of this other, [self-consciousness] . . . takes this nothingness *for itself* as the truth of the other; it negates the independent object and thereby gives itself self-certainty, as *true* certainty as such, which has become so for it *in an objective way*."[14] Initially, self-conscious life involves a form of awareness that remains certain that its objects enjoy an independent existence, and thus self-consciousness retains within it the operations of naïve or mere consciousness. Yet, self-consciousness exceeds the dynamics of this more rudimentary form, and proceeds as a negation of this initial certainty that works to prove that consciousness' own intentional structures (and not the external world) form the ultimate epistemic and ontological condition of its objects.

But, self-conscious negation is not simply an abstract, theoretical exercise; instead, it forms a thoroughly practical, concrete activity of the situated, embodied agent. In order to attain self-certainty through the negation of our belief in the reality of external objects, it is not enough simply to entertain skeptical doubts about the ontological status of the world. Although such an endeavor might challenge our naïve certainty in things, it does not prove that our consciousness is itself independent. Rather, self-consciousness achieves certainty of itself only if it enters into practical relations with things in the world and accomplishes acts of negation that nullify the existence of its objects, thus proving its objects to be dependent on it. Hegel identifies the self-conscious processes of negation with the dynamics of desire, and he even claims that self-consciousness "is *desire* in general."[15] This is not to say that only self-consciousness is certain of the transience of things, nor to suggest that self-conscious beings are the only ones to express this certainty as desire. On the contrary,

> Even the animals are not shut out from this wisdom, but, on the contrary, show themselves to be most profoundly initiated into it; for they do not just stand idly in front of sensuous things as if these possessed intrinsic being, but, despairing of their reality, and completely assured of their nothingness, they fall to without ceremony and eat them up.[16]

While the independence of self-conscious beings requires that we attain self-certainty through the negation of objects we encounter in the world, both self-conscious beings and animals alike convey this process in their acts of desire.

However, on Hegel's view, experience teaches us that we win true self-certainty only in our desire to be recognized by another self-conscious being, not in our merely natural, immediate impulses. In Hegel's larger presentation of spirit, self-consciousness in its proper form first develops from out of a lower figure of awareness, a kind of proto-self-consciousness. As Kojève observes, this proto-self-consciousness can be compared to forms of animal life that are governed by more or less instinctual appetites, and, at this bestial level, self-certainty is sought primarily by means of basic drives, such as the appetite for consumption.[17] But, even though it initially appears as if true self-certainty might result from the indulgence of basic drives, the life of consumption actually turns out to be a dead-end that forces us to turn elsewhere for our satisfaction. The experience of eating something leads not to self-certainty, but rather confirms only the inscrutability of our objects of desire. In the process of ingestion, the object we eat is destroyed and the satisfaction we sought from our food is ephemeral, gone as soon as the meal is over. Ultimately, the pursuit of self-certainty through consumption turns into a relentless binge, until, as Judith Butler argues, quasi-self-consciousness "eats its way through the world" long enough to realize "that this mode of contending with difference is exceedingly tiresome."[18] Once quasi-self-consciousness reaches this point, it becomes clear that the appetitive life does not confirm our certainty of ourselves but, instead, simply reveals our chronic and ceaseless dependence on the presence of independent beings for us to eat. Such a discovery leads to the birth of self-consciousness in its proper form and to the insight that self-certainty must be sought elsewhere: in the satisfaction of our desire to be recognized by other self-conscious beings.

Recognition and Death

Why is it that self-consciousness proper achieves certainty of itself only in relationships of recognition with other self-conscious beings? Even if self-conscious life learns that the satisfaction of basic drives in consumption is fruitless, what is it about recognition from another self-conscious being that succeeds where a good meal fails? Hegel's answers to these questions turn on self-consciousness' unique talent for negation. "Due to the independence of the object" exposed in the life of consumption, Hegel argues, self-consciousness learns that "it can only achieve satisfaction insofar as [its] . . . object accomplishes a negation within itself."[19] Yet it is nothing other than self-consciousness that has the power of self-negation. To Hegel's mind, our deeply human capacity for negation allows us not only to pursue certainty of ourselves but moreover to recognize the self-certainty of another being through a certain act of self-abnegation. Relations of recognition exceed our connection to mere objects, for even though the binds that tie two self-conscious beings are their respective quests for self-certainty, each of them holds the key to the other's satisfaction.

Hegel maintains that self-conscious beings achieve self-certainty only if the relation of recognition is mutual. He writes that "action by one side would be useless because what is to happen can only be brought about by both."[20] Of course, Hegel's claim accords with our everyday experiences. It is much easier to recognize the people who recognize us—those who approach us as equals; and by the same token, it is all too easy not to recognize but rather *to resent* the people who deny us recognition—to wit, those who believe themselves to be our betters. "No man" after all, "is a hero to his valet."[21] Indeed, Hegel's larger commitments to the relation among independence, mutuality, and equality have led many scholars to compare Hegel's notion of recognition from the *Phenomenology* with his early concept of love from the Frankfurt period and assertions such as "true union, actual love, only appears among living beings equal in power."[22] The claim that self-certainty results only from *mutual* recognition is based on Hegel's conception of the structures and dynamics of self-consciousness. Thus, it is only in the reciprocal circulation of recognition between two self-conscious beings that self-certainty is assured. And further, in order to achieve independence through recognition, Hegel argues, it is necessary for both self-conscious beings to verify that their freedom is more important to them than their own lives.

If Hegel believes that the attainment of independence is possible only in relations of recognition, or love, then the achievement of this love, in turn, is contingent on a certain comportment toward death. As we have seen, both self-conscious beings' certainty of themselves as the ultimate condition of things is tied to the negation of material objects. But, in order for each of them to be recognized as the ultimate condition of the other's existence, each must put its own life on the line, and thereby risk the one object that conditions their relations to all other material things: the body, the seat of natural existence.

Hegel maintains that in its ideal or paradigmatic form, the achievement of recognition requires both self-conscious beings "to *prove* themselves and each other through a life and death struggle." Insofar as the relationship is mutual, both self-conscious beings must also "stake the life of the other, just as it stakes its own life, for the other counts no more to him than he to himself." In the mutual struggle for recognition, not only both self-conscious beings must gamble their own lives, but each must also pose the threat for the other that first makes the wager possible. Mutual recognition demands not only that we choose freedom over life but that we attempt (offer?) to kill the other, so that she may choose freedom as well.[23]

As we see, the relation among independence, recognition, and death, even if, as some commentators believe, it may be associated with a specific historical paradigms or model, nonetheless has its basis in the structure and dynamics of self-consciousness itself.[24] In his classic study, Hyppolite explains, "the struggle for independence is a category of historical life, not a specific, dateable moment in human history, or rather prehistory. It is a condition of human experience. . . ."[25] But, as Hans-Georg Gadamer points out, even though Hegel's account concerns general structures of self-conscious life, he nonetheless thinks of these structures as underlying cultural, social, and interpersonal practices, and in particular, the practice of the duel.[26] Of course in our day the duel is an anachronism, and by the turn of the twentieth century, the ridiculousness and even senselessness of the practice had already become an important theme in literary works such as

Arthur Schnitzler's *Lieutenant Gustl*. Whether or not Hegel, too, might have thought the duel to be shameful, he also saw it as a powerful and instructive expression of the struggle for recognition. In the traditions and rites associated with the duel, it appears that the interest in recognition unfolds primarily as a demand for the restoration of honor or respect. Important here is that if the duelers are to earn the respect of the other, then each must enter the contest to prove that they would choose respect over life, and each must also ensure that the other's aspiration for respect is credible.[27] Even if Hegel's speculative presentation of the independence of self-consciousness turns out to be a story of recognition, respect, or even love, it is nonetheless also, and perhaps foremost, a tale of the inexorable threat of death, and one that stands at the origin of all of our self-conscious relations to other self-conscious beings.

Independence and Dependence

Hegel believes that the demands of speculative philosophy require him not simply to elaborate on his conception of independence and the conditions that lead to it in the abstract, but moreover to explain the processes of historical development that work to bring about these conditions. For Hegel, the formation of relations of mutual recognition is possible only for highly sophisticated forms of self-consciousness that emerge from an extensive range of experiences. Thus much of his overall discussion of independence focuses on the cultivation of spirit that prepares us to enter into relations of mutual recognition and to choose freedom over death in our struggles with other self-conscious beings. Indeed, the educational itinerary that would lead to independence through fully reciprocal and equal relations begins in what he characterizes as the most unequal form of recognition, the liaison of mastery and servitude. On Hegel's view, the long path to independence through the establishment of mutual recognition originates from the life of servitude, and the monumental struggle of the servant to reverse the terms of her relation with her lord, as well as her potential to overcome her dependency, to achieve self-sufficiency, and to merit recognition from others.

But how, specifically, does Hegel characterize the relationship of mastery and servitude? And what, precisely, is it about the life of servitude that inaugurates our struggle for independence?

Hegel's *Phenomenology* should not be confused with a work of anthropology, and his discussion of mastery and servitude should not be read as an account of the primitive ages of the world or of some sort of Hobbesian world, as nasty and brutish as it is short. But Hegel's position does suggest that the relation of mastery and servitude is the most basic human relation and that higher forms of political, social, and interpersonal interaction that appear in the course of the development of spirit contain, in sublated form, the legacy of the ties that bind these two figures together. He characterizes the relation of mastery and servitude as a bond between two self-conscious beings wherein the recognition flows not reciprocally in both directions but rather only in one direction, such that the master is recognized by the servant but does not respond in kind. Hegel motivates his conviction that spirit's quest for independence must begin in relations of mastery and servitude by means of a kind of argument from extremes. He writes that the attainment of independence through completely mutual recognition

> may only be observed as its process appears for self-consciousness. Initially it will present the side of the *inequality* of each, or, the exhibition of the middle in the extremes, which, as extremes, are opposed to one another, only the one as the recognized, only the other as the recognizing.[28]

If the relationship of recognition reaches its highest perfection in complete mutuality, then it finds its lower, extreme limit in complete one-sidedness. Thus, while our many political, social, and interpersonal relations may embrace myriad forms of recognition that fall out along a spectrum between these two poles, our aspirations for independence have their remotest origin in the relations from the bottom end of the scale.

Hegel maintains that relationships of mastery and servitude arise because one self-conscious being, the one who becomes servant, fails to prove herself in a life and death struggle. As we have seen, the establishment of mutual recognition requires two self-conscious beings to verify that their independence means more to them than life—paradigmatically, in a struggle to the death. But, in confrontations that lead to mastery and servitude the crucible teaches one of the self-conscious beings, at least, that her life is just as crucial to her as her freedom.[29] Mastery and servitude emerge as the resolution of the conflict in which the one figure's newfound preference for life drives her to save her skin, to quit the struggle, to relinquish her desire for recognition, and to acquiesce to her opponent's demands to be recognized. Kojève, who translates '*Knecht*' not as 'servant' but as 'slave,' writes,

> The vanquished has subordinated his *human* desire for *Recognition* to the *biological* desire to preserve his *life*: this is what determines and reveals— to him and to the victor—his inferiority.... Thus, the difference between

Master and Slave is *realized* in the existence of the victor and of the vanquished.[30]

For Hegel the one-sidedness of the relation between master and servant is cast in the initial moment of its formation. The master's status as the independent self-consciousness who lives for herself is established by her defeat of the other, and the servant's status as a subordinate is set in the moment she surrenders.[31]

Hegel believes that at first the relationship between lordship and servitude, the master achieves a rudimentary form of self-certainty. The master receives recognition from the servant in a relation of exchange that is mediated by what Hegel simply calls "the thing," or, what might somewhat anachronistically be referred to as the goods and services that the master receives from the servant[32]—"The servant sets the master's table."[33] At this stage in the development of spirit, self-consciousness has already learned from the experience of proto-self-consciousness that it achieves only ephemeral self-certainty through the immediate destruction of its objects. Thus in mastery and servitude, the master does not seek its self-certainty in the immediate destruction (murder) of the servant but, instead, uses the threat of murder to seek self-certainty in a mediated way, through the consumption of the goods and services provided to her by the servant. So it turns out that in the relation of mastery and servitude—not unlike in the relation of proto-self-consciousness to its objects—the pursuit of self-certainty is centered on consumption. But in mastery and servitude, the master achieves self-certainty through the recognition of the servant, and the master's consumption of goods and services provided to her by the servant simply consummates the servant's sacrifice of her labors for the sake of the master.

Hegel's approach to the structural dynamics of the complex relation of master and servant speaks to a number of issues. For example, one of the aims of Hegel's discussion of self-consciousness is to build on, and, in his view, alleviate problems in, Kant's deduction of the unity of apperception from the first *Critique*. On such a view, it may be argued that to Hegel's mind it is the constituent elements of the relation of mastery and servitude that actually yields the genuine conditions of self-consciousness, or the unity of apperception, and, thus, if we are to follow Kant, of consciousness as such.[34] Moreover, if Hegel holds that the structural dynamics of self-consciousness demand the formation of relationships of recognition (implicitly present already even the one-sided relation of master and servant), then one of the important implications of his view is that the ultimate conditions of our awareness are intersubjective, interpretive, and practical in nature.³⁵ From this standpoint, it becomes clear that the reliance of the master/servant relation on the mediation of the thing is a complex matter. For, insofar as the circulation of recognition requires the thing, it is not enough to conceive of a thing as an unsituated, bare entity. Rather, it must be conceived in the most robust terms as an intrinsically relational and symbolic phenomenon that is always already bound up in networks of power, desire, and meaning.

In the relationship of mastery and servitude, it is not that the master derives satisfaction from the items produced for her, as, for example, they satisfy her tastes, or, in the case of something to eat, because of, say, their vitamin content. Rather, the nutrition that the master draws from the consumption of things provided by the servant is principally emblematic in nature. The principle that guides the master's consumption of things provided by the servant is the desire for recognition and, in this light, consumption may be understood to take on the form of a sort of *Ersatz*-murder, a semantic stand-in. Here, the master achieves self-certainty not through an actual struggle that would lead to the murder of the other, but, rather, through the performance of an intersubjectively understood act which *signifies* the subordination of the servant. Indeed, initially at least, it appears certain that the implementation of meaningfulness becomes a powerful tool of oppression that enables the master to achieve enduring satisfaction, insofar the invocation of the symbolic allows for the master constantly to repeat, and thereby to sustain, its achievement of self-certainty.

Hegel believes that the political, social, economic, and interpersonal dimensions of the life of spirit reverberate with many more- or less-pronounced dynamics of mastery and servitude, and his approach suggests that elements of mastery and servitude may be seen to pervade even modern forms of spirit. It should come as no surprise that many scholars inspired by Marx find Hegel's thought to provide a powerful resource to explain and critique forms of oppression and estrangement in diverse aspects of modern, bourgeois life. Yet, Hegel's discussion of mastery and servitude not only presents a powerful explanation of the logic of subjugation but also offers important insights into the processes that lead to our liberation. In order to elaborate on our prospects to achieve freedom from out of a history of oppression and estrangement, Hegel turns once again to the notion of 'reversal.'³⁶ However, on the surface, at least, this reversal does not appear to form a tragedy, but rather a triumph of spirit. Hegel maintains that our struggle for independence originates in a reversal within the dynamics of mastery and servitude that leaves the master a dependent, and puts the servant on the path to freedom.

Hegel maintains that this reversal in the relation of the lord and her subordinate results from the parameters or patterns that emerge in the experience of their interaction, and he even claims that while at first the relation is dominated by the master's certainty of herself, it will turn out that "the *truth* of independent consciousness is . . . *servile consciousness.*"[37] For the lord's part, Hegel asserts, the reversal embedded in experience reveals that she is not a sovereign, but, rather, a dependent, and, indeed, ultimately a sort of slave to her more natural desires. It is not only that the master wins recognition from a mere dependent, but also that the structure of the master/servant relation requires the master to seek recognition in the consumption of things, a practice which, Hegel's account seems to indicate, leads to gluttonous habits.[38] Initially it appears certain that the master's position affords her not only with dominion but also with a certain freedom from the vicissitudes of nature and the problem of scarcity—insofar as the master secures goods and services from the servant. To the extent that the life of mastery is focused on the achievement of recognition, however, it turns out to focus almost entirely on the sheer enjoyment of the things that the servant provides, a life dominated not by *production* but rather entirely by *consumption*,[39] one, we might extrapolate, that unfolds as a decadent and relentless orgy of gratification that softens and weakens the master, diminishes her power to fend for herself no less than it augments, expands, and engrains her uncultivated, immediately natural appetites. Thus, despite the master's certainty of her freedom, over the course of time she becomes, in truth, a dependent on a dependent whose life is guided not by the desire for true independence and mutual recognition but, rather, by her insatiable and brutish craving for something *more* to eat.

Although it may be argued that certain elements of master-consciousness re-emerge later in Hegel's presentation of spirit, one of the principal lessons of the reversal in lordship and bondage is that mastery involves a pyrrhic logic, and thus forms something of a dead-end in the history of spirit.[40] But, it also reveals that the life of servitude prepares the way for our emancipation from the exigencies of nature and from multiple forms of subjugation. At the outset, it appears certain that the servant is not only completely dependent on the master for her life and thus has no command over her fate, but also that she finds herself in this position as she recoiled from the threat of death. In truth, the life of servitude provides us with lessons that prepare us to achieve self-sufficiency and thus also control over our destiny. Perhaps most visibly, the life of servitude prepares us to achieve freedom from our dependence on nature. Whereas the conditions of mastery unfold under the rubric of mindless enjoyment, the servant's life of labor turns on disciplined, or "*inhibited* desire," and the development of her craft or skill to form things.[41] Hegel maintains that in the course of our spiritual development, the lessons we learn through labor ultimately give us the power to understand and control nature and thus to provide for ourselves.

This achievement of self-sufficiency, in turn, prepares us to overcome relations of domination and thus to win certainty of ourselves through recognition. As we have seen, the attainment of mutual recognition requires two self-conscious beings to prove that their freedom means more to them than their lives. And servants find themselves in their condition because they favor life. Yet, once the servant is in bondage she must dedicate her life and labor to another, a form of mortification that accustoms her to renouncing the very life she originally sought to preserve. In the course of its development, spirit internalizes and deepens its capacity for renunciation until it has finally prepared itself for the ultimate sacrifice and is thus ready to attain true independence and to choose freedom over death.

In the world of spirit, our hopes to attain freedom lie in the life of sacrifice, service, and labor. Whereas Marx may be said to indicate that our long history of struggle for liberation unfolds in a series of revolutions that result from changes in the material basis of society, the mode of production, Hegel maintains that spirit's long path to freedom has its basis in the self-conscious demand for self-certainty through recognition. However, Hegel, in anticipation of Marx, maintains that the attainment of independence through recognition emerges from a decisive (we might even be tempted to say revolutionary) reversal in the condition of servitude, itself a life of production that leads to our emancipation from nature, subjugation, and estrangement.

The Tragedy of the Master

Hegel's discussion is oriented by his interest in independence, and this leads him to focus more on the life of servitude and its larger consequences for the life of spirit than on the fate of the master. But is there not, perhaps, something tragic about the reversal in the life of mastery? After all, Hegel maintains that the story of the master begins prior to the establishment of her relation to the servant, in the life and death struggle, and that it gets off to a rather magnificent start. The master first achieves her status because she chooses freedom over life, an act that requires valor and strength, extraordinary courage, even abandon, in the face of death. In order to achieve independence through recognition, self-consciousness must "show that it is tied to no particular *existence*, certainly not to the universal singularity of existence, that it is not tied to life."[42] Masters arise from the conflict as masters because they demonstrate their readiness to part with life, they invite risk, and demonstrate steadfast certainty of themselves amidst danger. Yet, once the relationship of mastery and servitude is put into place, the life of the master turns brutish, sloth-like, and soft. All former splendor and daring forgotten, the master's existence unfolds as one long binge of consumption, until, one day, she awakes to find herself dependent on her dependent. If the Hegelian reversal in lordship and bondage forms a victory of the servant over her own condition, does it signal a sort of tragic downfall for the master?

Some have wondered. If many scholars, and, perhaps among them those with more Marxian leanings, take inspiration from Hegel's discussion, then others, perhaps especially those indebted to a certain Nietzschean heritage, take issue. Of course, none of Nietzsche's works offer any thematic or sustained discussion of the Hegelian presentation of mastery and servitude. But, there is an important vein of continental Hegel studies that is deeply influenced by Nietzsche's view (in texts such as the *Genealogy of Morals*) that the highest potentials of human freedom arise in the noble ranks, in the powerful displays of the sovereign, in the active life of the warrior.[43] From this more Nietzschean standpoint, we might argue, the Hegelian figure that best represents our aspirations for freedom is not the submissive and timid servant but, instead, the figure in the life and death struggle that becomes master. From this vantage point the interpretation of Hegel's reversal in mastery and servitude would not unfold as an account of our liberation from oppression, but rather appears under the auspices of a Nietzschean 'slave revolt.' Cast in this light, the mollification and pacification that results from the master's life of consumption would signal the breakdown, decay, and ultimately the demise of genuine freedom, while the successes of the servant would suggest the birth of an epoch of slavish mediocrity pervaded by sickness, mortification, inhibition, repression, and docility.

Perhaps one of the most provocative and innovative heirs of the Nietzschean approach to Hegel's discussion of mastery and servitude is the young Derrida.[44] Of course, Derrida's project is not simply to reconstruct Hegel's intention, that is, his thematic view, of the independence of self-consciousness, but, rather, to enter into an interpretive engagement with Hegel's text that reads both with and against Hegel in order to release original perspectives from his text, which, as we shall see, provide new insights into the finitude of human freedom.[45]

Derrida is nothing if not an original thinker, and although there can be little question that his works on Hegel are imbued with a number of Nietzschean themes, Derrida's approach to the Hegelian discussion of mastery and servitude exceeds many of the confines of Nietzsche's project in the *Genealogy of Morals*. In the essay, "From Restricted to General Economy, A Hegelianism without Reserve," Derrida approaches Hegel indirectly by means of an interpretation of Georges Bataille's work on Hegel, and, as Heinz Kimmerle notes, Derrida construes his approach to Hegel's discussion of mastery and servitude as an effort to "correct Bataille's interpretation."[46] Even so, Derrida shares in both Bataille's Nietzschean intuitions about freedom and Bataille's misgiving that Nietzsche never completely grasped the Hegelian view of mastery and servitude. Derrida cites from Bataille's *L'experience intérieure*:

> Nietzsche knew of Hegel only in the usual vulgarization. The *Genealogy of Morals* is the singular proof of the state of general ignorance in which remained, and remains today, the dialectic of master and slave, whose lucidity is blinding. . . .[47]

Even though Derrida wishes to maintain a certain critical distance from Bataille, Derrida, like Bataille, not only approaches Hegel in a Zarathustrian idiom but also suspects that not even Nietzsche himself fully appreciated Hegel's master/servant relation.

Like many of his earlier writings, Derrida's "From Restricted to General Economy" is in part programmatic in nature, and one of his chief purposes in this piece is to elucidate crucial tenets of his own conception of interpretative practice, deconstruction.[48] In light of this, it is no surprise that Derrida focuses on implications of Bataille's reading that speak to the features of Hegel's account that concern signification and meaning. Derrida's interest is guided by the insight that in the Hegelian conception of spirit, it is self-consciousness' demand for self-certainty that first gives rise to intersubjective interpretation and understanding, and, in particular, to a certain form of signs.[49] For Hegel, relationships of recognition emerge because self-consciousness learned through experience that in order to achieve satisfaction, it must not only enter into relations with another self-conscious being, but also have the operations of recognition mediated by a 'third term.' In the case of mastery and servitude, the relationship is mediated by the things that the lord receives from her dependent. But, the employment of such a third term constitutes a certain birth of the symbolic in the life of spirit, given that the thing carries a spiritual import, which exceeds its material form. In the initial case, for example, the things provided to the master by the servant are not simply 'something to eat,' but, more importantly, they 'say,' something, namely, that the satisfaction of the interests and desires of the master form the purpose of the servant's existence.

Derrida's elucidation of his conception of deconstruction takes its cue from a distinction, which Bataille developed in his interpretation of Hegel between 'general economy' and 'restricted economy.' Derrida develops his approach based on what he sees as a slippage in Hegel's account between 'sovereignty,' on the one hand, and 'lordship,' or 'mastery,' on the other.[50] In Derrida's piece, the notion of 'sovereignty' refers to the condition of the figure that is ready to choose freedom over life in the struggle with another for recognition. By contrast, 'mastery' refers to this same figure, but once she suddenly finds herself to be a master bound up in a relation to the servant. To Derrida's mind, the life of sovereignty unfolds in Zarathustrian fashion, for the sovereign's radical openness, even abandon, in the face of her own death, constitutes an unrestricted form of affirmation that exceeds not only self-consciousness' demand for self-certainty, but also, and by the same token, the limits of sense as such.[51] Once the relationship of recognition is established in the aftermath of the struggle, however, the master becomes a dependent. For Derrida this is not simply because the master comes to rely on the servant for her bread (although this is true). More crucially, it is because in the transition to a relation of recognition, the master trades in her radical openness to the utter loss of life and sense for the certainty of self she gains through the recognition by the servant. Thereby, the master submits to the demand for self-certainty as a law to guide and restrict all forms of signification.[52]

Derrida discerns a trace of the more Nietzschean vision of aristocratic, warrior-like freedom in the text of the *Phenomenology* and recasts Bataille's insights into an excessive, free play of desire in semantic terms. Bataille, in regard to somewhat different concerns, considers the notion that society must from time to time break out in a supersaturated, open-ended, general economy of expenditure because life gives rise to desires that exceed more restricted economies of exchange.[53] Bataille believes that this general economy is exemplified in the cultural practice of many Native American peoples: the potlatch, ritual of superabundant, overflowing, even outlandish expenditure, or "the exchange of gifts, in which the givers try to outdo each other in the giving-away of their own wealth."[54] Derrida, for his part, envisions deconstructive practice itself as a sort of "potlatch of signs" guided by the radical freedom of the sovereign, her readiness to stake the absolute loss of life and sense, an expenditure without reserve, all for the sake of nothing but the risk itself, for free play, and the affirmative production of semantic displacements.[55] For Derrida, Hegel's most prescient insights into our prospects for freedom exceed his intention and thus have little to do with the Hegelian vision of an independent subject, liberated both from the condition of servitude and from nature. Instead, our greatest aspirations lie in sovereignty and in the unrestricted expenditure that puts the very possibility of the subject in play.

From the more Nietzschean standpoint that Derrida creatively appropriates, the reversal in mastery and servitude must be seen as both more and less than tragic, perhaps even quasi-tragic.[56] First and foremost, the transition from what Derrida calls the condition of sovereignty to the life of the master must be seen to have something tragic about it, since it forms a decisive turning point that signals the eradication of genuine affirmative, free play in the sphere of practical life and of interpretive practice. Yet, to the extent that the notion of tragedy, even in its varied senses, connotes a sort of representation or disclosure, the transition from sovereignty to mastery must be seen as beyond tragedy. This becomes clear if we consider Derrida's claim that sovereignty forms the "repressed origin" of mastery.[57] On the one hand, the life of sovereignty forms the source for mastery, as the sovereign's openness to the loss of life forms a necessary condition of the struggle that brings about the relation of mastery and servitude in the first place.[58] But on the other hand, this origin remains repressed in the sense that the sovereign's initial openness, her staking of her own life, is inexpressible. This is not only because the radically free act of the sovereign itself is logically and temporally prior to the establishment of a relationship of recognition that would first give rise to the very possibility of intersubjective meaning in the first place, but also because this free act is itself in violation of the structural dynamics of recognition that work to govern signification and stabilize the relation of signifier and signified.

From the Derridian standpoint, the transition from sovereignty to mastery forms much more than a tragic reversal, in the sense that it comprises a loss of freedom so complete that it cannot even be memorialized in language. One of Hegel's thematic intentions in the *Phenomenology* is to show that it is only in relationships of mutual recognition that it is possible to achieve true independence. On Derrida's deconstruction of Hegel, however, the establishment of any relationship of recognition, even the bare relation of lordship and bondage, constitutes not only the loss of sovereign freedom but, moreover, the loss of the loss, for it necessarily recedes into inarticulate oblivion. Yet by the same token, there is a sense in which the transition from sovereignty to mastery is also less than tragic, since it never appears. In Derrida's view, the tragedy of the sovereign is only discernible in traces and forms a drama that is impossible to stage. Hegel's reversal of mastery and servitude is so tragic that it is not tragic at all, and the larger life of spirit unfolds not as a long path to independence but, instead, as a long process of development guided by radical forms of alienation and repression.

The Tragedy of the Servant

On his thematic view, Hegel believes that the human spirit is indexed to the achievement of independence, and that the reversal in the life of servitude forms the triumphant first step in our liberation from subjugation and estrangement. But, whereas figures such as Derrida wish to subvert this Hegelian picture by considering Hegel's silence on the tragic aspects of the sovereign, the one who becomes master, it is also possible to discern novel insights into finitude and freedom in reference to certain tragic elements in Hegel's portrayal of the servant. Certainly, the discourse on sovereignty that emerges from the constellation of Nietzsche, Bataille, and Derrida (and others) makes an important contribution to current efforts to mine post-modern possibilities from Hegel's discussion of self-consciousness. However, even if Hegel's overall picture of the path to independence inaugurated in servitude stands among the great intellectual monuments of modern optimism, it is nonetheless animated by the tragic themes of absurdity, anxiety, pain, and loss. Moreover, as commentators such as Hans-Georg Gadamer emphasize, the kind of freedom suggested by Hegel's account of servitude is inextricably tied to the servant's relation to death.[59] From this standpoint, Hegel's depiction of the tragic side of the reversal in the servant's fortunes point to a vision of human prospects for freedom guided neither by the apparition of independence, nor, for that matter, by the more Nietzschean portrait of the sovereign's unrestricted risk and play. Rather, it suggests what Gadamer refers to as a finite freedom of ability (*Können*), characterized by the constant presence of the specter of death, as well as by insuperable limitations on our efforts to achieve self-certainty and to transform the conditions of our existence.

In order to illuminate this side of Hegel's account, it is crucial to remember that for him, the reversal in the life of servitude not only gives rise to a progressive, forward motion that places the servant on the path to independence, but also throws the servant back on herself and forces her to come to terms with her own mortality and its consequences for her existence. For, we recall, the servant first finds herself in the condition of bondage precisely because she is dedicated not to freedom and to struggle but rather to the preservation of her own life, and to the pursuit of her more natural and immediate desires. Yet, Hegel maintains that once the master/servant relation has been created, the lord maintains her authority over her subordinate by means of the continuous threat of death. If the servant submits to her condition certain that this will protect her life, experience teaches her that the reverse is true. Under the tyranny of the master and as a result of her constant intimidation, the servant

> has not had anxiety in this moment or that, but instead in its entire being; for it has sensed the fear of death, the absolute master. It is thereby utterly undone, has been set atremble through and through, and everything fixed in it has been shaken to the core.[60]

The reversal in mastery and servitude forms a testament not only to independence and liberation but also to the more tragic fate of the humble figure who, though she wished for nothing more than to live, is consigned to a life reigned by and shot through with the one thing she feared most.

To Hegel's mind, all of spirit's progress beyond servitude, our further cultivation of discipline and skill, and our long struggle for liberation are contingent on the servant's tragic surrender of her commitments to natural life. And Hegel argues that the relationship of recognition forms the chief condition of our independence, because recognition results from a crucible that forces us to choose freedom over existence. The relation of mastery and servitude arises because the servant eschews this choice. But, the circumstances of servitude nevertheless open the path to freedom because the threats of the master force the servant to renounce her ties to her natural existence after all. Gadamer explains,

> Thus the reason why it [i.e., self-consciousness] must put its own life on the line is not that it is unable to become certain of itself without annihilation of the other and accordingly without a conflict with the other, but rather that it is unable to achieve true being-for-self without overcoming its attachment to life, i.e., annihilation of itself as mere 'life.'[61]

Although the relation of mastery and servitude arises from the servant's failure to choose freedom and to surmount her fear of death in the struggle for recognition, the condition of bondage leads her nonetheless, and by the logic of a certain tragic necessity, to disavow her natural existence.

Indeed, Hegel's emphasis upon the presence of the absolute master might lead one to argue that the more tragic side of Hegel's approach to servitude, elicited here by Gadamer, might suggest a relation of freedom and death that in some regards speaks to the depths of human finitude at least as fully as even Derrida has. Certainly, Derrida takes human finitude seriously, and, as we have seen, he maintains that the attainment of sovereignty is predicated on an affirmation of the ubiquitous and constant possibility of death. For him, the sovereign is openness to the unrestrained play of meaning is possible only on the basis of her readiness to risk the absolute extinction of sense and life. As we have seen, Derrida associates one of the summits of human freedom with the sovereign readiness to expend life and sense without reserve, to risk absolute loss for the sake of the transitory, productive play of meanings. Further, he indicates, the relationship of recognition in mastery and servitude comprises a restricted economy that forecloses the effectiveness of this play, a condition of slavishness that infects the existence of both master and servant. Thus, Derrida's concern for finitude leads him, too, to point out a certain kinship of freedom and death, insofar as he believes that the attainment of sovereignty is contingent on an affirmation of the ubiquitous and constant possibility of death.

Yet, despite Derrida's wish to show that sovereign freedom is foreclosed by the restricted economics established in the relation of mastery and servitude, the more tragic side of Hegel's account of servitude itself suggest that its freedom, too, is conditioned by the finitude exposed by our susceptibility to death. For the presence of the absolute master, the threat of death, is a constitutive and constant condition of the life of servitude as such, and one that creeps into every fiber of the servant's being until it 'undoes' her. Contrary to Derrida, who suggests that the relation of mastery and servitude suppresses and obviates the genuine affinity of freedom and death, it appears that the dynamics of the relation set up circumstances under which the presence of death as a condition of freedom first emerges.

On his thematic view, Hegel remains firm in his conviction that the human spirit is bound to a sense of independence that would liberate us not only from relationships of dependency, but also from the constraints imposed on us in our more uncultivated, immediate state. Nonetheless, the implications of the more tragic side of Hegel's account of servitude suggests a notion of finite freedom, characterized by incompleteness and transience, and the achievement of only provisional and temporary forms of self-certainty that arise from our merely partial ability to modify and adapt conditions of our existence through labor. In the reversal of mastery and servitude, it is precisely the master's reliance on the threat of death to exercise her dominion that, ironically, operates to loosen the master's hold on the servant. This is because it is nothing other than the constant presence of the absolute master in the servant's life that throws her back on herself, and wrests her from her certainty that her human master determines her reason for being. Moreover, the servant's new perspective, in turn, allows her to understand the fruits of her labor not simply as means to recognize her master, but, rather also as a form of self-expression. Again, Gadamer:

> although it appeared to be foreign to itself in labor for the master (and, as service, truly was) . . . consciousness that serves becomes conscious of itself insofar as it surrenders to labor as labor—and not simply to the master. Insofar as it 'puts out' the form as its own, i.e., produces, it knows itself in the therein and thus in labor is its *own*: "That I can do!"[62]

It is finally under the directive of the absolutely other, death, that the servant absolves herself of being-for-another, the master, and learns to live for herself. This relationship to death, in its turn, releases our powers to create for ourselves, a 'can do,' or, ability (*Können*), and enables her to discover herself in the things she produces.

Some of Hegel's thematic hopes about our prospects for independence notwithstanding, his conception of the presence of death in the life of servitude points to an aspect of the finitude in human freedom, understood here as ability. Perhaps not unlike Heidegger's *Dasein*, the self-consciousness of ability finds itself always already thrown into a world, and, in the Hegelian frame, a world in which it is always already subjected to the logic of subordination and to potentials for mortal violence that force it to surrender itself to the wishes of another. However, precisely these constituent features of (Hegelian) thrownness free up this self-consciousness' ability, and enable it to project itself onto its possibilities for being itself. Certainly, we might doubt if it is within the scope of our powers ever to overcome dependency, subjugation. Moreover, to read with Hegel's emphasis on the presence of death in our lives, even if thereby to read against some of the assumptions of his overall view, his account draws out that our efforts to achieve self-certainty in labor are as transitory as they are fractional. For the self-consciousness of ability, one might infer, freedom is not only enabled, but also limited by the presence of death, in that the imminence of the possibility of our own death delimits the scope of our powers to transform the conditions of existence, threatens to interrupt all our projects, and also to transform the meaning of our projects and thereby to subvert our intentions.

Of the numerous heritages of Hegel scholarship concerned with his consideration of self-consciousness, independence, recognition, and the relation of mastery and servitude, many from nineteenth- and twentieth-century continental thought coalesce around a desire to release relevant and novel insights into freedom from Hegel's account that exceed many of his own tenets. From such standpoints, the idea seems to be that "one can think better without Hegel," as one commentator puts it, "by thinking with him."[63] But, despite the influence of Derrida's deconstructivist approach, with its emphasis on Hegel's blindness to the tragedy of the sovereign, perhaps some of the deepest insights into finitude and freedom are won by focusing on what I have referred to as some of the more tragic aspects of Hegel's depiction of servitude. Certainly, as we have seen, Derrida's "From Restricted to General Economy" essay points to important ties to freedom and death. And yet, in Derrida's approach, perhaps not entirely unlike in Nietzsche's approach to sovereignty in the *Genealogy of Morals,* "First Essay," the kinship of freedom and death might be said to indicate much less about the limitations of our powers than about what could be construed as a sort of unlimited power to affirm ourselves and to produce the new. By contrast, the tragic mien of Hegel's servant reminds us that human freedom is shot through with limits, and that constraints imposed by relationships to other self-conscious beings, subjugation, and even natural life all comprise inescapable conditions of our possibilities as such. Hegel's discussion of the tragedy of the servant associates the origins of our productive practices not with our prospects to achieve sovereignty, but instead with the more humble insight that our possibilities for freedom are actually subject to, and born of, our limits.

3

The Tragedy of Ethical Life

Hegel's *Phenomenology* culminates in the views not only that the human spirit is destined to attain an absolute form of self-knowledge, but also that it is indexed to its potential to achieve independence. Yet, Hegel's dedication to the project of speculation requires him not simply to entertain these spiritual possibilities in the abstract but also to explain their emergence from out of actual developments in our conscious lives. In each discussion, he depends on the resources of tragedy to illuminate our most monstrous encounters with finitude in the course of our struggle to understand what and who we are, our place in the world, and our abilities to transform the conditions of our existence. But, the speculative approach further demands that Hegel also elucidate political, social, and ethical questions in concrete, historical terms, and his discussion reaches one of its highest summits in his account of ethical life (*Sittlichkeit*). Hegel's depiction of ethical life in the *Phenomenology* is among the most difficult to unpack because Hegel will associate it not only with an important stage in the development of self-conscious rationality, but also with the historical period of ancient Greece, as well as with a range of issues of community life, state power, factions, family, gender and sex, war, epochal change, and tradition.

But one of Hegel's chief purposes in his discussion of ethical life, a concern that is interwoven through all of the others, is to elaborate on consciousness' struggle to come to terms with a certain crisis it encounters in its efforts to find its place as a rational being in a larger world of political, social, historical, and filial relations. His consideration of ethical life is much more comprehensively oriented by questions of tragedy than either his treatment of experience or his treatment of freedom, in which his use of tragedy was restricted primarily to a single concept, that of tragic reversal. In his portrayal of ethical life, by contrast, Hegel not only incorporates other important ideas from Aristotle's *Poetics* but also relies extensively on Sophocles' *Antigone*—its central themes, its dramatic structure, characters, and action—as a sort of template for his presentation as a whole. Of course, it is difficult not to see a certain logic to the intensification of Hegel's interest in tragedy as his presentation progresses. Hegel believes that as the history of spirit unfolds, consciousness expands its awareness of itself and thus, we might extrapolate, also of the forms of difficulty, tension, anxiety, pain, and failure that animate its affairs. So, if Hegel understands the most poignant of these encounters with finitude as matters of tragedy, then it makes sense that consciousness' education would unfold, at least in part, as a broadening and deepening of its insight into the tragic aspects of its life.

It should also make sense to us that Hegel would associate questions of political, social, and ethical concern with Sophocles' *Antigone*, and Hegel's interest belongs to the heritages of modern European philosophical, scholarly, artistic, and political thought deeply influenced by the drama.[1] The pervasive attention given to the *Antigone* not only extends into the postmodern age from out of the modern period, but also spreads over a number of disciplines, to include not just philosophy, but also psychoanalysis, literary criticism, and feminism. No doubt the heightened interest received by the *Antigone* is due at least in part to its resonance with current and modern sensibilities about the dangers of state power, male domination, and, perhaps even more broadly, the sanctity and freedom of the individual.[2]

Hegel, too, understands that the *Antigone* is one of the great testaments to the dangers of authoritarian political power and to the imperative that we defy it. One important dimension of Hegel's view, which finds one of its more innovative and recent uses in Christoph Menke's *Die Tragödie im Sittlichen*, is that the *Antigone* gives expression to a crucial, initial stage in the formation of the modern, free individual as it emerges from the crucible of consciousness' struggle against state power and the authority of custom.[3] But, it would be reductive to suppose that Hegel's concern for the *Antigone* in the chapter on ethical life is reducible to issues of the epochal shift beyond antiquity. Hegel sees the *Antigone* as a rich and fertile ground to treat a number of interrelated issues, and his purpose in the *Phenomenology* need not be grasped solely as a characterization of consciousness' efforts to establish a sense of the individual under the threat of state power. Rather, it may also be seen as an inquiry into what it means for consciousness actually to embrace a number of broader political, social, and ethical commitments while allowing for an individual to remain true to itself. In this light, Hegel employs the *Antigone* primarily to depict consciousness' efforts to reconcile its awareness that it has ineluctable and legitimate duties to fulfill the demands placed on it by its community, its heritage, the law, and family with its knowledge of itself as a genuinely rational being that must give itself the principles it uses to guide its life and actions.[4]

Yet, as we shall see, consciousness' experience of ethical life exposes that it simply cannot harmonize all of its divergent commitments. Hegel's reliance on the *Antigone* as a matrix for his presentation results in the insight that even consciousness' most principled actions may turn out to be criminal, and, ultimately, that all of a rational agent's actions are inextricably bound up with a certain guilt. Indeed, Hegel will hold that because the rational agent's guilt is inherent in action as such, it cannot be interpreted as a simple moral or ethical failure. But, neither will Hegel evoke a doctrine of original sin to trace back the rational agent's guiltiness to a failure of some first free choice. Instead, I will suggest, Hegel associates guilt with a certain interpretation of the Greek notion of ἁμαρτία, waywardness, or errancy. Hegel is well aware that this notion plays an integral role not only in Aristotle's *Poetics* but also in much of sixth century Attic tragedy, and he will introduce it into his discussion to suggest that actions are bound up with guilt not because the agent fails to act properly, but because even the most proper action is susceptible to multiple forms of failure. In ethical life, consciousness is forced to learn that we release our purposes into the world through action like prodigal sons, or daughters, always with the danger that their consequences will contravene our plans for them, and with the potential for devastating results. The experience of ethical life teaches that even rational beings who act on sound principles may unavoidably and inadvertently become embroiled in conflict, strife, and violence.

It is true that for Hegel, consciousness comes ultimately to triumph over this form of vulnerability, insofar as it overcomes guiltiness by means of sublation in the dialectical development of spirit. Yet, Hegel's larger view suggests that it is only in the highest phases of consciousness' development, in the achievement of higher-order, reflective experiences of philosophy, religion, and art, through the experience of forgiveness, that it comes to unify its experiences of the difficulties of practical life, such as those that emerge from ethical life. Hegel's *Phenomenology* "could only see a redeemed ... form of life," as Pinkard puts it, in contemplative activity, and not in the arenas of raw, practical action.[5] From this standpoint, it is possible to suggest that even though Hegel believes that certain reflective forms of life allow us to make peace with the more hostile aspects of our practical affairs, his treatment of guilt nonetheless poses significant and enduring questions about *praxis*. With this in mind, we shall see that Hegel's association of guilt with errancy both anticipates and sheds new light on important themes in existentialism, such as Sartre's notion of abandonment.

Ethical Life and Rational Agency

Hegel's conceptions of ethical life and agency are bound up in his vision of the ancient Greek world, and much of his presentation may be seen to form a sort of speculative response to a number of his contemporaries' views of antiquity. At the dawn of classical Germany, many important intellectuals maintained what now appears to be a decidedly artificial conception of antiquity and imagined that ancient society formed a highly perfected, beautiful, and harmonious whole. Important strands of intellectual discourse in this period may even be seen as being shadowed by a certain nostalgia for what was perceived as the greatness of Greek political, social, and cultural life.[6] Hegel's conception of antiquity is informed by an extensive and rich knowledge of Greek history, politics, culture, arts, and language, but there can be no question that he also holds a rather stylized view of the ancient world, based on fantasy as well as fact. Not unlike a number of intellectuals of his day, Hegel, too, holds up ancient Greece as a certain ideal form of spiritual life. But, whereas some in Hegel's generation may have been persuaded that the Hellenic ideal formed a genuine alternative to the conditions of the modern world, Hegel argues that despite initial appearances, the ethical life of the ancient polis is fractured and fraught with internal tensions.[7] As we shall see later in the chapter, Hegel further argues that the majestic splendor of the Greek world disappears from the face of the earth not because it is overrun by external powers, or due to extraneous, or arbitrary circumstances; rather, it falls into oblivion because it collapses under the weight of its own dialectic.

But how does Hegel characterize the ethical life of the Greek polis? What does his view tell us about rational agency?

Hegel maintains that as our spiritual development arrives at the stage of ethical life, one of consciousness' deepest concerns is to reconcile its conception of itself as a rational being with its knowledge that it belongs to a world larger than itself. Consciousness begins to feel the burden of this bifurcation of its self-understanding as the result of a number of experiences that expand its awareness, consciousness learns that it is governed by its capacity for reason, and, because of this, that the subject's synthetic relation to the world, both in its theoretical and practical endeavors, is drawn to the assertion of general laws.[8] In the arena of practical affairs, consciousness' discovery of its affinity for the universal has led it to recognize, as the result of a dialectical progression inaugurated in its experience of 'the actualization of rational self-consciousness through itself,' that it is the inviolable legislator and arbiter of the laws it must rely on to guide all of its endeavors.[9] Schmidt explains, "[t]his means simply, as Kant had shown, that consciousness lays down the law in each and every deed; each of its actions has the weight of a universal action."[10] It is true that Hegel treats some important features of Kant's view under the rubric of conscience, an advanced stage in its development that comes well after ethical life. But, he claims that even before our consciousness arrives at ethical life, it has already learned of the centrality of reason for its life and, thus, that all of its affairs must be governed by laws of its own making.[11]

In ethical life, consciousness is dedicated to the harmonization of its knowledge of itself as a legislative being with the awareness that its life is also guided by multiple commitments and conditions that it does not author. Hegel's presentation indicates that consciousness's perception of its larger world is informed by a number of issues of political life, sociality, and nature. In its awareness of ethical life, its view of things is oriented first and foremost by questions of historicity and tradition, or, in a current idiom, what we might call cultural heritage.[12] For Hegel, the ancient Greeks had a profound sense of history and Greek society sustained and preserved itself by means of the continual renewal of traditions and customs. In this light, he defines the ethical life of an ancient Greek polis primarily in terms of the societal efforts made in its present to uphold what he calls its "*ethical substance*," its customary body of ethical laws (*Sitten*).[13]

Hegel's basic idea is that this customary body of law, in turn, prescribes an organic nexus of official duties or, perhaps, offices (in the sense of the original Latin *officium*—as a function or charge). In the ethical life of a people, these duties are assigned to specific individuals in the political sphere, who, in turn, work to perpetuate their heritage through their fulfillment of their responsibilities. Figures such as Philippe Lacoue-Labarthe and Jean-Luc Nancy have characterized the dynamics of ethical life as a form of 'autopoesy,' a process by which a people continually restores its sense of identity to full presence through the appropriation of the central myths, beliefs, and values from its heritage.[14] For his part, Hegel defines the ethical life of a people as a "general work [*Werk*] that is engendered by the *activity* [*Tun*] of one and all as their unity."[15] Hegel envisions ancient societies as self-sustaining creations, though, of course, this is not to say that he sees them as the handiwork of some divine craftsman or demiurge. Rather, he believes that the polis unfolds under the auspices of a sort of self-sufficient life, which persists of its own efforts in its chronic revival of its traditions. Hegel's notion of Greek ethical life might be seen to owe debts to Kant's account of nature as an 'internal teleology' in the third *Critique*, and Hegel holds that the ethical life of Greek society is both an end and a means to itself, generated (and thereby conserved) by the particular rational agents allotted to uphold its most time-honored ethical laws.[16]

What conception of rational agency and action emerge from this depiction of ethical life? Charles Taylor places Hegel's conception within a family of 'qualitative' theories of action that arise within the post-Kantian continental European tradition in response to more mainstream, 'causal' accounts that can be found in both the Cartesian and empiricist traditions. Taylor maintains that causal views are characterized by a strict and clear separation between an agent's motives—the purposes, intentions, beliefs, and desires that give rise to her actions—and the actions that follow on them. Within a Cartesian schema, the separation between an agent's motives and actions is calibrated to an ontological split: mind, or immaterial substance, forms the seat of our intentions, whereas our actions unfold within the spatiotemporal realm of material substances. Certainly, many empiricists of the seventeenth and eighteenth centuries held out hope, perhaps not unlike proponents of reductive materialism in our day, that scientific research might someday reinterpret certain mental phenomena such as intentions and desires as physical events and thus overcome Cartesian-style dualism. But, even so, many who have accepted a more physicalistic framework continue to maintain a distinction between the motivation that guides an agent and the actions that result.[17]

By contrast, Hegel rejects the idea that our motivations *cause* our actions and believes instead that there is a sense in which our purposes actually *constitute* the actions that flow from them. Taylor explains, a rational agent's "actions are what we might call intrinsically directed. Actions are in a sense inhabited by the purposes that direct them...."[18] Whereas causal theorists maintain that an agent's purposes are antecedent to her actions, Hegel believes that purposes and actions are co-primordial, even co-constitutive. This Hegelian conception of rational agency rests not on Cartesian or empiricist assumptions but, instead, is influenced by the effective history of the Aristotelian notion of informed matter, and Hegel maintains that our purposes suffuse our actions and give shape to them. From this standpoint, there is no ultimate disparity between a rational agent's purposes and her actions, and thus all of our actions must be understood not as the effects, but rather as expressions of intentions. To Hegel's mind, motivations do not lie 'behind' our actions; rather, our purposes are 'in' our actions as what gives them direction.

Just as important to Hegel's view is the claim that the cultural heritage of a people, in the shape of its ethical substance, plays a decisive role in the formation of the purposes that govern individual agents' endeavors. The presumption of Cartesian-style dualism makes it easy to suppose that the individual enjoys a power to determine her intentions that is separate from her historical situation. But, on the Hegelian position, there is no ontological gap between the domain of intentions, purposes, beliefs, and desires, and the world of concrete affairs. Owing to this view, he is able to see that ostensibly external sources, such as the principles, beliefs, and values inherited from the past, help to determine even our deepest aspirations and desires. Moreover, for the ethical life of a Greek people, Hegel holds, the realization of the people's ethical substance is understood to be universally effective and binding, the "*ground* and *point of departure* for the activity of all."[19] Thus, although it is ultimately the force of tradition that assigns specific offices to rational agents in the polis, these agents experience their charges not as coercive or arbitrary impositions, but, instead, as legitimate duties compatible with their own powers of legislation. It is a Hegelian claim put well by Terry Pinkard:

> There was no discontinuity between how individuals understood themselves as individuals, and how they understood society. . . . The Greek individual understood himself in terms of his social role; his individuality is filled out by his social role, not by any idiosyncratic and contingent features of himself.[20]

In the Greek world, consciousness' twofold conception of its commitments to a larger world and to itself is opened up by a certain awareness of its historicity, and, specifically, of the ethical substance embedded in cultural heritage. For Hegel, the rational agent is governed neither by abstract rules nor by physical impulses. She is rather an expressive and permeable subject guided by the purposes that originate from a world that is beyond herself and yet her own.

Does Hegel believe that a rational agent's knowledge of her purposes is 'corrigible?' Taylor maintains that since the Hegelian agent's intentions always permeate her actions, it is impossible for her ever completely to lack at least some sense of her purposes. Yet, an agent's purposes become entirely manifest only as they come to fruition through action, and for Taylor, this implies that on Hegel's view, even an agent herself must revise and correct her knowledge of her purposes as her endeavors unfold. As one recent commentator on the corrigiblist position explains, "an agent's experience . . . [of] what she understands herself to *intend*, may, for example, change in the course of the action or may be adequately understood only when the action has been completed and seen in its full context."[21] On the basis of such a view, Taylor argues that whereas causal theorists may imagine that rational agents enjoy a sort of incorrigible, immediate knowledge of their motives 'before' they act on them, Hegel's view reveals that we do not fully know what we wish to do until we have done it. Before we complete our actions, we may have some sense of our purposes, but they may remain "dim, inarticulate, or subliminal. . . ."[22] Is this picture of Hegelian agency accurate? Surely, Hegel believes that consciousness, at the stage of ethical life, has not yet achieved complete self-conscious awareness, and, thus, in a sense, remains at this level only incompletely aware of itself and its ends. Certainly, too, the overall tenor of Hegel's approach would recommend that the consciousness of rational agents, like consciousness of all kinds, increase their self-knowledge only by means of experience, so that it would only be possible to develop a more robust sense of one's own intentions in the course of practice.

Yet, even if Hegel's view suggests that an agent's knowledge of her purposes may be corrigible, it does not necessarily imply that it may be said categorically that her initial sense of her intentions is indistinct, unformed, or vague. For in the ethical life of the Greeks, it would seem, rational agents enter into the arena of practical affairs with a sound sense of the offices assigned to them by their heritage, and thus also of the purposes that must guide them if they are to fulfill their duties. It is this view that will later allow Hegel, in his discussion of the principal agents of the dialectical unraveling of the Greek ethical world, to claim of their ethical action that it is guided by genuine, law-governed duty, and is not characterized by indecision, nor by arbitrary desire or passion.[23] Although in ethical life rational agents do not yet enjoy complete self-awareness, and thus remain in some sense only dimly aware of their vocation and of the stakes of their endeavors, they are nonetheless fully aware of the universal form, and substantive content, of the purposes prescribed to them by the ethical substance of their people.

The Crisis of the Ethical World

Although the ethical life of the Greeks, in its initial stage, is summoned to sustain and preserve itself by means of the constant revivification of its traditional ethical substance, Hegel holds that as consciousness' experience of ethical life begins to unfold, the opposition between its awareness of its more global ties to the world around it and of its sense of itself as the author of the law will come to a head, until it is forced to concede that the "simple substance of spirit divides itself. . . ."[24] With this insight, consciousness shifts its focus from an awareness of the general character of ethical life (*Sittlichkeit*) to more specific aspects of the actual Greek ethical world (*die sittliche Welt*).[25] In this transition, consciousness' broader interest in ancient society's ethical substance undergoes a certain distillation, and it telescopes in on what it comes to see as the polis' two most essential laws. Hegel writes, "the plurality of ethical moments becomes the duality of a law of singularity and of universality."[26] As consciousness moves from an awareness of ethical life to the ethical world, it moves beyond questions concerned with the conservation of a people's ethical substance and comes to see that this substance contains two indispensable but antithetical laws that embody its twofold commitments to itself and to its larger world.

Hegel's presentation of the Greek ethical world is profoundly influenced by Sophocles' *Antigone*, and although Hegel hardly mentions the tragedy directly in this section of his discussion, he uses the storyline and characters of the drama as a sort of speculative script for his portrayal of consciousness' experience of the collision between the law of universality and the law of individuality. Hegel will return to Sophocles' play more explicitly later in his presentation of spirit, to elaborate on its speculative significance as a work of dramatic art.[27] But, in his depiction of ethical life, Hegel treats the drama primarily as an artistic reflection of the actual structures and dynamics of political and social life in antiquity. Hegel, like Sophocles, contends that the tensions between the laws of universality and of singularity manifest themselves most explicitly at a precarious and peculiar site within society, one that cleaves our lives and draws us at once toward communal, civic life, and toward more private affairs: the family.[28] If ethical life has its deepest origins in questions of cultural heritage and tradition, then the ethical world's deepest wounds are cut across our natural ties to others, our blood relations. Hegel recognizes that the opposition between the two laws permeates all the important aspects of family life and that it expresses itself in the institution of marriage, in the acquisition of family capital, and in the education of children.[29] But, the structure of

Hegel's presentation, forged in large part on the model of Sophocles, suggests that the mutual repulsion of the twinned laws reaches its most extreme and clearest form in the guise of a collision between the 'human law' and the 'divine law' over the issue of burial.[30] Of course, quite a lot has been said, and said quite well, about Hegel's account of this collision, much more than could fruitfully be treated here. In what follows, I wish only to reiterate and develop certain themes of his account that will prove relevant to the questions of tragedy and agency I raise in this chapter.

In this light, one of Hegel's chief claims about burial is that the customary performance of last rites is a spiritual effort to achieve political and social unity and cohesion through the memorialization of the dead. The observation of the interment ceremony and, we might infer from Hegel's exposition, other rituals that surround it, help to inscribe the corpse with significance in our thoughts, so that the deceased may, in a certain sense, be reintegrated into society. Through burial,

> the blood relative supplements the abstract, natural movement [of the corpse's destruction through physical decay], in that [she] adds the movement of consciousness to it, interrupts the work of nature, and rescues her kin from destruction. . . .[31]

Hegel's dedication to the speculative approach leads him to what we might call a holistic stance on burial, and his view suggests that if society is to be complete, it must embrace not only the living but also the dead by incorporating the memory of those from the past into its present. Certainly, one can argue that the completion of rituals such as the preparation of the corpse, the death knell, the funeral, the eulogy, the dirge, the shroud, the wake, and the entombment are significant for a wide range of reasons and that customs associated with death afford those who remain alive important occasions to grieve their loss. Hegel does not consider such matters at any length in his account of the ethical world, but focuses rather on what he takes to be the speculatively decisive need: to spiritualize the dead through the act of mourning, and thus to offset the processes of nature that precipitate the dissolution of the corpse into oblivion.

In this light, as consciousness initially enters in the ethical world of the Greeks, it interprets the human law as the greatest embodiment of its larger political and social commitments, and it finds that the highest meaning of the human law comes to the fore in the law's ramifications for questions of burial. Hegel identifies the human law primarily as a sort of self-conscious, higher-order law that commands us to respect all other laws of our society as law; or, put another way, the human law universally compels every individual to submit, or, to recognize, the universal scope and binding force of the legal code itself.[32] The fulfillment of the human law is charged to the government (on the model of the *Antigone*, ultimately, to its supreme governor, the monarch) and the regime discharges its duty to this law in its continual efforts to promulgate and enforce society's ethical law.[33] On this view, the human law forms an absolute expression of consciousness' awareness of its broader commitments because of its heightened relation to the universal. The human law charges the government to establish universal recognition of the universal force of law; and as a result, it introduces a powerful, cohesive force into society, one that induces a people to coalesce, bind, and unify.

Hegel's account of the human law is keyed to Sophocles' depiction, and in Hegel's presentation, too, the demands of the human law for the universal and for societal cohesion reach one of their highest summits in the regime's use of its power to prohibit the interment of those who, in life, betrayed their people, that is, national traitors, such as Polynices. For Hegel, the human law forms an ineluctable and legitimate component of community life, and thus he denies that there is anything sinister about its enforcement. This is a conviction implicit in claims he makes about the *Antigone*, posed in a somewhat different context, that "Creon is not a tyrant, but rather just an ethical power. Creon is not unjust."[34] From the standpoint of the human law, traditional burial rituals are preeminently a legal and societal matter, aimed to incorporate our memory into the life of the polis, and our entitlement to last rites rests ultimately on our status as subjects of the law. Thus, the logic of the human law dictates that members of the polis who recognized the binding force of law in life receive proper burial. But, by contrast, members of the polis who refuse to recognize the universality of the law of the land—that is to say, traitors: those who reject the binding force of her people's ethical substance as such, and who not simply transgress one law or other—must be left unburied. Thereby, the human law safeguards the cohesive unity of the people by means of a prohibition on burial that effectively excludes and erases the traitor's transgression from the memory of society. The human law, as Sophocles' Creon put it, prescribes that the government's treatment of individuals should be "never the same for the patriot and the traitor," not only in life, but even in death.[35]

Hegel's explanation of consciousness' interest in the divine law is multilayered and nuanced, and concerns a number of issues derived from matters of Greek religious and social life.[36] If he maintains that consciousness interprets the human law as the highest embodiment of its broader political and social ties, then one of his chief claims about the divine law is that consciousness embraces it as one of the deepest expressions of the singular. Whereas the human law demands that the state assert its legal authority over burial practices and treat the dead as subjects of the law primarily as the indirect result of its more general charge to uphold society's ethical substance, the divine law's object of the singular focuses it explicitly focused upon the issue of burial.[37] The divine law commands that society's obligation to bury the dead is universal, so that the last rites must be performed for all people, regardless of whether, in life, they were patriots or traitors. Moreover, in the Greek ethical world, tradition assigns the duty to fulfill the divine law not to the state, but rather, in each case, to the families that survive their deceased relative.[38]

Consciousness' education thus far has already prepared it to recognize the connection between itself as a self-legislating being and its relation to death. Hegel recognizes that in this phase of its development, consciousness conceives of itself preeminently as a rational agent, and thus even its sense of self is inextricably bound up with the universal, in that rational agents understand that their actions must be governed by universalizable principles. However, as a self-legislating being, consciousness knows itself to be a singular being because its efforts to lay down the law must be carried out under the sign of a certain 'mineness,' since its assertion of law flows in each case from an irreducibly spontaneous, first-person act.[39] But, as Schmidt observes, consciousness already knows that its spontaneity and singularity are bound up with its relation to death from its experience of servitude, for in this phase of its development, we recall, consciousness learned that both its own spontaneous freedom of ability as well as its sense of self as a self-conscious being originated in the process of singularization that resulted from its experience of the absolute master.[40]

Hegel is dedicated to the belief that the divine law's focus on singularity interpenetrates every aspect of the family's duty, and it is really this conviction that guides what is by now one of Hegel's most notorious claims: that within the family, the obligation to inter the corpse falls on the women. Hegel's speculative approach typically leads him to resist unreflective stereotypes and commonsense views, and his interpretation of issues of gender and sex is in fact informed by extensive and original research.[41] Although his purpose in this portion of the *Phenomenology* is to present speculatively consciousness' experience of the Greek ethical world and not to use external standards to criticize it, it would be difficult to ignore that his discussion of family life and of women resonates deeply with bourgeois, sexist values of nineteenth-century Germany. Hegel's thought seems to be that the divine law favors the family's women because whereas the preeminent and proper place of men is the world of political and economic affairs, the purview of women is domestic life or the home.

Yet, difficult as it is to separate Hegel's genuine insights into the divine law, family life, and women from his unforgivably obvious blindness to issues of gender and sex, his discussion nevertheless illuminates important features of rational agency, and also sets the stage for both creative appropriations and critical responses in feminism.[42] Hegel conceives of filial life primarily in terms of power relations and gender roles, and he maintains that the family women must achieve a certain equality of power to perform last rites properly. Hegel believes that from among all of the family women, their potential to reach equality culminates in one figure in particular, the sister, and, once again, plainly, he has Antigone, the courageous and powerful sister of Polynices, Eteocles, and Ismene in mind. Indeed, Hegel's discussion appears to be guided by one of Antigone's statements from near the end of the drama, though he does not cite it directly. Just before Sophocles has Antigone go to die, he has her pronounce,

> Never, I tell you,
> if I had been the mother of children
> or if my husband died, exposed and rotting—
> I'd never have taken this ordeal upon myself,
> never defied our people's will.[43]

Antigone's explanation of the privileged status of a woman's role as sister over that of mother or that of wife is enigmatic, but it appears to focus on the irreplaceability of the sister's bond to her brother. Antigone states that insofar as a woman may be a mother, she may replace a dead child with another, and insofar as she may be a wife, she may replace a dead husband through remarriage. Antigone then says that for a woman whose parents are dead, as hers are, is it impossible, as sister, to replace a dead brother.[44]

Hegel's conception of the exemplarity of a woman's role as sister also turns on issues of irreplaceability, but from a subtly different point of view. For Hegel, the divine law favors the sister because in contrast with all other filial women, only she is able to treat the dead as an irreplaceable, singular, and unique being. Hegel focuses on filial relations between wife and husband, parent and child, and sister and brother. (He has not much to say about other possible family relations, such as, for example, blended family relations, same-sex partnerships, or, for that matter, brother-brother or sister-sister relations.)[45] His position indicates that husbands typically hold sexual power over their wives, and that parents typically maintain a kind of natural authority over their children until the children come of age, so that fathers hold sway over their daughters.[46] But, he argues that because the dynamics of power between sister and brother are guided neither by sexual power nor by parental authority, they have the potential to reach an "equilibrium."[47] Due to this, Hegel reasons, a family's sisters have more freedom to fulfill the divine law than its other women. For the divine law requires the family to treat the dead as fully singular beings; but since men's place in society is more than in the home, and since husbands and fathers subject their wives and daughters to male domination, only the sisters' commitments are unmixed, and thus only sisters are able to mourn the dead suitably.

Hegel's discussion of the affinity between the divine law and the singular reaches its summit in his treatment of the object of the sister's labors: her brother's lifeless body, the corpse. From the standpoint of the divine law, not only does the sister's duty to perform burial rites extend beyond the purview of the human law, but also the corpse itself forms a singularity that stands outside of the human law's jurisdiction. Hegel writes that whereas in life a Greek society's inhabitants are "actual and substantial," in death the individual becomes a merely "irreal, pithless shade."[48] While still alive an individual is, whatever else it is, always a member of the larger society's political, social, and economic life, and, as such, all of its endeavors remained within the domain of the human law, the force of government, and the pull of social cohesion. From the standpoint of the divine law, however, an individual's death releases her from all duties to the human law, and what remains is nothing other than the unqualified uniqueness of the former individual. Jacques Derrida, indefatigable in his attention to matters of difference and singularity, explains,

> The family . . . has as its object only the singular, the essentially singular, that which, without reaching the universality of the city [i.e., the polis] strips itself of every empiric characteristic. This pure singularity, stripped but incapable of passing to universality, is the dead— . . . the corpse.[49]

Under the sign of divine law the corpse is regarded not simply as a legal subject but rather as a unique being, absolved of the political, social, and ethical status of its former self.

Hegel believes that consciousness' experience of the Greek ethical world leads it into a tragic crisis. As consciousness initially reaches this stage in its development, it longs to reconcile its awareness that it has indispensable political, social, and ethical commitments with its equally indispensable sense of self as the unique author of its own principles. And consciousness identifies its dual loyalties, respectively, with the human and divine laws. Yet, as experience unfolds, consciousness is forced to learn that even though it sees both of these laws as imperatives, they are nevertheless, at root, mutually incompatible. For the human and divine laws charge their agents in the political sphere, the monarch and the sister, with duties that will collide over questions about the burial of those who, in life, betrayed their people's ethical substance. From the standpoint of the human law, entitlement to last rites is restricted to those who, in life, respected the people's traditional legal code, whereas, by contrast, the divine law dictates that everyone deserves proper burial not because of their loyalty to the people or to law in life, but, on the contrary, due to the fact that in death, they are the sheer remains of singular beings.

Hegel maintains that although consciousness eventually comes to terms with this crisis of burial as its education unfolds, it ultimately does so only in the higher-order activities of philosophy, religion, and art, achieved in the aftermath of its development of conscience and the capacity for forgiveness. But, his presentation suggests that consciousness' confrontation with the crisis of burial reveals a fundamental, and implacable, rupture of practical life. Consciousness' awareness of its conflicted commitments to the universal and to the singular proves to be a recalcitrant feature of its broader development, even if the tension comes to assume different, more subtle and complex, shapes over the course of its educational path. Indeed, even in the ethical world of the Greeks, the collision of the laws of the universal and of the singular comes to form what Hegel (famously) refers to as an "eternal irony."[50] Hegel associates this irony with family life and with the feminine, and, certainly, figures such as Luce Irigaray have shown us that Hegel's association of this irony with questions about domestic life, women, and sex deserves careful attention.[51] Perhaps one of the most important provocations that arises from Hegel's claim, however, is that practical life is grounded not in a potential for cohesion and unity, but, instead, an insuperable paradox, an ineradicable fault line, of our broader ties to the world, and our sense of ourselves.

Rational Agency, Guilt, and Errancy

Hegel turns to Sophocles' *Antigone* as a sort of matrix for the ethical world of the Greeks, and his use of the tragedy centers on the unavoidable and irresolvable crisis that arises from the collision of the law of universality, expressed by the human law, and the law of singularity, embodied in the divine law. Of course, Hegel believes that consciousness' experience of the ethical world, like all of its experiences, leads it to transform itself, to grow, and to attain a higher level of spiritual development. In the aftermath of consciousness' encounter with the ethical world and its discontents, Hegel has spirit's journey advance from the epoch of classical Greece to the epoch of Rome, and, with it, to an awareness of the Roman legalistic interpretation of human beings as persons.[52] This transformation from classical Hellenic society and culture to the Roman Republic may be seen as one of the most important epochal shifts in the sweep of the history of spirit, as consciousness' discovery of personhood forms an important anticipation, albeit in an impoverished, abstract, and crude form, of the modern, free individual.[53]

Yet, Hegel maintains that the emergence of the Roman world is ultimately enabled by the downfall of Greece, and he claims that the Greek ethical world collapses because the collision between the human law and the divine law reveals a decisive limit of our powers to find our place in the sphere of political, social, and filial life as self-legislating, unique beings. He argues that consciousness' encounter with the Greeks culminates in the tragic insight that as participants in a larger arena of practical affairs, rational action is, by virtue of its own structures and operations, inviolably bound up with guilt (*Schuld*). In the aftermath of its encounter with the ethical world, consciousness is forced to see that a rational agent, through her action alone, or, "by the deed," alone, "becomes guilt," and that "innocence is therefore simply non-action, like the being of a stone, not even that of a child."[54] Hegel's reliance on the *Antigone* to discuss the Greek ethical world reveals that the lives of rational agents are pervaded by finitude—insofar as rational action itself is essentially indexed to a peculiar form of failure.

But, what is it about consciousness' experience of the collision between the human law and divine law that leads it to believe that rational action is inherently ridden with guilt? What does Hegel mean by guilt in this context?

Some of Hegel's most important answers to these questions turn on the lessons we learn from the tragic structure of consciousness' encounter with the collision of the human law and the divine law. For on Hegel's presentation of the Greek ethical world, consciousness' encounter with traitor's corpse reveals that the protection of either the human or divine law results in the violation of the other. In research on a somewhat different topic, Lore

Hühn explains that Hegel conceives of the "basic figure" of tragedy as the collision of

> two equally legitimate powers that never attain any advantage over one another because both inhere in each other as one of the other's moments. This means that from a theoretical standpoint on tragedy, each side brings the unity of the whole to presence such that the doer and victim collapse into one.[55]

In the Greek ethical world, both the human law and divine law prescribe legitimate and necessary duties, and thus the agents who are assigned to uphold the laws, the monarch and the sister, are bound by reason and custom to fulfill their duties. But, in practice the two laws prove to be mutually intertwined, entangled, and repellant, until the claims they stake on the landscape of our ethical commitments come to form a sort of speculative Catch-22. Confronted with the traitor's corpse, neither agent is able to avoid guilt, for the action each takes to uphold one law serves to disobey the other.

One of Hegel's most provocative conclusions is that consciousness' confrontation with this enigma of the ethical world compels it to the view that not only rational agency on behalf of the human and divine laws but also all rational agency, is intrinsically guilty. Hegel's explanation of why consciousness draws this conclusion is complex, but it is possible to argue that his view suggests, in part, that the lessons we learn from the conflict of human and divine laws reveals a general rule of rational action. The purpose of the law of universality, the human law, is to enforce respect for the universal scope and binding force of law and, thus, there is a sense in which the human law guides all law-governed actions. Moreover, the government and the male citizens of the community who adhere to their duty to this law cannot help but remain blind to the claims made on them by the divine law. At the same time, this divine law of the singular also interpenetrates the practical arena, making its claim on the figure of woman, who must also in a certain sense remain blind to the demands of the human law.[56] So if the laws of universality and of singularity suffuse all agency in the ethical world, and if these laws prove to be mutually incompatible and antithetical in the crucible of concrete practice, then, the argument would go, all rational actions leads to guilt.

Even if we were to accept such claims, is it right to say that rational agents become guilty simply because their law-governed actions turn out to violate some other law? It seems natural to object that rational agents should be held accountable only for what is more or less directly under their purview and control. From this viewpoint, it might be argued that although we often have good reasons to hold agents accountable for their purposes, intentions, beliefs, and desires, there is at times much less reason to condemn agents for the unintended repercussions of their actions. Since Antigone, for example, is guided by a time-honored and rational law, she seems to be basically innocent, even if the fulfillment of her purposes fortuitously leads her to violate Creon's decree.

Yet, this sort of objection fails to address the central tenets of Hegel's qualitative theory of action. Hegel maintains that, in contrast with more causal theories of action, there is no ultimate ontological or epistemic disjunction between an agent's intentions, purposes, beliefs, and desires and the actions that flow from them. Thus on the Hegelian view, the measure of an agent's innocence or guilt turns on her purposes, her efforts to bring them to bear on the world, as well as their deliberate and unintended consequences taken as a whole and not on her intentions alone, abstracted from the sphere of actual, concrete affairs. He writes, "the deed is its *doing*, and the doing its inmost nature," and, because of this, "the agent [*das Handelnde*] cannot deny the crime or his guilt; —the deed is this: to set into motion what was unmoved and to bring forth what was first locked up in possibility. . . ."[57] For Hegel, rational agents must answer to more than is immediately before them in consciousness, or is under their influence and control, and guilt results from the structure of action itself and not merely from the election of an illegitimate or inadequate intention.

Since Hegel contends that human beings' propensity for failure in practical affairs is ineluctable, his conception of guilt points to a deep ontological structure of action. However, even though Hegel's view thus elicits comparisons to the doctrine of original sin, it is fruitful to keep in mind differences between Christian and Greek sensibilities.[58] For although the Hegelian view of (Greek) guilt, not unlike a standard notion of original sin, suggests that the condition of guilt is an inevitable and unavoidable result of human action, Hegel will identify it primarily as an implication of finitude and not as the consequence of an original evil act. Of course, discourses about original sin are highly developed and sophisticated. But, in the most general terms, broadly Augustinian, a basic account might be said to start with the idea of the human being in a perfected condition, in which it is possible to act freely and responsibly, and to avoid evil. But, due to God's just punishment for original sin, human beings now live in a fallen state, and are condemned to a life marked by what Augustine, for example, eventually described in reference to terms such as ignorance and difficulty.[59] But, even if such a characterization of original sin might be associated with a conception of guilt that is intrinsic to human being, it nonetheless appears, at least, to involve a notion of a prior type of human being that is not yet infected with sinfulness.

Of course, Hegel's position differs from the Augustinian model of original sin along a number of lines. Most salient for the present matter, however, is that on Hegel's account of the Hellenic notion of action, there is no condition in which human beings are free from guilt. On Hegel's approach to the Greek view, human beings are always already guilty, and not guilty simply as the consequence of any punishment or fall. The Greek experience of ethical life turns on the insight that practical action is simply subject to a certain finitude, and that an agent's encounter with guilt results not from a previous sin but from inescapable structural tensions that emerge in our efforts to participate in a larger practical world as unique beings.

If Hegel's account of guiltiness resists both the more mainstream, modern assumptions of the causal theory as well as the main lines of the Christian doctrine of original sin, then, I suggest, it registers a deep affinity for the ancient Greek notion of ἁμαρτία, waywardness, or errancy. Hegel introduces the concept of tragic errancy into his discussion only obliquely, in a quotation from Sophocles' drama, but the idea nonetheless plays a decisive role in Hegel's conception of guilt. Hegel claims that the rational agent's guiltiness is similar to Creon's and Antigone's guilt, and then, to clarify what this guilt is, he enlists a passage from the drama in which Antigone reflects upon the nature of her failure. Hegel cites Sophocles' character Antigone, "*because we suffer, we recognize that we have erred.*"[60] Given that the rest of Hegel's discussion of the Greek ethical world makes only circuitous use of Sophocles' drama, Hegel's direct quotation of the text stands out as an especially salient moment in his treatment. Indeed, Hegel's citation of the *Antigone* gains more emphasis when we notice that the form of his argument here, namely, that Hegel clarifies his own position based on the quotation of another text, is extremely rare within the *Phenomenology*. Hegel quotes directly from only a few poetic works in his entire book (another, from Friedrich Schiller's *An die Freude*, forms the final passage of Hegel's text).[61] Hegel's quotation from the *Antigone* illuminates his conception of guilt because the passage contains the verbal form of a word from the same family as the substantive ἁμαρτία: the English '... *erred*' is a translation of the German '... *gefehlt*,' in turn, in Sophocles' drama, '... ἁμαρτάνουσι.'[62]

In discussions of Attic tragedy the notion of ἁμαρτία is typically associated with a drama's tragic hero or protagonist, and, perhaps due in part to the continuing influence of a long heritage of efforts to place a moral frame around the notion, it is still relatively common to identify ἁμαρτία not as errancy, but, instead, as something that emerges from a sort of failure of moral fiber.[63] It is possible to argue, however, that in the Greek imagination ἁμαρτία had little to do with an agent's moral rectitude. Hegel enlists the passage from the *Antigone* to help to distinguish his conception of guilt from more modern and Christian interpretations, and, in this light, ἁμαρτία singles out not something like an agent's improper use of the free will or vulgar disposition but, rather, an involuntary tendency to err, to go astray, in all of her actions. Yet, the original sense of ἁμαρτία differs not only from the idea of character flaw but also from that of happenstance or bad luck.[64] While the Greeks thought that an agent's penchant to miss the mark is involuntary, this errancy does not result from external, fortuitous, or arbitrary circumstances. Instead, our proclivity in life to drift wayward forms an intrinsic, if unintended, aspect of our actions as actions.

On Hegel's discussion of the ancient world, consciousness' efforts to reconcile its awareness that it belongs to a broader world with its knowledge of itself as a rational agent result in collision and crisis and, ultimately, shed light on a crucial aspect of human finitude. Hegel's conception of antiquity is complex and intricate, and his account weaves together debates among his contemporaries about Hellenic culture, a speculative interpretation of Sophocles' *Antigone*, issues of cultural heritage and the law, family life, gender and sex, memory, and death. Some of the central lines of Hegel's treatment of Greece turn, however, on consciousness' efforts to come to terms with the question: what does it mean to participate in a political, social, and ethical world comprised of other rational individuals yet to remain true to oneself as a legislative being? Hegel concludes that one of the deepest meanings of rational agency is guilt—that, as rational agents, all of our efforts to realize our ends result in a certain failure, regardless of the rightness of our purposes, the strength of our character, or the conviviality of our circumstances. Human beings, as rational agents, are subject to a certain finitude of vulnerability, not simply due to external forces or to our reliance on external goods but, rather, by virtue of our own nature as errant.

From Errancy to Existence

Surely Hegel's insistence on our prospects to achieve the absolute, and his overall emphasis on our synthetic powers to unify our experience, strains all connective tissues between Hegelian speculation and existential philosophy.

Yet, despite the more triumphant, thematic strand of Hegel's thought, his use of Sophoclean tragedy to associate rational agency with errancy nevertheless anticipates a number of important themes in existentialist thought.[65] We are tempted to ask ourselves, for example, if Hegel's association of consciousness' experience of rational agency and guilt with errancy might not reverberate in Heidegger's existential analytic in *Being and Time* and Heidegger's account of *Dasein*'s encounter with guilt. But provocative though this issue might be, the relationship between Heidegger and Hegel is as profound and intricate as it is ambiguous, and it lies beyond the scope of our work to flesh it out in any detail.

Perhaps one of the deepest resonances between Hegel's account of rational agency and existentialist philosophy would lead us not only to Heidegger's *Being and Time* but also to Jean-Paul Sartre and, in particular, to his 1946 lecture, "Existentialism is a Humanism." There may be some reason for caution about this piece, at least in part because it is susceptible to interpretations that misrepresent Sartre's position as commensurate with a sort of voluntarism. But, Sartre's "Existentialism is a Humanism" forms a concise statement of his view, and, moreover, reveals unmistakable, if somewhat oblique, ties between Hegel's discussion of rational agency and the existentialist view of human action. Of course, Sartre consistently characterizes the project of existentialism in opposition to Hegelian speculation, and many of the differences between Sartrean existentialism and Hegel's thought are decisive. Still, as many scholars recognize, Sartre's thought is profoundly influenced by Hegel, and often more so than Sartre himself admits.[66]

In "Existentialism is a Humanism" Sartre proposes to defend existentialism against its many critics and to explain in straightforward language the meaning of the existentialist motto, 'existence precedes essence.' Sartre first defends existentialist philosophy against the charge that it leads to subjectivism and, in particular, against the claim that the existentialist position leads to the view that moral or ethical choices rest on nothing more than individual impulse or caprice. On the existentialist view, a human being chooses her essence in every deed, and all of our actions unfold under the sign of universality, not idiosyncratic whim. Sartre introduces the notion of 'anguish' to characterize the indefeasible and decisive form of responsibility placed on us by virtue of the universal aspect of each of our endeavors. He writes,

> When a man commits himself to anything, fully realizing that he is not only choosing what he will be, but is thereby at the same time a legislator deciding for the whole of mankind—in such a moment a man cannot

> escape from the sense of complete and profound responsibility. There are many, indeed, who show no such anxiety. But we affirm that they are merely disguising their anguish or are in flight from it.[67]

Sartre maintains that on the existentialist view, and to this extent his position remains consistent with Hegelian and Kantian frameworks, it is universalizable principle, not whim, that not only determines what and who we are but also governs every one of our actions, even though we wish, often enough, not to acknowledge it.

Yet, Sartre further argues that for existentialists, there is no ultimate court of appeals that can tell us what universal principles we must allow to guide our actions. For existentialists, there is an insurmountable disjunction between humans as legislative beings and the impenetrable thickness and arational sheen of the world, so that although it is impossible for us to relinquish our anguish, it is just as impossible for us to determine what purposes we should have, or, for that matter, to know if the purposes we do have will bring about our desired effects. For Sartre, the absence of any ultimate arbiter or *a priori* basis for the principles of our actions results in 'abandonment.' He explains,

> There can no longer be any good *a priori*, since there is no infinite and perfect consciousness to think it.... Dostoevsky once wrote "If god did not exist, everything would be permitted"; and that, for existentialism, is the starting point.... [M]an is in consequence forlorn, for he cannot find anything to depend upon either within or outside himself.[68]

Since there is no divine being or any other power to ensure that the grounds of universality are cut to fit the world, we find no inviolable link between the two, and, as a consequence, there is no *terra firma* from which we might view the principles of our actions. For Sartre, existentialism teaches not only that universal principles necessarily govern our actions but, moreover, that it is impossible to verify the credentials of the principles we choose to follow.

The Sartrean conception of human existence relies on Heidegger's thought and other developments of post-Hegelian German and French philosophy, and Sartre's position forms a radical departure from the Hegelian view that the speculative unity contains within it rationality, history, and their opposition. But, Sartre's vision of the ramifications of abandonment exhibits remarkable parallels to Hegel's conceptions of rational agency and errancy. Sartre registers one of the deepest points of contact between his position and Hegel's in a story he recounts to illustrate the notion of abandonment. Sartre tells of a student who, during the war, sought his advice about whether to travel to England to join the Free French Forces or to stay in France to care for his languishing mother.[69] "Consequently," Sartre observes, his student "found himself confronted by two very different modes of action; the one concrete, immediate, but directed towards only one individual; and the other an action addressed to an end infinitely greater, a national collectivity. . . ."[70] Sartre claims that there are no ethical resources that might help the student come to a decision—not Christian doctrine, not the Kantian categorical imperative, nothing. Thus the student experiences not only anguish due to the universal weight of his choice but also abandonment, in that his decision must be made entirely without the guidance of any eternal verities or certain principles to guide him.[71]

The parallels between Sartre's anecdote about his student to illustrate abandonment and Hegel's use of the *Antigone* to examine guiltiness, or errancy, cannot be denied. It is true that Sartre's story unfolds not in antiquity but rather in modern day Europe, and that it addresses itself to Kantian moral philosophy and Christianity. It is also true that Sartre's story focuses not on an irreconcilable collision of two rational agents in the political sphere but rather on an irresolvable dilemma faced by a single individual.[72] Yet, in both Sartre's and Hegel's accounts, questions about rational agency gravitate toward our awareness of our dual commitments to the broader world and to our more immediate matters; and for both Sartre and Hegel, the incompatibility of these two concerns reaches one of its most tenacious expressions in the collision of our loyalties to the state and to our families. Moreover, both Sartre and Hegel believe that our encounter with this conflict forces us to confront an important aspect of the finitude of our powers as rational agents. Taken together, Sartre's and Hegel's views complement one another and help us to form a broader picture of the essential limitations we face in our practical affairs. For if Sartre's discussion of abandonment emphasizes a form of finitude we encounter in our efforts to adjudicate our intentions or purposes, then Hegel's account of guilt reminds us that whichever purpose we choose, our fulfillment of our intentions is subject to errancy.

The instructive similarities between Sartre's "Existentialism is a Humanism" and Hegel's discussion of ethical life underscore the *rapprochement* between important themes in post-Hegelian philosophy and themes that emerge in Hegel's own thought as a result of his reliance on Greek tragedy. If Hegel's speculative philosophy forms a certain summit of philosophical movements in the Western tradition, then it is perhaps no surprise to find that similar questions animate the thought of figures such as Sartre who stand in its aftermath. Although Hegel's more triumphant, modern vision of the human spirit leads to the view that we ultimately find reconciliation in the consolations of philosophy, religion, art, and forgiveness, his reliance on the *Antigone* to discuss agency not only marks a return to the remotest origins of the Western heritage but also points beyond the trajectories of the very traditions that Hegel wishes to complete. For Hegel's reliance on the resources of tragedy to elaborate on ethical life and rational agency, not unlike his uses of tragedy to discuss human freedom and experience, reveals that although speculative thought announces itself as a philosophy of infinite identity, its dedication to the incorporation of multiplicity, disunion, difference, and strife perhaps tells us no more about our relation to the absolute than it speaks to our finitude.

4

Tragic Wisdom

Nietzsche's thematic purposes in the *Birth of Tragedy* center on his interests in the significance of ancient Greek drama and reveal his early hopes for the revival of a culture of tragedy in modern Germany. But in point of fact, he devotes a great share of his focus in this text to the critique of Socratism, one of his first names, we might suggest, for the impulse he sees behind philosophical tenets that profess to achieve transcendence, to discern permanence and identities, to attain wholeness and unity.[1] For whatever ostensible purposes they may have, Nietzsche tells us in this work, philosophers in the West have always been directed by "the Socratic delight in knowledge and the delusion that through it we will be able to heal the eternal wound of existence."[2] Nietzsche's pronouncement recommends itself as evidence for those detractors discomfited by his alleged romanticism, and, years later, even Nietzsche himself conveys the regret that the *Birth of Tragedy* was "marked by every defect of youth."[3] But one of the chief upshots of this book—and it is one that will continue to permeate his more mature thought—is that philosophical attempts to establish a complete and coherent picture of things characteristically amount to little more than so many masks for a subterranean, reactive need to avoid, or even to deny, what has typically been perceived as "the terrible, icy current of existence."[4] Thus, Nietzsche's repudiation of Socratism can be seen as an important, preliminary statement of his celebrated suspicion of metaphysical, epistemological, and ethical theories that purport to systematize, unify, and in this manner, to mend the wounds of the disjointedness and variegation of life.

Nietzsche's diagnosis of the philosophical heritage of the West is meant to be comprehensive in scope, and he declares, for example, that the entire history of thought since the fifth-century B.C.E., to include the philosophical climate of his times, continues to stand in the ever longer shadow of Socrates.[5] But as Gilles Deleuze (and others) point out, Nietzsche directs crucial aspects of his critique of the tradition against tenets of Hegel's thought, such as, for example, Hegel's notion of dialectic.[6] In light of this, it perhaps comes as no surprise that the choice of words Nietzsche uses to admonish Socratism might also be cast as a sort of critical parody of a passage from Hegel's *Phenomenology*. Ironically, the phrase of Hegel's appears in his discussion of self-renunciation and forgiveness, important issues of human finitude. Nonetheless, as if to substantiate Nietzsche's claim that Hegel's thought is infected with an acute case of Socratism, Hegel not only asserts that consciousness surpasses these experiences of limits, but further announces that "the wounds of spirit heal and leave no scars behind."[7]

It remains unclear whether, and to what extent, Nietzsche himself may be said to overcome the Socratic impulse he so readily finds in others; and some scholars argue that despite all of Nietzsche's efforts to outstrip Hegel, it is ultimately Hegel's critical relation to the tradition that is the more compelling and radical of the two.[8] In any case, Hegel's identification of his project in the *Phenomenology* with a sense of unity that aims to doctor the wounds of spirit comes into sharpest focus in his discussion of the last phases in the development of spirit. Finally, near the end of its career, consciousness has become explicitly aware of its speculative nature, and has thus also come to recognize that its greatest hopes to synthesize its experience lie in higher-order practices of reflective life, and not in the more raw arenas of, for example, ethical action and labor. In chapter 1, we considered Hegel's association of the perfection of self-conscious reflection with absolute knowledge, and, in the final chapter of his presentation, Hegel identifies speculative philosophy as the seat of this achievement. But, as we shall see, for Hegel speculative philosophy is itself only the highest form of 'absolute spirit,' and derives from other, lower forms of reflective life, emerging from a dialectic that passes through consciousness' experience of the 'revealed religion,' or Christianity, as well as its predecessor, the Greek 'religion of art,' and, more originally still, through natural religion.[9]

Insofar as the attainment of the absolute constitutes the organizing principle of this dialectic as a whole, Hegel's discussion of philosophy, religion, and art may be seen as the culmination of the more triumphant, modern aspirations of his project in the *Phenomenology*. With this in mind, one is perhaps led to wonder whether the conclusion of Hegel's account might actually counter his, otherwise, intense interest in the tragic, serving not to deepen, but rather to mitigate, temper, perhaps, even undermine his previous sensitivity to the scope and weight of the tragic side of spirit. Yet, despite the stress of the absolute in Hegel's presentation of the dialectical advance to philosophy through Christian, Greek, and natural religion, his discussion of 'absolute spirit' nonetheless draws him once again within the vicinity of the tragic. For even though he holds that the Greek religion of art is superceded by more advanced forms of consciousness, his elucidation of ancient art comes to focus on the tragic drama of the Attic period, and on the roles played by tragic drama in the religious and civic life of Hellenic society.

In this last of Hegel's uses of tragedy in the *Phenomenology*, he considers tragic drama, for the first time, explicitly as a form of art, and not simply as a template of model for another form of experience. Although Hegel's conception of tragic drama is intricate and complex, it will not be difficult to see similarities with some hermeneutical views to art, such as the one developed by Gadamer.[10] Hegel's approach is governed by the belief that, like philosophy, the tragic art of antiquity was animated by a speculative directive. From this standpoint, the vocation of tragic drama would have been to represent foundational contours of the Greek spirit: roughly, what might be called the basic truths of the historical time and place in terms of which human beings of the age understood their world and themselves. Thus, on this view, the spectators of a performance of tragedy would have been met with an occasion not simply to experience a fiction, but, moreover, to reflect on fundamental conditions of their lives. For Hegel, the speculative significance of the tragic work of art will be determined neither by its capacity to entertain, divert, or produce pleasurable affects, nor, for that matter, by its adherence to formal rules or other standards set out by the aesthete or art critic.[11] Rather, his discussion will indicate that for the spectators of antiquity, the performance of tragic drama unfolded above all as an interpretive event that culminated in the disclosure of a certain form of tragic knowledge.

So, even if Nietzsche's diagnosis of Hegel's Socratism caution us to be beware of Hegel's faith in the healing power of the absolute, Hegel's account of the insight offered by tragic art may nonetheless point to important aspects of finitude. In comparison to speculative philosophy, which Hegel believes to supercede all restrictive conditions, we shall see that tragic art remains dependent on a number of historical, material, and cultural conditions. Moreover, if philosophy is supposed to involve a form of purified thought that completely unifies our experience, tragic art will offer an only attenuated sense of unity that remains wedded to image and affect. Yet, perhaps what will strike us most about Hegel's view is its implication that in antiquity, the religion of tragic art led not to pessimism or cynicism, but, instead, to what appears to be an affirmative, even beautiful, relation of life. For, as we shall see, Hegel concludes that for spectators in antiquity, tragic drama led to a sense of acceptance, or repose, that allowed them to embrace, perhaps even to love, the forms of vulnerability and suffering they watched on stage.

It may be said of Hegel, as it may also be said of many other philosophers before and after him, that his view associates the perfection of knowledge with the notion of wisdom. In his celebrated lectures on Hegel, Kojève argues that Hegel's conception of wisdom has a number of facets.[12] But it is safe to say, minimally, that Hegel associates his notion of wisdom with the consciousness of the absolute achieved in speculative philosophy. Certainly, as Kojève points out (and as I hint at near the outset of chapter 2), there is a sense in which Hegel's speculative philosophy is no longer philosophy at all, to the extent that the term 'philosophy' may be used to designate not the full *possession* of wisdom, but, rather, its ongoing *pursuit*.[13] It is, furthermore, not difficult to discern in Hegel's wisdom of the absolute a number of presumptions of modernity whose credentials have been lost. Yet, even if important aspects of Hegel's official view of wisdom no longer appear plausible, his consideration of tragic drama may nevertheless provide insight into a different, more ancient, perhaps even Delphic, and, too, also more sustaining vision of wisdom operative in his text. In what follows, I would like to open up this other, more tragic vision of wisdom, suggesting that it turns not on the attainment of an absolute form of knowledge, but, rather, on a certain acknowledgement of limits, and, indeed, an acknowledgement that exposes the hubris in Hegel's own, thematic belief in the power of thought to remove the scars left by the wounds of spirit.

The Theoretical and the Theater

What does Hegel mean by his claim that speculative philosophy, as well as both religion and art, are forms of reflective life? In what sense does the purpose of reflection inform the Hellenic experience of tragic art? Scholarship on Hegel's notion of 'absolute spirit' admits of a greater range of interpretations that would be fruitful to consider here.[14] Perhaps at least one of Charles Taylor's claims about Hegel's approach captures a more common thread in the literature. For Taylor, the purpose of philosophy, religion, and art is to permit spirit "to come to a full . . . knowledge of itself."[15] From this standpoint, all three forms of absolute spirit may be seen as *self-referential* aspects of spirit, which, Taylor argues, involve self-conscious forms of cognition that serve as the "vehicle" in virtue of which spirit comes to know itself.[16] Thus, in its highest forms, spirit as it were folds over and in onto itself, and culminates in the performance of a certain interpretive circle. On the one hand, it is spirit, by means of the self-conscious activities of philosophy, religion, and art, that serves in the role of interpretive subject, of knower, poised to achieve new awareness and insight. On the other hand, in these absolute forms of spirit, it is of course also none other than spirit itself, now taken in the historical totality of its substantial elements, which comprises the interpretive object, the phenomenon that is to be known.

Yet, even though Hegel envisions the attainment of spiritual self-knowledge as the highest and, thus, *last* stage in the development of spirit, he also maintains, at the same time, that philosophy, religion, and art play a *foundational* role in the constitution of spiritual life. In the mainstreams of recent Hegel studies, Terry Pinkard is among those who capture the point nicely. Pinkard's description of philosophy, religion, and art as forms of "absolute reflection" echoes the idea that they aim to achieve spiritual self-knowledge, and he holds that this type of reflection is governed by the demand of spirit to achieve "authoritative" knowledge of its own essence and goals.[17] But for Pinkard, further, each of Hegel's three forms of absolute reflection may be seen as "a type of practice that has come to count in . . . [a] community as being itself warranted to articulate what else in that community is definitive for it."[18] Not only does Hegel view philosophy, religion, and art as the highest flowers in the development of consciousness, but he also maintains, at the same time, that these practices fulfill a mythopoetic function, constituting the spiritual fundaments of a community.

Some of Hegel's most basic sensibilities about the purpose of philosophy, religion, and art may be discerned, too, in connotations that arise from his association of them with the term 'speculation' itself. Jacques Taminiaux asserts that the first, extensive, thematic use of the term in modern philosophy appears in Kant, and he notes that Hegel's extensive and positive use of the word may in part be seen as a kind of rejoinder to the pejorative sense Kant often ascribes to it.[19] But Taminiaux also calls attention the fact that Hegel's employment of the term exploits its etymological origins in the Latin *speculum*.[20] On this view, to associate speculation with philosophy, religion, and art, is to emblemize them as forms of spiritual self-mirroring. Furthermore, Hegel associates this speculative mirror-play with a certain modern revision of the ancient Greek notion of θεωρία, which Taminiaux translates as the "beholding [of] beings as they truly are."[21] Surely, Hegel would affirm that there is much about philosophical practice, religious experience, and both the production and reception of art that appear, on the surface at least, to diverge from any interest in self-reflection or θεωρία. Yet, Hegel's view indicates that properly grasped, the highest goal of all three forms of absolute spirit is to establish an authoritative, foundational account, in a special sense, a 'theory,' of what spirit itself *is*.

One of Hegel's chief claims is that spirit's efforts to achieve this theoretical insight, or self-knowledge, reach complete adequacy only in philosophy, and not in religion and art. So, even if an identical theoretical drive guides all three forms, it is finally only in philosophy that this need is satisfied fully.[22] As is well-known, Hegel places his view on a historical matrix, such that philosophy is said to reach its apotheosis in modernity (and in particular, in the culmination of German Idealism in his own system); religion in Christian Europe; and art in ancient Greece.[23] But the general lines of Hegel's distinction between philosophy and the other forms of absolute spirit also incorporate some staples of modern critiques of religion. Now, the difference should not be reduced to an opposition between enlightenment and superstition, as Hegel treats this antagonism as a discrete and nuanced stage in the development of consciousness.[24] But philosophy, he tells us, culminates in systematic and rigorous science (*Wissenschaft*), whose rationality and legitimacy is embodied in the concept (*Begriff*), itself independent of all restrictive conditions.[25] By contrast, religious consciousness (which, in the *Phenomenology*, includes both the Christian religion and the Greek religion of art) is inadequate. For, although it is the same theoretical interest that governs all forms of religion, religious and artistic practice result not in the complete and direct conceptual expression, but rather only in incomplete, dependent forms of depiction. Hegel characterizes the lower, religious forms of expression as mere "*representation*" (*Vorstellung*), insofar as they remain wedded to sensation.[26] Moreover, whereas philosophical reflection is completely self-conscious, religious and artistic practice, foremost in their Christian and Greek forms, remain bound by the unreflective recapitulation of traditional beliefs, customs, and myths.[27]

Does Hegel's identification of philosophy as the perfection of theory, or science, mean that he believes it to achieve a 'transhistorical' point of view? Hegel's characterization of speculative philosophy as a genuine science suggests that he believes his position to conform to the belief, typical of modernity, that science must meet legitimate standards of objectivity and certainty.[28] Yet, Hegel would differ from those who hold that justification in science turns on the establishment of proper criteria for induction.[29] For, to Hegel's mind the objectivity of philosophical reflection, of science, depends on the achievement not of a *trans*historical perspective, but rather of an *omni*historical stance. Here, the perfection of science does not depend on attaining a standpoint that purports somehow to remove itself completely from conditions of history. Instead, spirit achieves an objective view of itself as the result of an exhaustively historical form of reflection that recollects the entire range of experiences that have contributed to its own development. Of absolute knowledge, Burbridge writes, for example, that it is "the awareness, at a more encompassing level, of the process of experience and learning that has marked each stage of the phenomenological odyssey."[30] Hegel is concerned with the modern drive for objectivity and certainty. But in contrast with many of his contemporaries and predecessors in modernity, his view suggests that the perfection of knowledge is won not in the flight from history, but rather in an exhaustive, even totalizing engagement with it.

Important for Hegel's view is that once the education of spirit reaches its fruition in the modern period in philosophy, religious practice and the work of art lose their authority as occasions for speculative reflection. Hegel maintains that in the modern age of philosophy, it is no longer a "highest need" of spirit that directs our interest in religion and art, such that "however much we would like to find the Greek divine images pertinent [*vortrefflich*], or to see the Holy Father, Christ, and Mary reverentially [*würdig*] and consummately [*vollendet*] presented, it does not matter, we of course no longer bend our knee."[31] From this modern vantage, we come to see art as "a thing of the past" (*ein Vergangenes*).[32] Of course he does not mean by these assertions that once spirit achieves the level of philosophy, religion and art disappear from the face of the earth; nor does he mean that believers suddenly lose their faith and artists cease to create, nor that the seminaries, churches, the art galleries, and auction houses promptly empty out. Rather, his contention is that part and parcel of the ascension of philosophy in the modern period is the demise of religion and art as the highest sources of meaning for spirit.[33] Philosophical reflection, due to the completeness, robustness, and transparency of the knowledge it provides, comes to supercede religion and art as the touchstone of our knowledge of what and who we are. As a consequence, in the historical age of philosophy, religion and art are reduced to a speculatively secondary and derivative status.

Several important figures in twentieth-century continental European philosophy, such as Heidegger, Gadamer, Derrida, and, more recently, Giorgio Agamben develop an ambiguous relation to Hegel's contention, and recognize a grain of truth in Hegel's claim that the modern age has seen the displacement of religion and art from their once prominent position within society.[34] Yet, these figures disagree with Hegel about the cause of religion's and art's demise, and Gadamer, for example, associates the marginalization of art not with the rise of German Idealism, but rather with the historical consciousness, diagnosed early on by Nietzsche, that begins to take hold in the deterioration of traditional Christian and humanist cultural forms.[35] Some twentieth-century figures will also agree with Hegel's related claim that the gradual downfall and demise of religion and art in modern times coincides with the birth of the modern museum, though, to be sure, they explain the reasons for this birth along very different lines than Hegel will. Gadamer, again here among those to see in Hegel's position a challenge, characterizes the emergence of the museum in modern times as a symptom of the estrangement of art and of the dislocation of art from its important position in political, social, and religious life, relegating it to an artificial, even derivate social space.[36] The phenomenon is not difficult to reconstruct. On a recent journey through the Alsace, for example, I visited a museum in Colmar to see the Grünewald altarpiece housed there.[37] Magnificent and powerful as the work was, my encounter with it in a museum was cut off from its original world of signification, its place in the church and its rituals, as well as the central role these played in the community life of the period. Due to this, the experience of the piece inevitably lost some of its fullness, and, indeed, appeared at least as much as a historical artifact as it did a work of art.[38]

Although Hegel finds the ascendancy of philosophical science and not the leveling of the life-world responsible for the death of religion and art, he, too, conceives of the modern museum first and foremost as a sort of mausoleum designed to house and preserve religious and artistic works from the past. His philosophical interest in the museum reaches its height during the time he lived in Berlin in the 1820s, and some of his convictions appear at least as visibly in his practical affairs as they do in his written works or his lectures from that time. As Andreas Grossmann maintains, the Hegel of this later period became concerned that the dissolution of our speculative need for religion and art might lead modern societies to neglect their heritages of religious and artistic works, spurring in him an interest in the possibility of a museum to house the *monumenta nationum historica*.[39] Hegel believes that while modern society gives rise to an indubitable and exhaustive form of philosophical reflection and thus progresses beyond all speculative need of religious ritual, mythic icon, and artistic image, he nonetheless recognizes a need for a kind of archival space that would allow us to conserve and catalog the remnants of world history.

Yet, despite the fact that Hegel's more triumphant view of philosophical science leads to the foreclosure or, as he puts it, the "remission" of the relation between our pursuit of absolute knowledge and our concern for art, his speculative approach to the work of art actually opens up new paths of inquiry that continue to play an important role in research now.[40] For notwithstanding his claims about modernity and the dissolution of our speculative need for art, Hegel nonetheless defends in his discussion of the absolute art of ancient Greece the affinity between our aspirations for knowledge and the resource of art. Thus, even if Hegel's doctrine of the pastness of art poses a decisive challenge to current inquiries into the significance and function of art—and, indeed, a challenge that has drawn the attention of galactic figures of post-Hegelian continental thought—his conception of the speculative impulse that guides art might nonetheless shed original light on the potential of art, in tragic drama, at least, to provide insight into the conditions of finitude that inform historical life.

Readers of Hegel's *Lectures on Aesthetics* will know that in his later years he developed an expansive body of work on the subject, which addresses, among other things, both the history of art and its forms, numerous aesthetic theories of beauty and art, and an enormous number of individual artworks.[41] Although Hegel's *Phenomenology* approach to the religion of art is largely consonant with his later views, the interest that guides him is somewhat different, and his treatment is much more condensed.[42] It would not be fruitful for purposes of the present inquiry, however, to focus on the relation of Hegel's *Aesthetics* to the *Phenomenology*, nor, for that matter, to delve too deeply into the capillaries of his approach in the *Phenomenology* itself, as my principal focus here is to consider the implications of Hegel's general approach to art for the notion of tragic wisdom that emerges from it. To this end, it will suffice to outline in broad strokes some of the principal features of the view that arises from Hegel's discussion. A more general picture of the notion of art at issue here begins to take shape in some of the suggestions made by Hegel about the production and reception of art; one of the important rationale behind the special status he affords to tragic drama may be drawn from some of his views of artistic genre.

Production—Genius versus Expert

It would be reductive to assert that Hegel's approach to the production of art is completely opposed to romanticism, and it is possible to argue that he appropriates and reconfigures romantic themes into his own view.[43] One aspect of Hegel's creative use of a standard of romanticism is found in his claim, asserted expressly in the *Lectures on Aesthetics*, but consistent with his account in the *Phenomenology*, that imaginative genius is required by the artist who produces spiritually significant art. Hegel defines imaginative genius as "the *general* capacity to produce the true work of art, as well as the energy by which it is trained and applied."[44] Here, the power of the artist to create works of art is thought to derive from an intrinsic gift for expression, which, though it may be cultivated through the development of technical expertise, cannot be instilled in a would-be artist from whole cloth. Hegel writes, again in the *Lectures on Aesthetics*,

> Certainly, to all of the arts there belongs expansive study, incessant industriousness, and manifold polished skill; however, the greater and more extensive is the talent and genius, the less it knows of arduousness in the acquisition of the facilities necessary for production.[45]

Hegel would not deny that expertise is required for the production of art, but holds that distinct from, and deeper than, the artist's technical skill is the genius she simply finds in herself. On this view, the ultimate powers of an artist to create derive not from her intentional efforts to master her craft, but to a serendipitous dispensation of talent.

But Hegel holds that the production of art is of speculative significance, and he rejects the idea that works of art express only, say, the mystical or inward feelings of the artist. Rather, Hegel's view suggests that it is one of the hallmarks of genius to produce works of art that actually express general truths of spirit. Hegel's vision of the production of art might thus also be said to turn on a notion of inspiration, insofar as creations of genius reflect something larger than the subjective, interior world of the artist. Furthermore, in contrast with some prevalent currents of romanticism in his time, as well as the Kant of the *Critique of Judgment*, Hegel believes that it is the larger world of spirit, and not of nature, that issues forth in the fruits of the genius' labors. Similar in some regards to Hegel, Kant also associates the production of great art with genius. Yet, Kant characterizes the genius as a "favorite of nature," whose special gift is "the inborn temperament (*ingenium*) *through which* nature gives the rule to art."[46] By contrast, Hegel holds that it is not the foremost features of the extra-spiritual world of nature, but, rather, the fundamental aspects of spirit itself that 'give the rule' to art. From the Hegelian angle, the artist may be cast as something of a medium through which the basic structures and dynamics of spirit itself come to be represented in a concrete, tangible form. Of course,

Hegel's attention to the tragic aspects of spirit remind us that many of these structures and dynamics are imbued with rupture, conflict, violence, loss, and the exposure of limits. It may be in part for this reason that the Hegel of the *Phenomenology* refers to the artist, whose genius brings her to express such crises of spirit in her art, as "the vessel of its sorrows."[47]

Reception—Festival and Work

How does Hegel conceive of the reception of artworks created by imaginative genius? Although he provides no explicit 'reception theory' in the *Phenomenology*, we shall see that he makes many of his most direct claims about the matter in his discussion of the spectators' relation to the performance of tragic art in antiquity. However, some of the most provocative and instructive ideas Hegel has about the reception of art may be derived from implications of his overall account of the dialectical process by which the Hellenic religion of art develops. Hegel locates tragic drama as the second of three forms of 'spiritual art,' which itself is his name for the highest phase in the development of the Greek religion of art. But he holds, further, that 'spiritual art' arises from two previous phases, first, the 'abstract work of art,' and then, in turn, the 'living work of art.'[48] In the broadest terms, one of Hegel's labors in these sections is to present the dialectic by which Hellenic artistic practice developed more and more self-conscious spiritual means of producing an adequate expression of the idea. In regard of this, Hegel conceives of the Greek religion of art as a dialectical progression in which spirit comes to learn that the representation of the idea unfolds as something human beings produce or make. Here, the representation of the idea is no longer grasped, as it was in the religion of nature, as something indeterminately and vaguely symbolized in something seen as outside or beyond.[49]

Hegel outlines the advance of the tradition of Hellenic art to its zenith in the 'spiritual' forms of epic, tragic, and comic poetry through a number of lower stages, and he discusses as one of the early phases of this tradition the emergence of the Greek statue, which he interprets as an originary production of spirit that embodies the image of spirit itself.[50] Some of the richest connotations of his view arise, however, from his conviction that the development of the ancient religion of art as a whole must pass through a phase that centers on the performance of religious and civic festivals. In his discussion of the 'living work of art,' Hegel turns to forms of spiritual practice that employ spiritual means to produce not an abstract image of spirit, but rather an immediate, direct expression of it. Here, he tells us, spirit, ultimately, the entire people, becomes a collective form of practice that serves to represent itself.[51]

Hegel's discussion circles in on three shapes of 'living art,' which, though historically more or less contemporaneous, nonetheless fall out in a dialectic of increasingly more robust forms. In the course of his treatment, he specifies as an initial type of living art the religious mysteries of Demeter and Dionysus, and then considers, in turn, the famed athletic games held in the period.[52] But the cairn of his account focuses on the festival (*das Fest*), exemplified in the sanctioned, public processions that surrounded events such as not only the Olympics, but also the performance of epic and dramatic art.[53] Grasped as 'living art,' the celebration of these festivals unfold as occasions in which spirit, in the figure of the community as a whole, becomes an artist that depicts to itself its own organic structure and basic aspects. In the processions, H. S. Harris summarizes, "*every citizen lives out the experience of identity with the divine subject of the City's substance.*"[54] As living art, the festival may, in short, be construed as a large-scale form of civic self-expression.

Hegel's conception of the difference and relation of 'spiritual' and 'living' art is complex and nuanced. But, even though he would argue that spiritual art is a discrete and higher form than living art, his presentation nonetheless raises the idea that the performance of spiritual art, such as tragedy, is predicated on the establishment of a broad-based, communal form of self-awareness. From such an angle, the reception of art, though itself governed by a speculative impulse, might nonetheless be seen as bound up with the creation of a politically and socially charged ethos, one of intense and common interest in the body politic. Thus, important features of the Hegelian framework suggest that the reception of art, or at least, in his lexicon, of spiritual art, could not be reduced to a private affair, and resists the assumption that the experience of art is a merely subjective, contingent matter. Instead, Hegel's connection of the work of art to the festival points to the possibility that the reception of art arises from an intersubjective milieu, guided by shared interpretive questions and presuppositions.

Genre—Dramatic versus Epic

Hegel's presentation of the religion of art maps the dialectical stages in the development of Hellenic art in reference not only to history, but also to genre.[55] Thus, although Hegel conceives of the development of spiritual art in historical stages, he also differentiates the forms of spiritual art with reference to the generic and specific differences of the forms of spiritual art. Hegel's presentation of Greek art reaches its dialectical summit in 'spiritual art,' and, in the *Phenomenology*, his discussion comes to center on three genres: the epic, tragedy, and comedy. But, the larger division that informs his account, however, is between epic poetry, on the one hand, and dramatic poetry, of which tragedy and comedy are species, on the other. In fact, Hegel's view of the central lines of the difference between epic and dramatic art may be seen as hearkening back to a distinction made already by Aristotle. In the *Poetics*, the demarcation of the epic from drama is cast foremost as a matter of their divergent manners or styles of presentation. Aristotle states,

> One may speak at one moment in narrative and another in an assumed character, as Homer does; or one may remain the same throughout, without any change; or the imitators may represent the entire story dramatically, as though they were doing the things described.[56]

Aristotle's position appears to owe debts to Plato's discussion of different poetic forms in Book II of the *Republic*, and suggests that whereas the manner of representation in epic poems unfolds (either in part or in full) as narration, dramatic representation takes shape in performance.

Hegel associates dramatic performance with a "higher language" than epic narration,[57] and his assertion may be interpreted as a certain progeny of Aristotle's view. But in Hegel, the distinction between performance and narration appears with a new significance. We have already seen that for Hegel, the vocation of philosophy, religion, and art is to arrive at unrestricted knowledge of the essential structures of spirit. Whereas in philosophy our knowledge of spirit reaches an omnihistorical and conceptual form as the result of exhaustive mediation, absolute art culminates only in a representation of this knowledge in immediate, sensuous intuition. Thus, in the idiom of a certain Platonism, Hegel might be said to believe that if philosophy offers us the genuine idea of spirit, art shows us only a likeness of it.[58]

Yet, even though Hegel never doubts that philosophy is superior to art, he nonetheless argues that drama offers a more perfect image than the epic. For on his view, dramatic performance gives its audience the impression of immediacy, while an epic reminds its listener (or reader) of the difference between the narration and the events it retells. Hegel's account accommodates the idea that a number of historical, cultural, and material conditions contribute to the success of a performance. He would be able to agree, for example, that the performance of tragedy is dependent on the aesthetic space created by the structures of the theater, the stage, and orchestra, even the scenery and props. But Hegel's discussion telescopes to one such condition in particular, the use of oversized masks by the actors on stage.[59] Indeed, Hegel conceives of the employment of these masks as an essential element of tragic drama, precisely because it contributes to the impression created by dramatic performance that we are confronted with characters and actions immediately before our eyes, and not in the idiom of narrative recapitulation.[60]

Earlier we noted Taminiaux's observation that Hegel associates the vocation of philosophy, religion, and art with a special sense of the Greek notion of θεωρία. Even if Hegel conceives philosophy as the perfection of this θεωρία, Taminiaux's discussion nonetheless helps to ground Hegel's contention of the 'theoretical' purpose that informed ancient Greek tragic drama, too. In the course of his discussion, Taminiaux asserts that with Plato, the notion of θεωρία often refers to the pure, philosophical contemplation of ideas. But Taminiaux suggests, further, that Plato's more technical use forms a contrast to a family of ordinary Greek words that associate θεωρία with dramatic art. He states, "The Greek work for theater, *theatron*, means a place for seeing. The Greek word for seeing is *theorein*. Prior to Plato, *theoria* meant beholding a spectacle, and the theorists par excellence were the spectators in the theater."[61] If Hegel aligns speculative philosophy with a sense of θεωρία that might be closer in spirit to a Platonic employment of the word, then his conception of the speculative vocation of tragic art, in turn, could be said to belong to a further, even more customary, Greek usage.

Message and Medium, the Riddle

But if Hegel's discussion suggests that absolute art reaches its height in the experience of Attic tragedy, what, specifically, does he think this tragic art showed? If his overall account points to the importance of tragic performances for Hellenic life, and casts tragic art as the vessel of the sorrows of spirit, what, after all, did the ancient Greek spectators of tragedy glean? In his classic lecture "Hegel's Theory of Tragedy," A. C. Bradley reminds us that on the Hegelian view, tragic drama not only produces sadness in us but also provides insights into the reasons for our pain. He writes,

> That tragedy is a story of suffering is probably to many people the most obvious fact about it. Hegel says very little of this; partly, perhaps, because it is obvious, but more because the essential point to him is not the suffering, but its cause, namely, the action or conflict.[62]

In Hegel, the speculative impulse that animates the experience of art directs its audiences to reflect on the specific forms the conflict presented on stage take, and to understand why they lead to anguish and pain. But Hegel's account focuses on the idea that the spectator's reflective comportment to a performance of a tragic drama is recreated within the drama itself, in the image of the chorus. He states, "consciousness of the spectator," or, "the crowd of spectators . . . have in the chorus their counterpart, or rather, their own thought expressing itself."[63] So, if the spectators fulfill the purpose of tragic art in their interpretive relation to the drama, and what this drama teaches them about their world, themselves, and their anguish, then the lessons they learn are duplicated by the expression of the chorus. Indeed, because it embodies this "wisdom" of tragic drama, Hegel refers to the chorus as the "*general ground*" of tragedy.[64]

Hegel's discussion of the chorus leads him to consider its specific role in the dramatic structure of Attic tragedy, and his approach could again be seen to owe a number of debts to Aristotle's *Poetics*. Hegel's *Lectures on Aesthetics* will characterize the work of art as a complex unity that integrates both formal and material elements. In the *Phenomenology*, Hegel's discussion suggests of tragic art that its organicity involves the synthesis of an internal opposition in the structure of the drama between the segments of the chorus (the parados, stasima, and exodus), and of the action (the episodes). One might even say that the *ontological* separation of the actual world of the spectators and the imaginary world of the drama is represented in the tragic work of art itself in the separation of the chorus and the action. Schmidt explains, "[t]he wellspring of the tragic is found in the antithesis between the acting subjects of the drama, who confront the world as a reality to be negated, and the chorus, who confront the action as a truth to be known."[65]

Hegel's insistence on the theoretical mission of tragic drama and on the relation of spectators and chorus elicits comparisons with other figures from the German heritage in which his view places him. Certainly, in twentieth-century continental philosophy, Gadamer's and Heidegger's respective beliefs that the vocation of art is to reveal truth each owe a substantial debt to Hegel's approach.[66] But, Hegel's claims also show signs of the influence of aesthetic and dramatic theory written by number of his contemporaries, such as Schiller's claim in *On the Aesthetic Education of Man in a Series of Letters* that art answers to a need for cultivation.[67] Perhaps somewhat less directly, Hegel's ideas of art may also have been influenced Lessing.[68]

But, even if we accept the Hegelian picture of tragedy, what does he believe the chorus teaches us? What message, finally, do the spectators see mirrored in the knowledge expressed by the chorus? Hegel would surely agree that the tragic dramas of the period, as well as the lessons to be gleaned from its choral odes, are multiple. But the centerpiece of his discussion refers first of all to the collision of ethical powers depicted in Sophocles' *Antigone*.[69] Of course, this does not come as much of a surprise. Hegel's broader idea, after all, is that in ancient Greece, the religious and civic performance of tragic art provided the members of the *polis* with the chance to confront and think about the foundational features and dynamics of the world in which they find themselves. However, as we have seen, Hegel holds that the ethical life of the Greeks was dominated by the tension between the human and divine law, the government and the family. So, even if one of Hegel's aims is to consider the function of the chorus in general terms, he could choose no better representative of the lessons it was to learn than those represented in the action of the *Antigone*.

Hegel's discussion extends further, though, and he also considers the spectators' (and the chorus') reflection on the interpenetration of knowledge and ignorance that afflicts tragic heroes, not only in the *Antigone*, but it would seem, to tragedies more generally.[70] Hegel's idea is that as interpreters of the dramatic action, spectators and chorus are able to see that a tragic hero's knowledge of her own situation, motivations, and fate is one-sided and partial, whereas the tragic hero, as an agent, is bound to a form of consciousness whose knowing is, at once, also a not-knowing.[71] In the *Antigone*, for example, the spectators and chorus are able to tell that Creon's grasp of things is only half of the story, while Creon's action remains completely blind to Antigone's point of view.[72]

Perhaps the most provocative thing that emerges from Hegel's account is the connection it appears to suggest between this entanglement of knowledge and ignorance and the idiom of the riddle. Now, it is true that Hegel provides no explicit reason why he invokes the notion of the riddle at this juncture, nor does he explicitly define the term. Yet, in the course of his efforts to illustrate the conjunction of knowledge and ignorance in the tragic hero, Hegel refers to several celebrated dramas, and focuses on the riddles that face their protagonists. He refers, for example, to Sophocles' depiction of the riddle of the Sphinx in *Oedipus Tyrannus*, to the role of the Oracle at Delphi in the stories of Oedipus and Orestes, to Shakespeare's portrayal of the prognostications of the weird sisters in *Macbeth*, and to his representation of the demands placed on Hamlet by his father's ghost.[73]

Hegel's discussion of the spectators and the chorus touches on the issue of the riddle only indirectly and briefly, and it does not form a central theme in his account. Yet, the connection he suggests between the ambiguous knowledge of the tragic hero and the riddle is redolent and warrants further attention. If Hegel holds that the spectators and chorus learn something from their reflection on the knowledge and ignorance of the tragic hero, for example, what might it mean to associate this lesson with the riddle? As I wish to consider, it might be that the tragic riddle forms not only an expressive medium, but, moreover, a certain message. For perhaps whatever other insights the spectators and chorus are to gather from dramatic action, it is that in the throws of conflict and action, human beings inevitably become a certain riddle to themselves.

Although Hegel does not mention Aristotle's *Poetics* in this context, it is an influential and vital resource on the tragic use of riddles. In recent scholarship, Schmidt is among those who shed much fresh light on Aristotle's interest in the riddle as a form of diction that reflects, even redoubles, the substantial contents and themes of tragic plot.[74] As is mentioned in chapter 1, much of Aristotle's discussion in the *Poetics* flows from his claim that tragic drama contains six basic parts. Of the elements, Aristotle considers the plot and characters to be most crucial. Even though his analysis of diction is nothing if not thorough (he considers not only the characteristic poetic styles of tragedy but also their elements, all the way down to the syllable and the letter), it does not appear to be among Aristotle's most central concerns.[75] But Aristotle nonetheless insists that the form of speech best suited to tragedy is the riddle, (incidentally, he remarks, along with the joke), which he casts as an extreme type of metaphor. Aristotle writes that for the tragedian,

> It is a great thing, indeed, to make a proper use of these poetical forms, as also of compounds and strange words. But the greatest thing by far is to be a master of metaphor. It is the one thing that cannot be learnt from others; and it is also a sign of genius. . . .[76]

For Aristotle the formal style of the riddle, itself the most intense type of metaphor, is the pinnacle of tragic diction, such that it may be seen to square more fully with the spirit of tragic drama than other forms of speech.

But what is it about the riddle that grants it such a special status for tragedy? What about the riddle cuts it to fit tragedy so well? Certainly, Aristotle's discussion appears to imply that tragic art distinguishes itself from other genres in part due to the monstrousness and scope of the difficulties it depicts.[77] After all, even a cursory survey of the tragic plots of interest to Aristotle would reveal not only multiple instances of violent conflict, but also numerous tragic heroes confronted with unpredictable breeches in the rhythms of everyday life, ethical entanglements, paradoxes, and perhaps even absurdities. What Schmidt's approach emphasizes is that Aristotle's definition of the riddle offers a sort of semantic double of these tragic representations of action. Schmidt cites Aristotle, "the very nature indeed of a riddle is this, to describe a fact in an impossible combination of words (which cannot be done with a combination of other names, but can be done with a combination of metaphors)."[78] On this view, Schmidt argues, the riddle, as a figure of speech that interconnects opposites, intertwines irreconcilables, and thereby gives expression to the inconceivable, is exceptionally suited to express and enhance the tragic action of the plot.[79] In short, Schmidt cites J.P. Vernant and P. Vidal-Naquet, "the dramatist plays on this [i.e., the power of the riddle] to transmit his tragic vision of a world divided against itself and rent with contradictions."[80] From such a standpoint, Aristotle may be seen to cast the riddle as an acme of tragic diction due to the peculiar semantic force that allows it to reiterate, redouble, and sharpen the tragedian's portrayal of tragic events.

It would be a mistake to suppose that Hegel overtakes Aristotle's view wholesale, or even to assume that Hegel develops his view expressly in regard of the *Poetics*. However, Hegel's introduction of questions about tragic diction into his discussion of the chorus appears to suggest, too, that the formal style of the riddle encapsulates one of the principal lessons of tragedy. As we have seen, Hegel conceives of the encounter with tragic drama from a speculative standpoint as an interpretive event that unfolds as an occasion for its spectators, through the chorus, to reflect on the fundamental conditions of their lives. If what the spectators and chorus confront is the riddle, then one of the lessons they are to see is, perhaps, that human life itself is a riddle of sorts. Indeed, the tragic riddle may perhaps be seen as a certain motto of the inescapable ambiguities that guide the fate of tragedies' heroes, and, thus, a token of finitude.

If one of Hegel's wishes is to elucidate his vision of the riddle by means of illustrations, then among his allusions to tragic riddles, it is perhaps his reference to Sophocles' depiction of Oedipus that bears out the implications of Hegel's view the best. Indeed, as Schmidt suggests in the context of his discussion of Aristotle, it may be that Sophocles indicates something of a model of the riddle in his portrayal of the enigma that Oedipus comes to pose to himself.[81] The story begins, as we know, in the city of Thebes in the aftermath of its liberation from the Sphinx by Oedipus, who has been rewarded for his ability to solve the Sphinx's riddle with the throne. But, of course, something remains afoul in Thebes, and, as the action unfolds, it becomes clear that although Oedipus was able to solve one riddle about the human being, he nonetheless fails to grasp the riddle of his own fate. For, despite all of his efforts to outwit the prophesy that he would murder his father and marry his mother, he is foiled by his ultimate ignorance of his own identity. Oedipus, the only human being to discern that the correct response to the riddle of the Sphinx was 'human being,' fails to see that his answer itself actually points to another, even darker mystery: one that he himself exemplifies and embodies, but, yet, cannot decipher.

Tragic Wisdom

Hegel's conviction that the speculative philosophy of the absolute supercedes the forms of insight won in religion and art may be seen to counter, even to threaten, his otherwise extensive and careful attention to the tragic limits encountered by consciousness in its long course of development. For in the framework of Hegel's thought, the philosophical wisdom of absolute science finally serves to remainder religion and art, and, along with them, the tragic representation of the riddles of human finitude. Yet, Hegel's overall approach to tragic art may nevertheless be viewed as the summit of his concern for tragic limits in the *Phenomenology*, and his discussion of it culminates in a consideration of the greatest insight, the final wisdom, that the spectators and chorus take from their experience of tragic art. In contrast with his vision of philosophical wisdom, which might appear to harbor an impossible desire to surmount all boundaries, his depiction of this tragic wisdom, by contrast, encourages us to recognize and embrace the forms of finitude signified in the tragic riddles represented on stage. To the extent that the present age continues to stand under the sign of what the young Nietzsche referred to as Socratism, and to embrace the central tenets of modernity that he would see as growing from it, we might expect this more tragic sense of wisdom to be received as a negative or downbeat view of life. But not unlike Nietzsche's later vision of the tragic, Hegel's discussion of tragic wisdom points to a life-affirming and even beautiful view of things that would allow us to accept the forms of finitude that imbue human life.

As we have seen, Hegel maintains that whereas the knowledge we achieve in philosophical reflection is purely conceptual, the insight that the spectators glean from a tragic drama remains imbued with sensation. But Hegel's discussion suggests that our experience of this emotional insight distinguishes itself from other types of affect because it is communicable and may thus in some sense be shared among those who undergo it.

Despite the significant differences between Hegel's and Kant's views of aesthetic life, one is tempted to wonder if Hegel's description of the sociality of this emotional insight might elicit comparisons with Kant's notion of the *sensus communis* from his analysis of judgments of taste in the third *Critique*. Regardless, Hegel's overall vision does suggest lines of continuity between the *Phenomenology* and his Frankfurt writing on love. For, perhaps just as the Hegel of the *Phenomenology* describes the collective insights we win from tragedy as a socially shared, or, at least, sharable, emotion, so the younger Hegel of the Frankfurt period casts our communal bonds as a form of love. He writes of that love that it

> is a feeling, though not a single feeling; . . . in love the whole is not held together as in the sum of many individuals, or separated moments; . . . in love there is still the separated, but no longer as separated, [but instead] as the own, and the living feels the living.[82]

If Hegel's *Phenomenology* account of our tragic sense of the common retains features of his earlier belief, then the quickening of social bonds felt in response to tragic art may be seen to culminate in a complex affective relation. Illuminated by Hegel's earliest notion of love, the kind of togetherness forged among the spectators of tragic drama is predicated on the presence of individual difference. It is even possible to wonder if, in the constitution of such a bond of love, commonality itself might be constituted focally as a shared sense of separateness.

Even if the *Phenomenology* discussion of tragic wisdom appears to flow from his earlier interest in love, it unfolds along very different lines. For Hegel believes that our encounters with tragic drama reach a more positive insight only in virtue of our experience of the negative, painful emotions of fear and pity.[83] Hegel's enlistment of these terms place him one more time in Aristotle's debt, not to mention the heritages in poetics that draw on Aristotle's approach. But, from the speculative standpoint, the spectators' experiences of fear and pity, registered in the chorus, may be seen as a constitutive feature of the lesson that tragedy teaches. The members of the chorus, H. S. Harris asserts, "lead us, the audience, into the right ethical understanding" of what happens on stage.[84] Hegel's elucidation is compact, and his initial move is to acknowledge that the spectators' reflective affects of fear and pity find their echo not in every word of the chorus, but instead only in those portions of its odes guided by an "earnestness of the concept."[85] Hegel's explanation of this distinction, though brief, points to a number of issues. One of his chief aims is to cordon off the portion of the spectators' experience expressed in the chorus that aims at a complete, unified understanding of the plot. For much of a drama, he tells us, the spectators lack the reflective distance to gather together the meanings of the series of events presented to them. This experience, in turn, is expressed in those choral odes in which the chorus appears not to consider the entire round of action in its unity, but rather simply to respond or react to individual episodes.[86] Hegel's assertions suggest that spectators nonetheless eventually attain heightened moments of reflection, in which they summate the specific events of the plot and thereby grasp the tragic import of the action as a whole. Given expression in the chorus, it is just such a kairos that adumbrates the serious, synthetic force of the concept, even if only at the level of representation.

Hegel asserts that as the consciousness of the spectator reaches its summit, it comes to see itself as subject to a "foreign fate."[87] But, while he believes this knowledge to be rational, he nonetheless holds that it bears itself out as a complex affective response. The initial phase of this emotional dynamic is negative, and involves, first of all, an element, or, to employ a Hegelian idiom that he himself does not invoke in this case, a 'moment' of fear. Hegel's idea is that the culmination of the spectators' interpretive relation to the dramatic events portrayed in the episodes, the fulguration of their grasp of the meaning of the action, expresses itself as a shudder of horror. Hegel illustrates this view in reference to Sophocles' *Antigone*. As the spectators (along with the chorus) observe the episodes, their interpretive understanding of the action goes back and forth, until, at a decisive moment, they grasp that taken as a meaningful whole, the action represents the ineluctability of the collision of the "higher powers" embodied in the struggle between Creon and Antigone.[88] But the advent of this tragic insight expresses itself, Hegel's view suggests, in the spectators' experience of a sudden onset of fear in the face of these opposed ethical powers, their conflict, and the destruction that this conflict brings about.

The negative side of the spectators' affective response also entails a moment of pity. For Hegel, the crucial instant in which the spectators understand the meaning of the action as a whole brings on not just fear, but also compassion in the face of the monstrous suffering of the tragic heroes. Furthermore, the spectators' experience of this compassion also serves as a mutually felt empathy for themselves, since, Hegel tells us, they see that the terrible plight of the tragic hero is nothing else than a depiction of crucial conditions of their own lives.[89] The spectators of the *Antigone*, for example, feel pity for Antigone, condemned to a horrible death before her life had really begun; and, too, even for Creon, whose fulfillment of his duty to the human law leads him to lose everything dear to him.[90] In turn, Hegel would hold, the spectators would then also feel pity for one another and for themselves, since they would see that the story of Antigone and Creon is itself a poetic image of the fault lines of an ethical world in which their own lives unfold.[91]

But, Hegel's discussion suggests that the spectators' affective response results in a sudden turnaround or switch, a transport, in which the negative emotions of fear and pity give way to a positive sentiment. It would be hard to avoid the presumption that Hegel's conception of this positive outcome is patterned on Aristotle's notion of catharsis. But it is instructive that Hegel's *Phenomenology* does not appropriate Aristotle's language to denote the positive side of the spectators' affective response, even though Hegel expressly used Aristotelian terms to describe its negative aspects. For, Hegel's abstention from Aristotle's 'catharsis' might lead us to suspect he wished to avoid confusions that might arise from predominant interpretations in which catharsis is described along more or less medical lines of a kind of therapeutic release of emotions or a purge.[92] Of course, there is no reason to suppose that this is the only heritage of interpretive approaches to catharsis with which Hegel would have been familiar; but it is certainly one that runs contrary to his consideration of the purpose of art. Hegel's conviction is that a speculative need governs the encounter with art, and so even though he believes the spectators' response to tragic drama is affective, he nonetheless thinks of the emotions produced by tragedy to comprise a form of insight. Thus, in Hegel, the spectators' experience of a positive emotion brought about by fear and pity should not be cast as, say, a kind of curative discharge, but, instead, as the final, affirmative lesson of tragic drama.

Hegel identifies the spectators' experience of this positive, affective awareness as a sense of "empty repose" (*Ruhe*).[93] For him, however, this sensation of calm does not refer to, say, the relief that spectators must have felt once the terrible events of the plot had run their course and the dramatic tension had unraveled. Rather, he believes that the spectators' positive quiescence arises from their decision to accept the negative insights embodied in their experience of fear and pity. For Hegel, the spectators' repose unfolds as a "surrender to necessity."[94] Yet, Hegel specifies that the spectators' surrender is not to 'necessity' understood in terms of the obligation that guides the characters' action, which in the Greek ethical world, as we saw in chapter 3, derives from the ethical substance of a people.[95] But neither do the spectators see this 'necessity' as an "operation of the absolute essence."[96] Rather, Hegel's approach suggests a perspective on 'necessity' that refers to the recalcitrant resistance of the real that foils all human intention, effort, and skill. In this view, one might recognize a divergence from modern notions of the necessary, such as those that govern, for example, a Newtonian image of the universe, and a return to the much more ancient sense of ἀνάγκη. On this view, the spectators' ultimate emotional response turns on the composure that comes over them when they acknowledge the causes of their fear and pity cannot be controlled or changed, but rather only endured.

For Hegel, then, the highest lesson of tragic art teaches us to acquiesce to the painful fact that spiritual life is imbued with potentials for catastrophe, collision, and conflict over which we are powerless. It might be that Hegel's conception of speculative philosophy is infected by a hidden desire to reinscribe control over life, to the extent that it turns on a form of knowledge that is restricted by nothing foreign to mind. But Hegel's treatment of the spectators' complex and dynamic emotional response to tragedy indicates the possibility of an insight that speaks less to the masterful powers of reason than to the forms of finitude that pervade spiritual life. Indeed, Hegel's view points to the idea that the encounter with tragic art unfolds as an experience in which the spectators would be compelled to relinquish all pretenses of control. For, the spectators of tragedy are confronted not only by insuperable and destructive fault lines of spirit, but also their impotence to mitigate or to dissolve them.

Hegel's discussion of the education spectators received from tragic art in ancient Greece might be seen as a capstone of all his other uses of tragedy in his phenomenology of spirit. Hegel's elucidation of the consciousness of the spectator centers on Attic tragedy, and on Sophoclean drama in particular. But his discussion nonetheless points to implications that might be applied more broadly to his interest in tragedy. Throughout Hegel's presentation of its experience, one of consciousness' deepest needs is to integrate and unify its experience. In one of Hegel's more poetic turns of phrase, this aspiration is consciousness' desire to recognize itself as being at home in the world.[97] But as we have seen, in the course of consciousness' development, it is continually forced to concede that this destination of home remains beyond its reach, and, thus, that it remains a stranger in its world. If it were possible to extrapolate from Hegel's account of the spectators' response to tragic drama, tragedy might be thought of as a form of art that would enable us to gather together these tragedies of spirit, to suffer fear and pity in the face of them, and, in turn, to affirm them as ineluctable features of life. From this standpoint, the final wisdom of tragedy would emphasize not the scope of our powers to understand and transform the conditions of existence, but, rather, the transformation we ourselves undergo as we reflect on our limits.

Postscript. "Life Hangs in the Balance"

The influence of Hegel on subsequent movements of continental European, British, and American philosophy is so extensive that it is impossible credibly to question his importance for current discussions. However, one might worry that the past century has seen scholarly interest in Hegel drift from its once more prominent place both on the continent and in the Anglophone world. Moreover, it may also be that over the past half-century Anglo-American approaches to metaphysics, epistemology, value theory, and language attend less to historical figures and themes than their counterparts in the continental traditions of thought. Indeed, even if in more recent 'analytic' approaches historical figures have become more important, it could be suggested that figures in British empiricism and Kant, for example, have received more attention than Hegel.[1] Traditionally, continental heritages of philosophy, even those schools of thought directed by the aspirations to overturn traditional forms of philosophical inquiry, have typically endowed philosophers from the past with much more credence. But, even here it is possible to be concerned that some have begun to take a de-historicized approach to Hegel that treats him more as an icon of the wrong-headedness of modernity than as a crucial and rich resource to help us work through it.[2]

If the current status (and future) of Hegel's importance for philosophical research is shadowed by ambiguity, it might perhaps be in part due to warranted concerns about the grander side of his story of spirit, and this despite a growing body of scholarship that seeks to put Hegel's claims in a more 'modest' light.[3] After all, he believes that the education of spirit culminates in our philosophical reflection on an unconditioned, 'absolute' form of knowing, which unfolds as a thoroughly conceptual comprehension that supercedes the kind of insight won in religion and art. It is true that Hegel believes philosophical reflection to incorporate and contain within it consciousness' memory of the myriad forms of limit it encountered along the long path of experience. His position nonetheless suggests that philosophy achieves a form of knowledge that unifies our experience. For, although philosophical reflection does not operate to suppress or ignore the memory of its tragedies of spirit, it nonetheless diffuses their painful, rougher edges through an act of integration that incorporates them into a larger, comprehensible, and organic whole.

Recent scholarship suggests that for many, perhaps especially those beholden to more postmodern claims and sensibilities, Hegel's vision of philosophical reflection in the *Phenomenology* might stand not so much as a sign of mature thought, but as a symptom of a hubris of some kind. Yet, as we have seen, it is precisely Hegel's speculative ambitions that led him to tarry on the complexity and richness of the human experience and to grapple with an expansive range of phenomena. Hegel's belief in the affinity between the project of speculation and the resources of tragedy remains vital because it broaches questions and problems that emerge from our efforts to come to terms with the impenetrability of our condition, the pervasiveness of confusion, failure, and conflict in our lives, and the anxiety and pain that result. Although Hegel enlists a number of resources to develop his tragedies of spirit, it may fairly be said that Sophocles' dramas find a special place in his discourse. Of Sophocles' three Theban plays, Hegel's *Phenomenology* pays the most attention to the *Antigone*, and, also, pays heed to *Oedipus Tyrannus*. But, it may also be that some of Hegel's comments about *Oedipus at Colonus* from the later *Lectures on Aesthetics* add further perspective on the tragic side of Hegel's project in the *Phenomenology*.

Sophocles' *Oedipus at Colonus* is a multilayered and subtle work that treats a host of themes, such as the Greek cultic worship of mythic heroes, the political affairs of Athens, militarism, hospitality, and, too, the significance of Sophocles' other works, especially the *Antigone*.[4] Perhaps above all else, however, this drama portrays the unsurpassed tragic hero, Oedipus, now an old man, engaged in the paradigmatic tragic struggle: his encounter with his own death. The drama's plot is driven by a number of tensions, but of central importance is the relation between the gods and Oedipus; and throughout the course of action, we encounter a pensive Oedipus who awaits a sign from the gods that it is time for him to die. Of Oedipus' lines, he delivers one that captures the essence of a tragic sense of life the moment after the gods bring him the word. He states, "My life hangs in the balance. / I must not die in bad faith . . ."[5] If Hegel's later interest in *Oedipus at Colonus* may be seen as an afterimage of his earlier *Phenomenology* interest in the tragedies of spirit, then perhaps it leaves us with the idea that not only does life hang in the balance of conditions we can neither control nor even understand, but that we are called to face up to this fact and its consequences.

Death and Life

How might Sophocles' portrayal of Oedipus' final words inform our interpretation of Hegel? What is the relation between the tragic view of life and the rapport with death? On the one hand, maybe it should come as a surprise that Hegel takes up *Oedipus at Colonus* later in his life, more than a decade after his speculative faith in philosophy, modernity, and the concept had replaced his more youthful and radical concerns for tragedy. Then again, on the other hand maybe it should make sense that this drama would capture his attention at a later stage: for, might not Hegel, as his own course of life drew toward its end, be drawn to the drama Sophocles wrote later in his own life about the theme of death? Hegel comments on *Oedipus at Colonus* at some length, in any case, near the end of his *Lectures on Aesthetics*. His discussion appears in the third and final part of his lectures, the purpose of which is to elucidate the system of what he understands to be the principal individual forms of art.[6] But, a number of his comments on the drama concern its place in the development of the history of religious and artistic consciousness.

Hegel devotes himself more fully to questions about the history of art not in the third, but rather in the second part of his *Lectures on Aesthetics*, and his approach is as grand in scope as it is precise in detail. At the most superordinate level, he organizes his account of the evolution of art from its earliest origins to the German art of his time into three phases: symbolic, classical, and romantic art.[7] The bright line he wishes to cut between romanticism and classicism operates to parse off the developments of modern, (and, more remotely, medieval and Roman) art from the art of ancient Greece.[8] As problematic as Hegel's speculative reinscription of the epochal fault lines between the modern and the ancient is, it permeates important aspects of his interpretation of *Oedipus at Colonus*. For, Hegel asserts that while *Oedipus at Colonus* still belongs to the classical period, it involves a sense of subjectivity that places it at the cusp of the modernity typical of the romantic period.[9] *Oedipus at Colonus* may then be seen to represent a highest stage in the evolution of Attic tragedy, and even to stand at a certain extreme limit of ancient art as such. Yet, from the speculative standpoint, and, in particular, in light of his doctrine of determinate negation, every limit not only forms the completion of one thing but also the transition to something new. In view of this, *Oedipus at Colonus* would not only express the cumulative tragic insights of antiquity but, at the same time, anticipate the romantic world of art as it emerges in the Roman and early Christian world.

Hegel's treatment of *Oedipus at Colonus* in this portion of the *Lectures on Aesthetics* focuses not upon the formal elements of the play but rather principally upon the significance of its substantial content; and despite the grandeur and scale of his conception of the history of art and the place of Sophocles' drama within it, his comments on the drama primarily concern the protagonist's comportment to the prospect of his own demise. His discussion suggests that the centerpiece of the play is what he calls Oedipus' "transfiguration in death."[10] Hegel maintains that Sophocles' *Oedipus at Colonus* anticipates the birth of the post-classical world because, in contrast with much of the Attic tragedy that precedes it, the conflicts that drive the plot turn not primarily upon broader ethical concerns of a historical people, but also upon issues of individuality and personality.[11] Hegel further offers that Sophocles' almost modern emphasis on the individual, coupled with his stress on the interrelation of Oedipus' redemption and death, might tempt us to interpret the drama as a kind of proto-Christian narrative. Hegel writes,

> One wants to find a Christian tone here, an illustration of a sinner whom God takes up into grace and of a destiny that unravels in finitude and is rewarded in death with bliss.[12]

From a Christian standpoint Sophocles' portrayal of Oedipus' transfiguration in death might suggest a story of redemption through repentance and eternal reward in the afterlife.

But, Hegel asserts that even if *Oedipus at Colonus* reflects a world in transition, it nonetheless remains a work of antiquity, which, thus, does not yet represent fantasies of a salvific afterlife, nor of a transcendent and transfinite soul but, instead, portrays the realities of *this* life. He argues,

> But Christian religious reconciliation is a transfiguration of the soul that, bathed in the source of eternal salvation, raises itself above actuality and action . . . and holds firmly onto the certainty of eternal, purely spiritual bliss. By contrast, Oedipus' transfiguration remains the product of an ancient consciousness that arises from the strife of ethical powers. . . .[13]

Whereas the Christian worldview characterizes transfiguration in death as the ascension of the soul of an individual to Heaven, Sophocles treats it as a profound issue for ethical life. Hegel's conception of the Christian vision of things might be captured by the image of, say, a St. Sebastian; but the Hellenic, tragic view of life, at the limit, might be said to be encapsulated by the figure of the elder Oedipus. Moreover, since death forms the ultimate limit of life, Oedipus' encounter with the prospect of his own end may be seen as a form of an emblem or motto for all tragic limits as such. In the *Phenomenology*, Hegel tells us that the principal lesson of tragic art is that we, like the Oedipus of *Oedipus Tyrannus*, are inscrutable to ourselves. His reference to *Oedipus at Colonus* in the third part of his *Lectures on Aesthetics* points to the idea that nothing reminds us of this riddle more than mortality, the specter of death.

In this light, Oedipus' transfiguration would concern not our ambitions to overcome death but, rather, our capacity to acknowledge death as an integral aspect of life. From such a point of view, Oedipus' assertion that life hangs in the balance might serve as a reminder that to live life properly and fully is, at least in part, to remain aware of the proximity of death. Oedipus' statement does not tell us that in order to achieve mercy we must prepare for the afterlife and atone for our sins before we die. Rather, his words may be seen as a gift for those left alive, advising that the perfection of this life, its dignity, value, and depth, depends on our awareness that death inhabits all human endeavors.

Preapprehensions of this Sophoclean transfiguration in death, as well as his insistence upon the interplay of death and life, may be sensed in each of the tragedies of spirit he presents in the *Phenomenology*. We have seen that one of Hegel's chief aims in his project is to present the absolute as it emerges in the history of spirit through experience. Although Hegel's broader concern for the absolute guides his account, his conception of experience nonetheless points to the insight that the most consequential moments of our lives are tied, if not to death proper, then, to multiple forms of demise and loss. Hegel tells us in his lectures on the philosophy of history that there are many periods of the past in which nothing much transpires, and he reminds us that the annals of time contain more blank pages than not.[14] Our knowledge of the absolute emerges only from our experience; but only the smaller share of occurrences count as experience. For Hegel, the expansion of our awareness ultimately results only from those occasions in life that transform our conception of ourselves, our world, and our past. Hegel identifies the principal structural feature of experience as a movement in consciousness from certainty to truth, and his characterization of this dynamic as a reversal remind us that maturation, growth, and change require us to relinquish our certainty of past views and to endure the anxiety and pain that accompanies such a loss. Hegel's doctrine of experience teaches that the highpoints in life, the most intense and fullest moments that reshape what and who we are, are those that remain closest to the death of purported certainties.

There can be little doubt that Hegel views independence as one of the greatest aspirations of human life. In his discussion of the remotest origin of the struggle for independence, the reversal in the relation of mastery and servitude, he recognizes that the aspirations for freedom are intertwined with our relation to death. For Hegel, the reversal of the servant's condition may be seen to comprise a crucial, initial step in the struggle for liberation. Whereas the sovereignty of the master dissipates as this figure becomes a slave to immediate, natural desires, the servant's life of labor actually begins a path to self-sufficiency, insofar as it forces the servant to cultivate discipline and skill. Yet, Hegel's discussion of mastery and servitude suggests that there is also a tragic side to the fortunes of both the master and the servant. We have seen that the reversal in the life of servitude, for example, has as its crux an intimate tie between freedom and death. For masters retain their power over servants by means of the threat of murder, and thus the servile consciousness, which entered into bondage precisely to avoid death, now finds its course of life guided by the prospect of its own demise. But, it is precisely *because* of the master's threats that the servant acquiesces to the master's demands and undertakes the labors that will awaken this figure's potential to be free. If Hegel associates the completeness of our lives with our freedom, then it might be said that the servant—the figure guided by death—lives most fully.

What about ethical life? Although Hegel's presentation of the Greek ethical world centers on questions of community, custom, and agency, his discussion as a whole is animated by a figure of death which he enlists from Sophocles' *Antigone*: the deceased brother. Hegel maintains that spirit reaches its explicit form in the communal and historical life of a people. Even if this spiritual world must be governed by principles and laws, however, the corpse reveals that universality and unity devoid of respect for the singular is empty. Hegel's discussion of ethical life could thus seem, at least, to indicate that the presence of death in the figure of the corpse does more to disrupt and destroy the polis than to sustain it. But, perhaps one lesson to take from the discussion of ethical life is that a community unable to come to grips with the tensions that emerge between the living and the dead is liable to fall into ruin.[15]

Hegel's account of our encounters with tragic art speaks to the kinship of life and death as well. He maintains that a theoretical interest guides our experiences of art, and he characterizes our reflection on art not as an activity divorced from life but rather as a highly concentrated and transformative aspect of living. Hegel argues that in Attic tragedy we come upon a form of art that in a sense challenges us and engages us more than all other forms of art, and he shows that our experience of ancient tragedy thus offers us some of the deepest insights into our condition as human beings. Yet, he recognizes that the lessons of tragedy concern the multiple forms of calamity and failure, destruction, limit, violence, and death that interpenetrate our lives. For Hegel, contemplative experience of tragic art unfolds as a festive occasion or kairos in the course of our lives, though it is a highpoint directed by a desire to reflect upon death and disasters in the neighborhood of death.

Whereas we may worry that Hegel's more thematic picture of the human spirit downplays, perhaps even represses, the interconnectedness of death and life, both his comments on *Oedipus at Colonus* and his earlier tragedies of spirit indicate that we carry out our lives in full view of the precariousness of their interplay.[16] Hegel's more tragic vision of spirit reminds us that the greatness of human life lies not in our masterful control of the circumstances of our existence, nor in our power to achieve certitude in knowledge but, rather, in our capacity to affirm our limitations. But, if there is beauty in the tragic side of Hegel's view, it is sustained by a certain foreboding, for it suggests that to embrace limits is at the same time to acknowledge the inestimable, the dangerous, and the unstable. Here, unexpected reversals of fortune would be the rule, in life as in art. In the spirit of figures such as Heidegger, Nietzsche, and many of the existentialists, the tragic side of Hegel's *Phenomenology* might call upon us to reject as deceptive excessive faith in calculative reason and its power to offer adequate shelter. The life turned away from death, as Hegel's tragedies of spirit seem to suggest, is diminished and incomplete. By contrast, the richest form of life, which is to say life in the preeminent or proper sense, would be one turned toward limits.

After and Before

Although the conclusions of Hegel's speculative idealism epitomize the presuppositions of modernity that many now call into question, there are nonetheless far-reaching and resilient connective tissues between movements in post-Hegelian philosophy concerned with human limits and the *Phenomenology*'s tragedies of spirit. Questions of human finitude are often associated with Nietzsche, Freud, the phenomenological and existential traditions, and philosophical hermeneutics. But no doubt, thanks in part to the French reception of Hegelian thought in the 1930s and 1940s, as well as Heidegger's revival of interest in nineteenth-century German philosophy, it has once again become possible to recognize deep ties between issues of human limit and Hegel's thought. As we have seen, claims to the contemporary relevance of the *Phenomenology* gain some of their greatest support from the study of Hegel's reliance on the resources of tragedy to elucidate the structures and operations of our limits in certain crucial aspects of life. Yet, the fruitfulness of our study of Hegel's tragedies of spirit points to further questions and urges us to expand out inquiry not simply to philosophers of tragedy that emerge after Hegel but, moreover, to philosophers, critics, and poets who develop original conceptions and uses of tragedy before him, in the intellectually imaginative, productive, but volatile years between the appearance of Kant's *Critique of Judgment* and Hegel's completion of the *Phenomenology*. If the philosophical projects of our day draw sustenance from the *Phenomenology*'s tragedies of spirit, then there are further resources that await in Hegel's earlier writings, in F. W. J. Schelling, in Friedrich Schlegel, and in Friedrich Hölderlin.

Hegel's *Phenomenology* and his later works may be said to associate the speculative unity, despite all of his innovations, with a heritage that traces itself back to Platonist accounts of the idea, even though, as we have seen, he enlists tragedy in the *Phenomenology* in his efforts to elaborate on the multiple forms of limit our consciousness encounters in the course of its development. In the initial phases of his intellectual life, however, especially in the Frankfurt and Tübingen periods and in his first years in Jena, Hegel appears to tarry on the idea that the speculative unity is actually more akin to the unity of art than anything else. Hegel points to the kinship between speculation and art at a number of junctures, for example, in preliminary versions of his Jena philosophy of spirit and in his Frankfurt essays on life and love.[17] It is difficult to reconstruct a complete picture of the young Hegel's concept of speculation from these pieces, not only because many of his claims about it in this period are formulated primarily as provocations and suggestions, but also due to the fact that portions of his early texts have been lost.[18] But, in one of his early extended and systematic essays, *On the Scientific Treatment of Natural Law, Its Place in Practical Philosophy, and its Relation to the Sciences of Positive Law* (1802), Hegel enlists the notion of tragedy to characterize the speculative unity of political life.

Hegel's essay on natural law is ambitious and he dedicates the larger portion of his discussion to differentiating a genuinely scientific or speculative view of natural law from other, merely abstract approaches.[19] One of the themes that emerges from Hegel's account is a rejection of the Kantian claim that the domains of practical reason and right are heteronymous, and his overall view involves the claim that rationality infuses the institutions and practices of the political and ethical spheres. In anticipation of the much later *Philosophy of Right*, the young Hegel suggests that it is the ethical life of a people that unites the political sphere; and, in addition, he argues that ethical life is a dialectical movement that synthesizes antithetical moments of political, social, and economic life.[20] In his 1802 view, he believes that the ethical life of a people is comprised primarily as a unity of two classes: the 'universal' class of political leaders that place rationality and the interests of the state ahead of their other desires (and thus live in freedom), and the 'particular class' of those dedicated to individual political, legal and economic gain.[21]

Throughout his philosophical life, Hegel characterizes the ethical life of a people as a complex and dynamic form of political and social unity comprised of and sustained by multiple forms of conflict. But the younger Hegel of the natural law essay associates the political unity achieved in ethical life not ultimately with the rationality of the concept, but rather with the structure of tragedy; and, in a celebrated turn of phrase, he maintains that the unification of the universal and particular classes unfolds as "the performance of the tragedy in the ethical."[22] In the same essay, he goes on to proffer Aeschylus' *Orestia* as something of a speculative image of the political, and he suggests that the conclusion of the drama—the transformation of the furies into good spirits through Orestes' trial—represents the tragic unity of ethical life in all of its dividedness, tenuousness, and fragility.[23] What difference might it make to assert that ethical life is burdened by conflict, one whose very constitution unfolds as a kind of tragedy? What is at stake in the distinction between Hegel's *Phenomenology* association of the structure of ethical life with the *Antigone*, and his Natural Law essay use of the *Orestia*?

If the Hegel of the 1802 natural law essay characterizes political life as a tragic drama, then the young Schelling, several years earlier, in his *Philosophical Letters on Dogmatism and Criticism* (1796), turns to tragedy as a model for nothing short of the ontological identity of reason and reality. Schelling maintains his speculative interest in art throughout his life. But the collection of ten *Letters* formed an important early publication, written while he was still a student at the *Stift* in Tübingen, and they may be seen to comprise one of his most provocative statements of the philosophical import of tragedy. The questions that guide the *Letters* concern the nature and unity of reason, and one of Schelling's chief aims is to articulate a rejoinder to the Kantian claim from the first *Critique* that our cognitive power of reason is essentially limited. Schelling endorses the Kantian view that the highest and proper vocation of reason is to represent the absolute unity of the subject and the world. He further subscribes to what he sees as the yield of the Kantian "Third Antinomy of Pure Reason," which, as we have seen, is that even our most rational efforts to establish a complete picture of the universe compel us to assent to two mutually antithetical and divergent views of the ultimate source of events in the phenomenal order: first, that everything in the universe is directed by powers of nature, and, second, that at least some events are guided by the spontaneous, free powers of the rational subject.[24]

Yet, Schelling claims that reason nonetheless forms a unity, and in his "Tenth Letter" he suggests that tragic drama, especially in its ancient Greek form, provides a synthetic image of reason that incorporates its antinomial aspect. Not unlike Hegel and others after him, Schelling recognizes that tragic drama is a form of art dedicated to the representation of irreconcilable difference, conflict, crisis, and catastrophe. But Schelling goes further to entertain the idea that the preeminent vocation of tragic drama is to represent the unity of reason itself. Schelling wonders at "how Greek reason could bear the contradictions of its tragedy," and proposes that one drama, Sophocles' *Oedipus Tyrannus*, actually forms an artistic view of the structure of reason itself.[25] Schelling believes that the plot of *Oedipus Tyrannus* unfolds in the conflict between the purposes of its protagonist and the recalcitrance of his circumstances. But, Schelling contends that "the *ground* of this contradiction lay in the strife of human freedom with the power of the objective world," and he argues that this tension forms an expression of human reason's divergent views of causation.[26]

From this standpoint, Sophocles' drama—the Oracle's prophecy, Oedipus' efforts to outwit his fate, the concatenation of events that lead Oedipus to fulfill his destiny—represents not simply a marvelous story, but the dynamic structure of human reason itself. For, Sophocles' tragic drama may be seen not only as a unity that integrates and joins together the two sides of the conflict that drive the plot. The dramatic tension of the work itself may be seen as being guided by the same antithetical claims of reason that Kant saw in his 'Third Antinomy.' From this standpoint, Oedipus' conviction that he may through his own actions avoid his fate forms an image of reason's view that the spontaneous and free subject is the origin of at least some events in the universe. But the Oracle's prophecy and its fulfillment suggest otherwise and serve to represent reason's other view: that the powers of the world that lie beyond the subject (though the Greeks might associate these powers not with causation, but the 'gods' or 'fate') guide everything.

About a decade before Hegel completed the *Phenomenology of Spirit*, Schelling indicated not simply that the world of human affairs is permeated by tragedy but that our greatest cognitive talent, reason, is itself tragic. He also suggested that reason's capacity to represent the unity of the subject and the world might unfold in tragic art. How might we conceive of the consequences of Schelling's tragic view of reason? What might it mean further to develop Schelling's tragic conception of human cognition? To what extent does Schelling's identification of rationality with the tragic inform the young Hegel's association of the speculative unity with tragedy?

Philippe Lacoue-Labarthe and Jean-Luc Nancy point out that the early German Romantics envisioned themselves as the intellectual avant-garde of the philosophical and literary culture of their day.[27] But a number of figures in the Romantic Movement devoted extensive attention to questions of antiquity and tragedy, and their innovation on "the romantic genre *par excellence*," the fragment, may be seen to reverberate with important formal elements of tragic art.[28] Of course, as Lacoue-Labarthe and Nancy indicate, the Romantics did not invent the notion of the fragment from whole cloth, and it has important precedents in the English and French traditions, such as the genre of the essay.[29] But, the early German Romantics, and, in particular, Friedrich Schlegel, developed the idea of the fragment as something of an autonomous and unique style of philosophical and literary criticism, which should be seen as different not only from more traditional forms such as the treatise, but also from the superficially similar aphorism, as well as from works of the past that have been partially lost to time, such as the writings of the pre-Socratics.[30]

Schlegel was a pivotal player among the Romantics thanks to his role in the *Athenaeum* and to his work as a translator in addition to his innovative and original contributions in the *Athenaeum Fragments*, *Critical Fragments*, and *Ideas*. The Romantics' collections of fragments concern a wide range of issues in philosophy, criticism, and poetry; they anticipate important aspects of our current views of knowledge, system, and history; and they provide provocative insights into themes such as friendship and religion.[31] Indeed, many of his fragments consider the specific character and virtues of tragic drama. But, we see perhaps Schlegel's deepest debts to the notion of tragedy in the stylistic structure of the fragment itself, and not in his explicit comments about tragedy. For the representational form of the fragment appears, at least in part, to be infused with the characteristic thematic lessons of tragic art, such that the fragment always indicates, whatever else it says, irretrievable absence and loss, incompleteness, ambiguity, and the tension between our affinity for wholeness and our confrontation with limits.[32] Is the fragment an heir of tragedy? If so, what does this tell us about the representational powers of the fragment? Of tragic drama? What might the concept of the fragment and its reliance upon the notion of tragedy teach us about the finitude of our capacity to represent our ideas?

The Most Joyous

Few of Hegel's contemporaries reflect upon the divide that separates modernity and its sensibilities from the Greeks and their culture of tragedy more pointedly than Hölderlin. Although Hölderlin is an extraordinarily innovative and original poet who develops a provocative and idiosyncratic vision of the Greeks, there is no doubt that he, like many German intellectuals of the period, imagined the Greeks to embody one of the highest points in human culture. Yet, whereas some of his contemporaries call for a revival of the Greek worldview in modern Germany, some of Hölderlin's work suggests that he questions not simply whether we moderns can embrace the lessons of tragedy but whether we are able to fathom them at all.[33] Have the triumphant visions of the modern philosophers; have two millennia of Christianity cut us off from the wisdom of the Greeks? Has the course of European history come to foreclose the insights of the Greeks?

Hölderlin sees questions about the continued viability of ancient tragedy as matters not simply of theoretical concern but rather of discursive, literary, and poetic practice.[34] Is it possible to create a modern German translation of an Attic tragedy? Would the modern tongue support the ancient tragic insights, or might the modern version offer nothing but an empty husk of the original? Further, would it be possible for a modern poet, today, not simply to translate but even to *create* an ancient drama? Hölderlin provides no easy answers to these questions; but one fears that the difficulties of his own labors as a translator and a poet suggest a response. He completed German renditions of Sophocles' *Oedipus Tyrannus* and *Antigone*, but the apparent idiosyncrasy of his versions might lead some to question their viability. In addition to his translations of Greek drama, Hölderlin attempted to write a modern tragedy whose protagonist is named after a Greek figure, entitled *The Death of Empedocles*. But the project appears to have proved complicated, too, as he has bequeathed to us three versions of the drama.

In the *Phenomenology*, Hegel, too, holds that we in the modern world cannot return to the sensibilities of the ancients, though for him this is because of the progress of our knowledge beyond the limits of consciousness in antiquity and not due to our irretrievable loss of the Greeks' original insights into the instabilities of human life.[35] Yet, as we have seen, Hegel returns time and again to the resources of tragedy in order to ensure his fidelity to the complexity and difficulty of life. Although we might question whether Hegel finally violates this trust, the cumulative result of his tragedies of spirit suggests a positive and human view of our condition. Despite the numerous differences between the two figures, Hölderlin, like Hegel, derives many of his ideas of the tragic from Sophocles, and it may be that a couplet penned by Hölderlin in Tübingen in 1801 offers a suitable last word on the core of Hegel's affinity for the tragic. Under the title, "Sophocles," Hölderlin writes,

> To no avail many have tried to say the most joyous joyfully.
> Here finally it expresses itself to me, here in mourning.[36]

For Hölderlin it is ultimately the voice of Sophocles, of the tragic, that speak of the most joyous. Certainly, we might wonder if Hegel's joy in the absolute runs counter to Hölderlin's joy in Sophocles, and, too, how Hegel's dedication to the absolute might color his capacity to mourn. But his deep concern for tragedy may nonetheless point to the different joy, one perhaps cognate to Hölderlin's, that arises for those who learn to accept that they belong to a world they cannot master and who come to see that their lives are governed by conflicts and tensions that cannot be reconciled.

Notes

Preface

1. Alfred Denker and Michael Vater, "Introduction," in *Hegel's* Phenomenology of Spirit, *New Critical Essays* (New York: Humanity Books, 2003), 8.

2. Although Hegel's conception of the philosophical treatment of the history of philosophy is in fact complex and nuanced, motivation for such a claim about Hegel might be found, for example, in his *Vorlesungen über die Geschichte der Philosophie*.

3. Hegel, *Differenz des Fichte'schen und Schelling'schen Systems der Philosophie*, in *Werke*, Volume 2, 16. I have used H. S. Harris' and Walter Cerf's translation, in Hegel, *The Difference Between Fichte's and Schelling's System of Philosophy*, trans. H. S. Harris and Walter Cerf (Albany: State University of New York Press, 1997), 86.

4. Ibid. Once again here, I have used Harris' and Cerf's translation, in Hegel, *Difference*, 86.

5. Ibid., 19.

Introduction

1. Hegel contributes to his elucidation of his conception of speculative philosophy as a demonstration of absolute unity at a number of junctures in the *Phenomenology*. See, for example, Hegel's association of speculation with "the rational and the rhythm of the organic whole," at Hegel, *Phänomenologie des Geistes*, in *Werke in 20 Bände*, Volume 3 (Frankfurt am Main: Suhrkamp, 1986), 55. Cf. Miller translation, 34/§ 56. See also Hegel's elucidation of the "speculative proposition" at Hegel, *Phänomenologie*, 61 ff. Cf. Miller, 38/§ 61 ff.

2. Of the figures associated with these approaches to Hegel, which are sometimes labeled as 'non-metaphysical,' or, 'epistemological,' see, for example, Robert Pippin. Although this trend in Hegel studies is multifaceted, it might be that one of the things at stake in it is to motivate the importance of, and thus also to stimulate new interest in, Hegel for current philosophical debate, sometimes, one might further suggest, with an eye turned toward more Anglo-American approaches to questions in fields such as epistemology, the philosophy of science, and the philosophy of language. A survey of the relevant literature might reveal that one of the aims of these approaches is to question whether the scope and

sweep of Hegel's metaphysical claims is as ambitious as many commentators have customarily thought. Once demythologized, the emphasis is shifted to more modest aspects of Hegel's thought that take up questions pertinent to many mainstreams of current research. In this vein, it might also be noted that a typical move is to turn to features of Hegel's thought that unfold as a response to Kant.

In his *The Company of Words, Hegel, Language, and Systematic Philosophy*, John McCumber approaches Hegel as a philosopher of language with affinities to Wittgenstein and Davidson, developing a number of issues including Hegelian notions of system and truth. As K. R. Dove notes, McCumber "displays an impressively wide acquaintance with much of the enormous Hegel literature in German, English, and French" (K. R. Dove, Review of John McCumber, "The Company of Words", *Journal of the History of Philosophy* 32, no. 4 (1994): 681, and his approach should not be reduced to any one school within Hegel studies. He recognizes the merits of non-metaphysical approaches to the extent that he views them as absolving Hegel of "several monstrously untenable ontological commitments" (John McCumber, *The Company of Words, Hegel, Language, and Systematic Philosophy* (Evanston: Northwestern University Press, 1993), 25–26). In light of this, it is perhaps not a surprise that his "Introduction" contains a series of interrogatives that could also be taken to be consistent with some presuppositions of the non-metaphysical option. He asks:

> What if (the real) Hegel was not an idealist or a metaphysician, but simply developed the empirical side of Kant's philosophy in a way that took seriously history and the sciences of his day? What if he were neither a 'realist' nor an 'idealist,' in the usual sense acceptations of these terms, but sought to develop an ontologically neutral philosophical vocabulary? What if Hegel did not deny the reality of rupture at all, so that his narrative of spirit, far from seamless, is compatible with all kinds of breaks and demarcations? (McCumber, *The Company of Words*, 2).

Of course, the appearance of interpretive approaches suggested by questions such as these represents a consequential and also highly productive development in Hegel studies.

Yet, it does not seem to me that there is enough reason to think that non-metaphysical views would somehow supplant the interpretive interests that guide many continental approaches to Hegel. One important concern in continental approaches to Hegel has been, roughly, that Hegel's thought forms a certain summit of metaphysical heritages that have become untenable, and, thus, must be approached critically and carefully. On the surface, it would seem that if Hegel is 'non-metaphysical,' then there is not so much to worry about as some in continental philosophy would seem to suppose. Once again, McCumber's "Introduction," contains a question that may be seen to get at the point: "What if Heidegger, Foucault, and Derrida all undertake to deconstruct something that Hegel never constructed, and thereby leave his real achievement untouched?" (McCumber, *The Company of Words*, 2). This is a provocative question, and one that deserves and has garnered much attention. It occurs to me, however, that while scholarship on the 'non-metaphysical' Hegel could be seen to pose challenges to some presuppositions of continental approaches to Hegel, continental approaches might equally be seen to pose challenges to proponents of the non-metaphysical approach. From this standpoint, continental approaches to Hegel might be seen to offer important critical resources to evaluate and delimit the plausibility and appeal of views that stem from non-metaphysical interpretations.

3. Indeed, perhaps many continental approaches to Hegel might be understood to unfold as what Paul Ricoeur would treat with reference to the hermeneutics of suspicion, which Gary Madison describes as "interpretive strategies . . . which seek to *reduce* the second-level [i.e., intended or explicit] meaning of symbolic expressions to some hidden dimension totally foreign to the subject's own interpretation and understanding, such as unconscious drives or social determinants . . ." See Gary Madison, *Hermeneutics of Postmodernity* (Bloomington: Indiana University Press, 1988), 93. In Errol E. Harris's helpful overview of the landscape of the twentieth century reception of Hegel, he observes that despite new interest in the possibility that Hegel may be of service to current debates, some may remain incredulous of Hegel's commitment to the absolute, and its implications for the rationality of the real. See Errol E. Harris, *The Spirit of Hegel* (Atlantic Highlands: Humanities Press, 1993), 17–18.

4. Stuart Barnett, "Introduction: Hegel Before Derrida," in *Hegel After Derrida*, ed. Stuart Barnett (New York: Routledge, 1998), 1.

5. Of course, Hegel recognizes that absolute knowledge does not alleviate or expunge the memory of spirit's painful experiences of disunity. Rather, he focuses upon a different sense of reconciliation brought about by the accomplishment of a form of knowledge that demonstrates the absolute unity that governs our experiences.

6. One of Hegel's more general criticisms of abstract thought, directed not foremost against philosophers, and written in a somewhat popular style, is found in "Wer Denkt Abstrakt?," in *Werke*, Volume 2, 575–81.

7. Hegel, *Phänomenologie*, 22. Cf. Miller, 9/§ 16.

8. Perhaps especially influential on the young Hegel were Schelling and Hölderlin. I briefly discuss some aspects of their interest in tragedy in the concluding chapter of this study.

9. Philippe Lacoue-Labarthe, *Heidegger, Art, and Politics, the Fiction of the Political*, trans. Chris Turner (Cambridge: Basil Blackwell, 1990), 41. Of course, the conviction that there is a disjunction between the current cultural milieu and the tradition it has inherited has been articulated in myriad ways in our time, though perhaps among the most celebrated remains Jean-François Lyotard's provocation made some decades ago now that the postmodern era finds itself in a situation of crisis, as "the grand narrative" characteristic of modernity "has lost its credibility." See Jean-François Lyotard, *The Postmodern Condition, a Report on Knowledge*, trans. Geoff Bennington and Brian Massumi (Minneapolis: Minnesota University Press, 1979, ninth printing 1993), 37.

10. John D. Caputo, "On Not Circumventing the Quasi-Transcendental: The Case of Rorty and Derrida," in *Working Through Derrida*, ed. Gary Madison (Evanston: Northwestern University Press, 1993), 148–49. Caputo's focus is on Rorty's claims that bourgeois liberalism should give up on enlightenment interests in foundationalism.

11. Although this continental sensibility is palpable in a number of schools of thought, perhaps it manifests itself most readily in Hans-Georg Gadamer's philosophical hermeneutics, for example, in his assertion of the inescapable role that prejudices (*Vorurteile*) from the past play in understanding. See, for example, Hans-Georg Gadamer, "Universalität des hermeneutischen Problems," in *Gesammelte Werke*, Volume 2 (Tübingen: Mohr Siebeck, 1993).

12. For an examination of Hegel's conception of the end of philosophy, see Stefano Franchi, "Telos and Terminus: Hegel and the End of Philosophy," in *Idealistic Studies* 18 (1998): 35–46.

13. Hegel, *Enzyklopädie der philosophischen Wissenschaften* I, in *Werke*, Volume 8, 58. In fact, Hegel insists on this notion of speculative philosophy as the fruition of the history of philosophy throughout his life, and already in the *Differenzschrift*. See Hegel, *Differenz des Fichte'schen und Schelling'schen Systems der Philosophie*, in *Werke*, Volume 2, 15 ff.

14. Friedrich Nietzsche, *Geburt der Tragödie*, in *Kritische Studienausgabe*, eds. Giorgio Colli and Mazzino Montinari, Volume 1 (München: de Gruyter, 1988), 148, 116.

15. Ibid., 129. Nietzsche develops the concept of decadence in, for example, *Genealogie der Moral*.

16. Nietzsche's reconsideration of Wagner is demonstrated most fully by Nietzsche's *Der Fall Wagner*, in *Kritische Studienausgabe*, eds. Giorgio Colli and Mazzino Montari, Volume 6.

17. Ibid., 128.

18. Ibid., 118.

19. Of course, psychoanalytic and feminist approaches to questions of tragedy are oriented by concerns distinct, if oftentimes related, to those in current movements of continental philosophy. I mention Lacan, Irigaray, and Butler here because some of their uses of tragedy are especially indebted, either creatively or critically, to Hegel's approach. See Jacques Lacan's lecture on the *Antigone*, collected in *The Ethics of Psychoanalysis*, trans. Dennis Porter (New York: W. W. Norton, 1992), Luce Irigaray, "Eternal Irony of the Community," in *Feminist Interpretations of G. W. F. Hegel*, ed. Patricia J. Mills (University Park: Pennsylvania State University Press, 1996), and Judith Butler, *Antigone's Claim, Kinship Between Life and Death* (New York: Columbia University Press, 2000).

20. Manfred Frank discusses the emphasis placed on these matters by commentators such as Philippe Lacoue-Labarthe, Jean-Luc Nancy, and Stanley Cavell in *Philosophical Foundations of Early German Romanticism*, trans. Elizabeth Millán-Zaibert (Albany: State University of New York Press, 2004). Schelling's assertion (which itself may find an echo in the first paragraph of Friedrich Schlegel's *Gespräch über die Poesie*, first appearing in 1800 in the *Atheneaum*) is found in F. J. W. Schelling, *System der transendentalen Idealismus*, in *Werke* (Stuttgart: Frommann-Holzboog, 1992), cited in Dennis Schmidt, *Germans and Other Greeks, Tragedy and Ethical Life* (Bloomington: Indiana University Press, 2001), 74.

21. Plato, *Republic*, trans. Allen Bloom (New York: Basic Books, 1991), 607b.

22. Of course, the project to overturn Platonism is not inconsistent with the revitalization of important Platonic themes. Jason Wirth, for example, suggests that Nietzsche, and before him, Schelling, by any measure a leading figure in the German intellectual scene at the dawn of the nineteenth century, associate their projects with the revitalization (and this means also transformation) of questions about the primacy of the good over the true: a decidedly important matter in Plato. See Jason Wirth, *The Conspiracy of Life, Meditations on Schelling and His Time* (Albany: State University of New York Press, 2003), 6.

23. Plato, *Republic*, trans. Allan Bloom (Basic Books, 1968, second paperback edition 1991), 53/376e ff.

24. Henry and Mary Garland, eds., *The Oxford Companion to German Literature*, Second edition (New York: Oxford University Press, 1986), 493.

25. Of the early German Romantics, for example, Philippe Lacoue-Labarthe and Jean-Luc Nancy claim that they comprise "In fact, and without any exaggeration the first avant-garde group in history." See Philippe Lacoue-Labarthe and Jean-Luc Nancy, *The Literary Absolute*, trans. Philip Barnard and Cheryl Lester (Albany: State University of New York Press, 1988), 8.

26. An important exception in the mature Hegel may be his reference to Sophocles' *Antigone* in the *Philosophy of Right*. See especially Hegel's reference to the *Antigone* in his discussion of the first moment of ethical life, the family. See G. W. F. Hegel, *Grundlinien der Philosophie des Rechts*, *Werke*, Volume 7, 319.

27. T. M. Knox, "Prefatory Note," in G. W. F. Hegel, *Early Theological Writings*, trans. T. M. Knox (Philadelphia: University of Pennsylvania Press, 1971, seventh paperback printing 1997), vi.

28. Probably there is no need to defend the claim that H. S. Harris' *Hegel's Development* forms a landmark in the historical development of studies on the early phases of Hegel's life. In Quentin Lauer's review of the first volume, for example, he praises that "like his scholarly predecessors [Rosenkranz, Haym, Dilthey, Asveld, Häring, and Lukács]—and perhaps even more successfully—Henry Harris has made excellent use of [the] . . . vast manuscript material [available from Hegel's early period] in presenting us with an absorbingly interesting account of these early years of development." Quentin Lauer, "H. S. Harris' *Hegel's Development: Toward the Sunlight, 1770–1801*: A Review," collected in *Essays in Hegelian Dialectic* (New York: Fordham University Press, 1977), 61.

29. Of the studies of the influence of the revolution at the *Stift*, see, for example, H. S. Harris, *Hegel's Development, Toward the Sunlight 1770–1801* (Oxford: Oxford University Press, 1972), especially pp. 64–65. Walter Kaufmann lends his insight into the story of the freedom tree in *Hegel, Reinterpretation, Texts, and Commentary*, 37. Harris mentions Hegel's lifelong celebration of Bastille Day, for example, in "Hegel's Intellectual Development to 1807," in *Cambridge Companion to Hegel*, 26.

30. Again, the extensive body of excellent research on Hegel's relation to Kant would render it superfluous to treat it at length here. Although any number of commentators might be consulted here, one might turn to the first chapter of Charles Taylor's *Hegel*, entitled, "The Aims of An Epoch."

31. I believe it may be prudent to express reservations about commentators who render '*Volksreligion*' as 'folk-religion,' on the grounds that this English translation might obviate connotations of nationality, if not nationalism, in the German word. Still, so as not unnecessarily to exaggerate the nationalistic overtones of the German *Volk*, I opt for 'people's religion,' over 'national religion.'

32. Harris, *Hegel's Development, Toward the Sunlight*, xxix.

33. Although numerous scholars of Hegel evoke his 'Hellenic ideal,' perhaps a classic source of the turn of phrase is Glenn Gray's, *Hegel's Hellenic Ideal* (New York: King's Crown Press, 1941). Again, there are many excellent accounts of Hegel's association of the potential of Christianity with Hellenic life. For now, suffice it to motivate Hegel's interest in the religious and cultural life of the Greeks to cite Richard Kroner's contention that "the young

Hegel would have liked to give up his own Christian faith and go back to the days of Greek paganism." Richard Kroner, "Introduction," in Hegel, *Early Theological Writings*, 4.

34. See, for example, Gray, *Hegel's Hellenic Ideal*, 17–34.

35. Philippe Lacoue-Labarthe, *Typography, Mimesis, Philosophy, Politics*, trans. Christopher Fynsk (Cambridge: Harvard University Press, 1989), 208.

36. Jacques Taminiaux, "Speculation and Difference," in *Poetics, Speculation, and Judgment, the Shadow of the Work of Art from Kant to Phenomenology*, trans. Michael Gendre (Albany: State University of New York Press, 1993), 42, 53.

37. H. S. Harris believes that he is able to put to rest claims against Hegel's authorship made by those who believe he did not write, but simply copied the text. See Harris, *Hegel's Development, Toward the Sunlight 1770–1801*, 249 ff. For accounts of the debates, see Hegel, *Frühe Schriften, Werke*, Band 1, eds. Eva Moldenhauer et al. (Frankfurt am Main: Suhrkamp, 1986), 628; Philippe Lacoue-Labarthe and Jean-Luc Nancy, *The Literary Absolute*, 27–28.

38. Hegel, "Das älteste Systemprogramm des deutschen Idealismus," in *Frühe Schriften, Hegel in 20 Bände*, Band 1, 235.

39. Peter Szondi, *Versuch Über das Tragische, Schriften*, Band 1 (Franfurt am Main: Suhrkamp), 157.

40. Obviously, my suggestion of these similarities comprises something more of a provocation than a fully articulated claim. But I nonetheless believe that a comparative study of these three conceptions of philosophy might prove fruitful, as it is suggested in each case, if in very different ways, that philosophical inquiry is bound up with purposes that require its practitioners also to employ artistic powers of expression. See Nietzsche, *Geburt der Tragödie*, 102. Heidegger, for his part, considers the relationship between the philosopher and the poet at a number of junctures, perhaps especially in certain texts from the 1930s and 1940s.

41. Taminiaux, "Speculation and Difference," 54.

42. Hegel's conception of the hierarchy of the various forms of art, and the place of tragic art within it, is complex, and unfolds along two different lines: first, his distinction among symbolic, classical, and romantic art; and, second, his distinction among what he understands to be the principal forms of art. See Robert Wicks, "Hegel's Aesthetics: An Overview," in *Cambridge Companion to Hegel*, ed. Friedrick C. Beiser (New York: Cambridge University Press, 1993), 348–77.

43. F. W. J. Schelling, *Philosophische Briefe Über Dogmatismus und Kriticismus*, in *Werke*, Volume 3 (Stuttgart: Frommann-Holzboog, 1992), 50.

44. John Toews provides a helpful outline of the transformation of Hegel's status from the margins to the center of German intellectual life in "Transformations of Hegelianism, 1805–1846," in *Cambridge Companion to Hegel*, ed. Fredrick Beiser (New York: Cambridge University Press, 1993), 381–82.

45. Of course, there is much debate about Hegel's political allegiances, both in Berlin and before, to say nothing of the implications of Hegel's political philosophy, whether it is conservative or otherwise, for the development of Marxian thought. Kenneth Westphal notes that critics often charge Hegel's mature political philosophy with conservatism, because he subscribes to a form of organicism that opposes individualism (Kenneth Westphal, "The Basic Context and Structure of Hegel's *Philosophy of Right*," in *Cambridge*

Companion to Hegel, 235–36). However, I believe my contention that Hegel becomes more conservative in his later years continues to be tenable even if we accept Westphal's position that Hegel should be understood not as a conservative, but as a reform-minded liberal. For, as Westphal notes, even if the mature Hegel's position would lead him to call for reforms in the Prussian monarchy, Hegel's political philosophy is animated not by a revolutionary spirit, but, rather, a reformist "institutional program [that] remains an idealized image of its age." (Westphal, "Basic Context and Structure," 264).

46. Even if Hegel's conception of the speculative unity may be said to shift over the course of his development, he remains constant in his belief that it forms a complex identity. Indeed, already in the "System Fragment" from the Frankfurt period, Hegel characterizes the speculative unity of life as a 'union of union and non-union.' Hegel, "Systemfragment," *Werke*, Volume 1, 422.

47. Hegel, *Vorlesungen über die Ästhetik*, *Werke*, Volume 13, 141, 25, respectively.

48. Andreas Grossmann, "Hegel, Heidegger, and the Question of Art Today," *Research in Phenomenology* 20 (1990): 119.

49. Hegel considers phrenology at *Phänomenologie*, 250 ff. Cf. Miller, 200/§ 331 ff. Hegel discusses the penis at *Phänomenologie*, 262. Cf. Miller, 210/§ 346.

50. See, for example, Hegel, *Phänomenologie*, 36. Cf. Miller, 19/§ 32, discussed in Chapter 1 of the present study.

51. In the *Lectures on the History of Philosophy*, for example, Hegel mentions that the path to speculative philosophy from the emergence of modern thought in Descartes involves much distance, though he also notes that "here [that is, in the modern period that begins with Descartes], we could say, we are at home, and could shout, like the seafarers after a long voyage on the stormy sea, 'land!' " Hegel, *Vorlesungen über die Geschichte der Philosophie* III, in *Werke*, Volume 20, 120. Jacques Taminiaux refers to Descartes, Galileo, and Hobbes as proponents of the *mathesis universalis* in "Speculation and Judgment" in *Poetics, Speculation, and Judgment*, 13.

52. Of course, as Hans-Georg Gadamer suggests, Hegel's work actually forms something of a swan song of this philosophical agenda of modernity more than anything else. Soon after the turn of the nineteenth century, the interest in a *mathesis universalis* had in large part already given way to the rise of new movements, by the second part of the century, of Neo-Kantianism and positivist schools. See Hans-Georg Gadamer, "Die deutsche Philosophie zwischen den Weltkriegen," in *Gesammelte Werke*, Volume 10 (Tübingen: Mohr Siebeck, 1995), 356–72.

53. Fyodor Dostoevsky, *Notes from the Underground and the Grand Inquisitor*, trans. Ralph E. Matlaw (New York: Meridian Books), 31.

54. Descartes, of course, stands at the center of modern projects that turn on the establishment of absolutely certain foundations for the sciences. See, for example, his celebrated opening remarks to his First Meditation. René Descartes, *Meditations on First Philosophy*, "First Meditation," in *Collected Writings*, trans. John Cottingham, Robert Stoothoff, and Dugald Murdoch (New York: Cambridge University Press, 1988), 76.

55. Hegel, *Phänomenologie*, 68. Cf. Miller, 46/§ 73.

56. As is well known, in the "Preface" to the *Phenomenology* Hegel characterizes this 'science of experience' as only the initial, first part of his system, to be followed by the 'science of logic.' Hegel, *Phänomenologie*, 39. Cf. Miller, 22/§ 37.

57. Hegel, *Phänomenologie*, 16. Cf. Miller, 5/§ 8.

58. Martha Nussbaum, *Fragility of Goodness, Luck and Ethics in Greek Tragedy and Philosophy* (Cambridge: Cambridge University Press, 1986), 78.

59. Jean Hyppolite, *Genesis and Structure of Hegel's* Phenomenology of Spirit, trans. Samuel Cherniak and John Heckman (Evanston: Northwestern University Press, 1974), 50.

60. Szondi, *Versuch Über das Tragische*, 173, 172, respectively.

61. Schmidt, *Germans and Other Greeks*, 9.

CHAPTER 1. THE TRAGEDY OF EXPERIENCE

1. Hegel, *Phänomenologie*, 14. I consulted Miller's translation extensively for my translation of this passage. See Miller, 3/§ 5. Cf. Kojève, "Philosophy and Wisdom," in *Introduction to the Reading of Hegel*, 75.

2. Ibid., 16. Cf. Miller 5/§ 8.

3. Commentators disagree about how advanced Hegel believes consciousness must be in order to grasp the necessity in the progressive stages of experience. Robert Bernasconi, who discusses the issue in an illuminating essay on the relationship between Heidegger and Hegel, and who himself holds that it is only in the achievement of absolute knowing that consciousness achieves the standpoint of this 'we,' provides an excellent summary of the history of the literature on this subject. See Robert Bernasconi, "We philosophers, *Barbaros mēdeis eisitō*" in *Endings, Questions of Memory in Hegel and Heidegger*, eds. Rebecca Comay and John McCumber, 85.

4. Hegel, *Phänomenologie*, 36. Cf. Miller, 19/§ 32.

5. Indeed, if Hyppolite's *Genesis and Structure* resonates with existential themes, then, as Leonard Lawler points out, Hyppolite's *Logic and Existence* speaks to the relationship between Hegel's thought and themes in structuralism and post-structuralism. See Leonard Lawler, "Translator's Preface," in Jean Hyppolite, *Logic and Existence*, trans. Leonard Lawler (Albany: State University of New York Press, 1997), ix ff.

6. Merold Westphal, *History and Truth in Hegel's* Phenomenology (New Jersey: Humanities Press International, 1990), 14.

7. I discussed these movements briefly in a footnote to the "Introduction" of the present study.

8. Hegel, *Phänomenologie*, 72. Cf. Miller, 49/§ 78.

9. As is well known, Hegel characterizes this form of divestiture as a movement from '*certainty*' to '*truth*.' He develops these terms, for example, in his discussion sensible certainty. See Hegel, *Phänomenologie*, 82. Cf. Miller, 58/§ 91.

10. John Burbridge, "Hegel's Absolutes," *The Owl of Minerva* 29, no. 1 (1997): 24. Burbridge's interpretation of absolute knowledge, the upshot of which is that Hegel's thought may form "more an affirmation of relativism than absolutism," provides a provocative

counterpoint to the interpretation I develop in the present study. Burbridge, "Hegel's Absolutes," 32.

11. Hegel rejects both of these would-be interpretations of the absolute, and, indeed, for the entirety of his philosophical life. Hegel's objection to romantic notions of the absolute is indicated in his contrast of his own position with those guided by "the unmatched enthusiasm, which immediately begins with absolute knowledge like a shot from a pistol." Hegel, *Phänomenologie*, 31. Cf. Miller, 16/§ 27. It is true that Hegel will later associate his speculative system with the encyclopedia, and he does not refer to the French encyclopedists in the "Preface" to the *Phenomenology* directly. But he often criticizes more positivistic approaches to knowledge as 'lifeless.' See, for example, Hegel's description of a positive form of knowledge of nature to "a table, which can be compared to a skeleton with scraps of paper stuck all over it. . . ." Hegel, *Phänomenologie*, 50. Cf. Miller, 31/§ 51.

12. Gadamer, "Wort und Bild, »so wahr, so seind«," in *Gesammelte Werke*, Volume 8, (Tübingen: Mohr Siebeck, 1991) 379. Of course, Gadamer is neither the first, nor the last, to note this basic sense of Hegel's notion of the absolute. Indeed, several years later, Burbridge, who also notes that Hegel derives his sense of the absolute at least in part in reference to Kant, proffers a similar insight in the aforementioned essay, "Hegel's Absolutes," 26.

13. Hegel begins to consider the notion of education at *Phänomenologie*, 31–32. Cf. Miller, 16/§ 28. In regard of the connection Hegel makes between this education and experience, see, for example, *Phänomenologie*, 38. Cf. Miller, 21/§ 36.

14. In Hegel, it is important for us to recall that the achievement of absolute knowledge does not ignore or repress the memory of those limitations consciousness encounters over the course of its education, but, rather, sublates, and, thus, in a sense incorporates them.

15. Schelling's relation to Kant is evident in a number of texts, such as the 1800 *System of Transcendental Idealism*, and even in his earliest work, the *Letters on Dogmatism and Criticism*. Hölderlin also develops his relation to Kant at a number of junctures; one might see, for example, Hölderlin's consideration of Kantian themes in his "Urtheil und Seyn," though, Hölderlin's relation to Kant in this text is mediated by figures such as Fichte and Reinhold (Frank, *Foundations of Early German Romanticism*, 101 ff. Hegel develops his relation to Kant throughout his philosophical life. Many of Friedrich Schlegel's fragments and writings concern Kant, and I might even submit that Schlegel's notion of criticism itself emerges in no small part as a response to Kant's notion of critique.

16. Notice from the *Fränkischen Staats- und Gelehrten-Zeitung*, March 1804, no. 49, 50. Reprinted under the title "Immanual Kant," in F. W. J. Schelling *Ausgewählte Schriften*, Band 3 (Frankfurt am Main: Suhrkamp, 1985), 19.

17. Paul Guyer addresses the chief aspects of these Hegelian critiques of Kant in his "Thought and being: Hegel's critique of Kant," in *Cambridge Companion to Hegel* (New York: Cambridge Companion to Hegel, 1993), 181 ff, 185. Cf. Otfried Höffe, *Immanuel Kant*, trans. Marshall Farrier (Albany: State University of New York Press, 1994), 71.

18. Immanuel Kant, *Kritik der reinen Vernunft*, in *Werkausgabe*, Volume 3 (Frankfurt am Main: Suhrkamp, 1997), 311, 309, 328 (AKA A299/B355, A295/B352, A325-26/B382).

19. Ibid., 330. Of course, not all commentators fail to see this connection. Recently, for example, Burbridge emphasizes the connection in his "Hegel's Absolutes," 26.

20. Kant, *Kritik der reinen Vernunft*, 335 (AKA 334/B391).

21. Ibid., 11 (AKA A vii).

22. Ibid., 565 (AKA A 644/B 672).

23. One of Hegel's more instructive, and early, discussions of his relationship to Kant is found in the "Vorerinnerung" to the *Differenz des Fichte'schen uns Schelling'schen Systems der Pilosophie*. See Hegel, *Werke*, Volume 2, 9 ff.

24. See Schelling, *Philosophische Briefe Über Dogmatismus und Kriticismus*, *Werke*, Volume 3 (Stuttgart: Frommann-Holzbook, 1992).

25. See Guyer, "Thought and Being," 171.

26. Henry Allison, *Kant's Transcendental Idealism*, 10–13, cited in Taylor Carmen, *Heidegger's Analytic: Interpretation, Discourse, and Authenticity in* Being and Time (New York: Cambridge University Press, 2003), 23.

27. Guyer, "Thought and Being," 171.

28. Kant, *Kritik der reinen Vernunft*, 145 (AKA B 146).

29. Hegel tells us, "the living *substance* is being, which is in truth *subject*. . . ." Hegel, *Phänomenologie*, 22. Cf. Miller, 10/§ 17. I cite Miller's translation here.

30. See, for example, Schmidt, *Germans and Other Greeks*, 5.

31. Hegel, *Phänomenologie*, 31. Cf. Miller, 15/§ 27.

32. Hegel discusses a classical notion of purposive activity at *Phänomenologie*, 26. Cf. Miller, 12/§ 22. He invokes the image of plant life at *Phänomenologie*, 12. Cf. Miller, 2/§ 2.

33. Hegel, *Phänomenologie*, 65, 72, respectively. Cf. Miller, 43/§ 70, 49/§ 78.

34. Daniel Dennett, *The Intentional Stance*, cited in Taylor Carmen, *Heidegger's Analytic*, 108.

35. Taylor Carmen, *Heidegger's Analytic*, 109.

36. For a classic study of the affinities and disparities between Husserl and Hegel, see Quentin Lauer, S.J., "Phenomenology: Hegel and Husserl," in *Essays in Hegelian Dialectic* (New York: Fordham University Press, 1977). In evidence of my suggestion that Husserl and Hegel differ in sensibility, see especially Lauer, "Phenomenology: Hegel and Husserl," 40.

37. Ibid., 46.

38. Anthony Steinbock, "Spirit and generativity: The role and contribution of the phenomenologist in Hegel and Husserl," in *Alterity and Facticity, New Perspectives on Husserl*, eds. Natalie Depraz and Dan Zahavi (Boston: Kluwer Academic Publishers, 1998), 166.

39. Hegel, *Phänomenologie*, 76. Cf. Miller, 52/§ 82.

40. Donn Welton, whose extremely illuminating discussion of standard interpretations of Husserl in *The Other Husserl, the Horizons of Transcendental Phenomenology* (Bloomington: Indiana University Press, 2000) informs much of my discussion of the relationship between Husserl and Hegel here, refers to this heritage of criticism against Husserl as 'deconstructive,' though he acknowledges that it includes figures associated with phenomenology, existentialism, hermeneutics, and critical theory, as well as (Derridian) deconstruction. Welton, *The Other Husserl*, 395.

41. Welton, *The Other Husserl*, 396.

42. John Caputo, *Radical Hermeneutics, Repetition, Deconstruction, and the Hermeneutic Project* (Bloomington: Indiana University Press, 1987), 57. Cited in Welton, *The Other Husserl*, 396.

43. One of the most celebrated figures to oppose Hegel to Husserl in this manner is Adorno. See Welton, *The Other Husserl*, 402.

44. Anthony Steinbock, "Spirit and Generativity: The Role and Contribution of the Phenomenologist in Hegel and Husserl," 166–67.

45. I am indebted to Steinbock for my overall account of Hegel's 'we' at this juncture, though it remains unclear to me whether he and I would agree on the claim I make here. Although Steinbock does not assert it expressly (and perhaps would not even assent to it), some of his comments nonetheless appear implicitly to associate Hegel's 'we,' or, as Steinbock puts it, 'the Hegelian phenomenologist,' with a form of theoretical disinterest. Steinbock writes, for example, that "the Hegelian phenomenologist must resist the temptation to manipulate the phenomena" and that the "role of the [Hegelian] phenomenologist is unbiased description." Steinbock, "Spirit and generativity," 167, 168, respectively. Although I agree with his point, I do not believe it follows that Hegel's 'we' is disinterested, since, after all, the overall purpose for its unbiased description is not to produce knowledge of an object in general, but is rather bound up with its driving concern to achieve insight into itself.

46. Of course, criticisms of Husserl raised in continental heritages are much more complicated than I am able to treat here, as are recent challenges to them. For a richer picture of the challenges, see, for example, Donn Welton's *The Other Husserl*, and Dan Zahavi's *Husserl's Phenomenology* (Stanford: Stanford University Press, 2003). Of course, such recent approaches also address debates on Husserl that emege in the Anglo-American context. For a concise account, see, for example, Dan Zahavi, "Husserl's Noema and the Internalism–Externalism Debate," *Inquiry* 47 (2004): 42–66.

47. Steinbock, "Spirit and Generativity," 176–77, 196 ff.

48. See Hegel, *Phänomenologie*, 73–75. Cf. Miller, 50–52/§§ 79–80.

49. Hegel, *Phänomenologie*, 75. Cf. Miller, 52/§ 81.

50. Of course, because Hegel believes that in absolute knowing, consciousness' cognition is ultimately adequate to phenomena, it would be misleading to claim that Hegel subscribes to what, following Jean-Luc Marion, might be treated under the rubric of the 'saturated phenomenon.'

51. Hegel, *Phänomenologie*, 72. Cf. Miller, 49/§ 78.

52. Hegel, *Phänomenologie*, 79. Cf. Miller, 55/§ 87.

53. Hegel, *Vorlesungen über die Ästhetik I*, in *Werke*, Volume 13, 31. See also Hegel, *Vorlesungen über die Ästhetik III*, in *Werke*, Volume 15, 474 ff.

54. Aristotle, *Poetics*, in *Complete Works of Aristotle*, Volume 2, trans. I. Bywater, ed. Jonathan Barnes (Princeton: Princeton University Press, 1984, fourth Printing 1991), 2320/1449b24–25.

55. Aristotle, *Poetics*, trans. I. Bywater, ed. Jonathan Barnes, *Complete Works of Aristotle*, Volume 2 (Princeton: Princeton University Press, 1984, fourth printing 1991), 2320/1450a9.

56. Ibid., 2320/1450a9, 1450a15.

57. Ibid., 2324/1542a22.

58. Schmidt, *Germans and Other Greeks*, 57.

59. Hegel, *Phänomenologie*, 74. Cf. Miller, 51/§ 80.

60. Ibid., 590. Cf. Miller, 492/§ 808.

Chapter 2. The Tragedy of Freedom

1. For an excellent treatment of the significance and role of freedom in Hegel's thought, including his interest in freedom in the *Science of Logic*, see Will Dudley, "Freedom in and through Hegel's Philosophy," *Owl of Minerva* 39, no. 4 (Fall 2000): 683–703.

2. Robert Pippen states, for example, "Although it is an arguable claim, it is not unreasonable to assert that much of what current academic practice characterizes as 'contemporary European philosophy' begins with and is largely determined by Hegel." Robert Pippen, *Hegel's Idealism, The Satisfactions of Self-consciousness* (Cambridge: Cambridge University Press, 1989), 1.

3. See Robert Pippen, *Hegel's Idealism*. Of course, it would be a mistake to suppose that emphasis upon Hegel's theoretical concerns somehow leads to the exclusion of the practical side of his account. On the contrary, Hegel's overall approach to self-consciousness suggests that he believes his speculative presentation, or, if we are to linger on the Kantian idiom, his 'deduction,' of self-consciousness to consist in not simply the analysis of theoretical cognition, but also of matters of practical life. The character of Hegel's presentation indicates that for him, questions about independence, the desire for recognition, and the relation of mastery and servitude are not extraneous to his deduction of self-consciousness, but, rather, comprise some of its constitutive elements.

4. It might be convenient to refer to such approaches to Hegel as 'deconstructionist,' but this might obviate important and nuanced differences among divergent approaches.

5. Friedrich Nietzsche, *Zur Genealogie der Moral*, in *Kritische Studienausgabe*, eds. Giorgio Colli and Mazzino Montinari (Munich: Deutscher Tachenbuch Verlag; Berlin: Walter de Gruyter, 1988), 268.

6. Hegel, *Phänomenologie*, 153. Cf. Miller, 117/§ 194.

7. As we shall see, it is Hans-Georg Gadamer who associates this finite form of freedom with ability. See Gadamer, "Hegels Dialektik des Selbstbewusstseins," in *Neuere Philosophie I, Gesammelte Werke*, Volume 3 (Tübingen: Mohr Siebeck, 1987), 60.

8. Of course, the range of figures in Hegel studies who take inspiration from Marx cannot be enumerated here, though, from continental heritages perhaps our first thought is of Alexandre Kojève, even if his debts are not only to Marx but also to Heidegger. Aimé Patri, "Dialectique du Maître et de l'Esclave," *Le Contrat Social* 5, no. 4 (July–August 1961), cited in Alexandre Kojève, *Introduction to the Reading of Hegel*, ed. Allan Bloom and trans. James H. Nichols, Jr. (Ithica: Cornell University Press, 1980, sixth printing 1996), vii.

9. One interesting defense of 'servitude' against 'slavery' as a translation of 'Knechtshaft' is found in Michael H. Hoffheimer, "Translating *Knechtschaft*," *Owl of Minerva* 32, no. 2 (2001): 169–75. Note that Hoffheimer also asserts reservations about 'bondage' as a translation of 'Knechtschaft,' stating, "I reject the once venerable 'bondage' because it, too, bears strong associations of enslavement that have contributed to the misunderstanding of Hegel's treatment of servitude" (Michael Hoffheimer, "Translating *Knechtschaft*," 169). Although I believe his point about 'bondage' has merit, I have decided on occasion to use it as a translation of 'Knechtschaft.' One reason for this is that the notion of bondage is tied to historical practices that focus on serfdom and labor. For another, I would submit, the English 'bondage' involves connotations that speak to the boundedness of the *Knecht* not only to the master, but also, in a different way, to the absolute master, and, perhaps in another way still, to natural life.

10. Karl Marx, *German Ideology*, in *Marx-Engels Reader*, ed. Robert Norton (New York: W. W. Norton, 1978), 197.

11. Allen W. Wood, *Hegel's Ethical Thought* (Cambridge: Cambridge University Press, 1990), 85. In addition to Allen Wood's work on the issue of recognition in Hegel, and his debts to Fichte, see also Andreas Wildt, *Autonomie und Anerkennung, Hegels Moralitätskritik im Lichte seiner Fichte-Rezeption* (Stuttgart: Klett-Cotta, 1982).

12. Peter Dews, *Logics of Disintegration, Post-structuralist Thought and the Claims of Critical Theory* (New York: Verso Press, 1987), 21.

13. See Hegel, *Phänomenologie*, 144. Cf. Miller, 110/§ 176. Here, Hegel asserts that the self-consciousness is a complex process, of which the pure 'I' is but one moment.

14. Hegel, *Phänomenologie*, 143. Cf. Miller, 109/§ 174. I borrow extensively from Miller's translation.

15. Hegel, *Phänomenologie*, 139. Cf. Miller, 105/§ 167.

16. Ibid., 91. This is Miller's translation. Cf. Miller, 65/§ 109.

17. Kojève, *Introduction to the Reading of Hegel*, 4.

18. Butler, *Subjects of Desire* (New York: Columbia University Press, 1987), 39.

19. Hegel, *Phänomenologie*, 144. Cf. Miller, 109/§ 175.

20. Hegel, *Phänomenologie*, 147. Cf. Miller, 112/§ 184. I have used Miller's translation here.

21. Ibid., 489. Cf. Miller, 404/§ 665. Although Hegel evokes this truism for slightly different purposes and in his discussion of consciousness, it may nevertheless be seen as relevant to his discussion of recognition in Chapter IV of the *Phenomenology*. However, it should be born in mind, as H. S. Harris points out, that Hegel's use of the phrase alludes to "the golden age of the ancien Régime." H. S. Harris, *Hegel's Ladder II*, 495.

22. Hegel, "Liebe," in *Frühe Schriften*, *Werke* 1, 245.

23. Hegel, *Phänomenologie*, 149. Cf. Miller, 113–14/§ 187.

24. H. S. Harris, for example, suggests that "Eteocles and Polynices are probably Hegel's own paradigm for the struggle to the death." in H. S. Harris, *Hegel's Ladder I: The Pilgrimage of Reason*, 355.

25. Jean Hyppolite, *Genesis and Structure of Hegel's* Phenomenology of Spirit, trans. Samuel Cherniak and John Heckman (Evanston: Northwestern University Press, 1974), 170.

26. Hans-Georg Gadamer, "Hegels Dialektik des Selbstbeusstseins," 56. Note that Gadamer himself illustrates the structure of self-consciousness' struggle for recognition with reference to another practice, the greeting. Ibid., 55.

27. Ibid., 56.

28. Hyppolite, *Genesis and Structure*, 147.

29. Ibid., 150.

30. Kojève, *Introduction*, 42.

31. Hegel, *Phänomenologie*, 150. Cf. Miller, 115/§ 189.

32. Ibid. Cf. Miller, 115/§ 190.

33. Gadamer, "Hegels Dialektik des Selbstbewusstseins," 58. Gadamer turns this phrase in order to sum up Kojève's view of the relation between master and servant.

34. John Russon offers an illuminating and thorough account of the relation between Hegel's discussion of self-consciousness and various aspects of Kant's Doctrine of Elements in the first *Critique*. See Russon, *Reading Hegel's* Phenomenology, perhaps especially Chapter 6.

35. In reference to the somewhat different, but by no means unrelated themes of communication and embodiment in Hegel's discussion of the master/servant relation, Russon argues, for example, that "to be a master means to be an interpreter," and, we might extrapolate, to be a servant means to be interpreted. See Russon, *Reading Hegel's* Phenomenology, 74.

36. Hegel, *Phänomenologie*, 152. Cf. Miller, 117/§ 193. Hegel uses the reflexive verb form, 'sich umkehren,' to indicate that the relation of mastery and servitude 'reverses itself.'

37. Ibid. Cf. Miller, ibid.

38. Hegel mentions the problem of receiving recognition from a dependent at ibid., 152. Cf. Miller, 117/§ 192.

39. I extrapolate this claim from Hegel's treatment of the relationship between mastery and enjoyment at ibid., 151/§ 190.

40. Although his use of the turn of phrase is somewhat different and more nuanced than mine, I owe the characterization of mastery as a 'dead end' to conversations with Dennis Schmidt.

41. Hegel, *Phänomenologie*, 153. Cf. Miller, 118/§ 195.

42. Hegel, *Phänomenologie*, 148. Cf. Miller, 113/§ 187.

43. See Friedrich Nietzsche, *Zur Genalogie der Moral*, in *Kritische Studienausgabe*, Volume 5, eds. Giorgio Colli and Mazzino Montinari (Munich: Walter de Gruyter, 1988).

44. In his illuminating essay, "Who is Nietzsche's Zarathustra? Of Fraternity, Friendship, and a Democracy to Come" John D. Caputo argues that Derrida's invocation of Nietzschean themes Derrida's *Politics of Friendship* (and, the suggestion is, perhaps in many of Derrida's other writings) rests upon a heterodox Nietzsche, "one, who flies in the

face of the fraternalistic, elitist, antidemocratic—let us say canonical—Nietzsche." Instead, Caputo argues that Derrida's Nietzsche in this text may be understood as "a kind of Dionysian rabbi, a Jewish, messianic Nietzsche," that has been "transcribed in terms of Blanchot and Levinas." (Caputo, "Who is Nietzsche's Zarathustra?," 193). I would suggest, however, that even if Derrida's Nietzsche in the "From Restricted to General Economy" essay exhibits traces of this heterodox Nietzsche, it also crucially involves what Caputo refers to as the more 'canonical' Nietzsche. For purposes of the present study, it is Derrida's debts to this latter Nietzsche with which I am concerned.

45. Karin de Boer, "Tragic Entanglements: Between Hegel and Derrida," *Bulletin of the Hegel Soceity of Great Britain* (2003): 35, 47–48.

46. Heinz Kimmerle, "On Derrida's Hegel Interpretation," in *Hegel after Derrida*, ed. Stuart Barnett (New York: Routledge Press, 1998), 230.

47. Georges Bataille, *L'experience intérieure*, cited in Jacques Derrida, "From Restricted to General Economy, A Hegelianism without Reserve," in *Writing and Difference*, trans. Alan Bass (Chicago: University of Chicago Press, 1978), 252.

48. In this essay, Derrida organizes his discourse not foremost around the term 'deconstruction' but, instead, 'writing.'

49. For an excellent extended discussion of the importance of questions of interpretation, language, and meaning for Hegel's account of self-consciousness, see John Russon, *Reading Hegel's* Phenomenology, perhaps especially Chapter 6, "Hermeneutical Pressure, Intersubjectivity and Objectivity," in Russon, *Reading Hegel's* Phenomenology (Bloomington: Indiana University Press, 2004), 81–95.

50. Derrida, "From Restricted to General Economy," 254. Derrida writes, further, that "Sovereignty . . . is more and less than lordship. . . ." (Derrida, "From Restricted to General Economy," 256).

51. Ibid., 264.

52. Derrida writes that in contrast with sovereignty, Hegelian lordship wants "to maintain itself, collect itself, or, collect the profits from itself its own risk . . ." (Derrida, "From Restricted to General Economy," 264).

53. Kimmerle, "On Derrida's Hegel Interpretation," 231.

54. Ibid.

55. Ibid.

56. Although this is perhaps not the proper place to consider Derrida's notion of the quasi-transcendental at length, it is nonetheless the right time at least to mention that what I describe here as the 'quasi-tragic' is not dissimilar from it. Commentators such as Karin de Boer notice that for Derrida, such self-withdrawing, or, perhaps, self-effacing, structures pervade Hegel's thought in general. She writes that from a Derridian standpoint, "Hegel can be considered to suppress a mode of negativity which *not only makes possible any self-actualization, but simultaneously threatens to make any kind of self-actualization impossible*" (de Boer, "Tragic Entanglements," 35).

57. Derrida, "From Restricted to General Economy," 255.

58. Within the Hegelian framework there is no other possibility. If neither self-consciousness risks her life, then no genuine struggle ensues.

59. See Gadamer, "Hegels Dialectik des Selbstbewusstseins," which provides the framework for much of my discussion here.

60. Hegel, *Phänomenologie*, 153. Cf. Miller, 117/§ 194.

61. Gadamer, "Hegels Dialektik des Selbstbewusstseins," 57. I cite Christopher P. Smith's translation here. See Gadamer, *Hegel's Dialectic, Five Hermeneutical Studies*, trans. Christopher P. Smith (New Haven: Yale University Press, 1976), 66.

62. Ibid., 62. Here I rely heavily upon Christopher P. Smith's translation. Cf. ibid., 71. Cf. also Jean Hyppolite, *Genesis and Structure*, 176.

63. Günter Figal, *Für eine Philosophie von Freiheit und Streit, Politik, Ästhetik, und Metaphysik* (Stuttgart: J. B. Metzler Verlag, 1994), 133. I use Wayne Klein's translation here. See Günter Figal, *For a Philosophy of Freedom and Strife*, trans. Wayne Klein (Albany: State University of New York Press, 1998), 141.

Chapter 3. The Tragedy of Ethical Life

1. George Steiner asserts, for example, that "Between *c.* 1790 and *c.* 1905, it was widely held by European poets, philosophers, scholars that Sophocles' *Antigone* was not only the finest work of Greek tragedies, but a work of art nearer to perfection than any other produced by the human spirit." George Steiner, *Antigones* (New York: Oxford University Press, 1984), 1.

2. A helpful collection of modern and early modern critical writings on Sophocles' dramas is R. D. Dawe, ed., *Sophocles, the Classical Heritage* (New York: Garland Publishing Co., 1996). Some influential psychoanalytic treatments of the *Antigone*, mentioned already in the "Introduction" of this book, are Jacques Lacan, "Seventh Lecture," and, with important implications for feminism, Luce Irigaray, "The Eternal Irony of the Community." In scholarship that emerges in recent feminist approaches, see Judith Butler, *Antigone's Claim* (New York: Columbia University Press, 2000).

3. Christoph Menke, *Die Tragödie im Sittlichen, Gerechtigkeit und Freiheit nach Hegel* (Frankfurt am Main: Suhrkamp, 1996), 77–78.

4. Of course, a full consideration of Hegel's notion of rational agency would have to consider not simply Hegel's treatment of consciousness' experience of ethical life and his use of the *Antigone* to describe it, but moreover consciousness' development of its awareness of practical reason and agency in its experiences of 'the actualization of rational self-consciousness through itself,' and 'individuality, which is real in and for itself.' See Hegel, *Phänomenologie*, 263 ff. Cf. Miller, 211/§ 347 ff. See also Schmidt, *Germans and Other Greeks*, 95.

5. Terry Pinkard, *Hegel's* Phenomenology*: The Sociality of Reason* (Cambridge: Cambridge University Press, 1996), 331.

6. See Jacques Taminiaux, "Nostalgia for Greece at the Dawn of Classical Germany," in *Poetics, Speculation, and Judgment, The Shadow of the Work of Art from Kant to Phenomenology*, trans. Michael Gendre (Albany: State University of New York Press, 1993), 73–92.

7. Terry Pinkard suggests that a number of Hegel's contemporaries conceive of the ancient Greek world as an alternative to modern life. See Pinkard, *Hegel's* Phenomenology, 137 ff.

8. Pinkard asserts, for example, "The section on reason attempts to narrate the dialectical history of [the] . . . attempt at establishing a self-justifying form of life by the application of various 'methods' in order to discover the general laws of nature and social life." Pinkard, *Hegel, The Sociality of Reason*, 81.

9. Hegel, *Phänomenologie*, 263 ff. Cf. Miller, 211/§ 347 ff.

10. Schmidt, *Germans and Other Greeks*, 95.

11. See Pinkard's discussion of Hegel's treatment of Kant in the discussion of 'reason as law-giver' and 'reason as law-tester.' Pinkard, *Hegel, The Sociality of Reason*, 124 ff.

12. I enlist the term 'cultural heritage' here because I believe it illuminates important aspects of Hegel's view and underscores the currency of his approach, even though it does not accord directly with Hegel's own usage. Of course, I trust that my readers will recognize that my use of 'cultural heritage' to discuss issues in Hegel's treatment of ethical life should not be confused with his use of the term 'culture' (*Kultur*) later in the *Phenomenology*.

13. Ibid., 325. Cf. Miller, 263/§ 438.

14. Philippe Lacoue-Labarthe and Jean-Luc Nancy, *The Literary Absolute, The Theory of Literature in German Romanticism*, trans. Philip Barnard and Cheryl Lester (Albany: State University of New York Press, 1988), 12.

15. Hegel, *Phänomenologie*, 325. Cf. Miller, 264/§ 439.

16. See, for example, Immanuel Kant, *Kritik der Urteilskraft*, "Analytik der telelogishen Urteilskraft" (§§ 62–68): 307–34 (AKA B 271/A 267–B 309/A 306).

17. Charles Taylor, "Hegel's Philosophy of Action," in *Hegel and the Philosophy of Action*, eds. Lawrence S. Stepelevich and David Lamb (Atlantic Highlands: Humanities Press, 1983), 2–3.

18. Taylor, "Hegel's Philosophy of Action," 4.

19. Hegel, *Phänomenologie*, 325. Cf. Miller, 264/§ 339.

20. Pinkard, *Hegel's* Phenomenology, 138.

21. Allen Speight, *Hegel, Literature, and the Problem of Agency* (Cambridge: Cambridge University Press, 2001), 4.

22. Taylor, "Hegel's Philosophy of Action," 2.

23. Hegel, *Phänomenologie*, 342. Cf. Miller, 279/§ 465.

24. Ibid., 328. Cf. Miller, 266/§ 444.

25. Ibid. Cf. Miller, ibid.

26. Ibid., 329. Cf. Miller, 267/§ 446.

27. Hegel, *Phänomenologie*, Chapter 7.

28. Ibid., 330. Cf. Miller, 268/§ 450. See also Schmidt, *Germans and Other Greeks*, 95.

29. Hegel, *Phänomenologie*, 330 ff. Cf. Miller, 268/§ 450 ff.

30. Hegel discusses the issue of burial in this context foremost as a filial duty. See ibid., 332. Cf. Miller, 270/§ 452.

31. Ibid., 333. Cf. Miller, 271/§ 452.

32. Hegel, *Phänomenologie*, 329–30. Cf. Miller, 267–68/§ 448.

33. Ibid. Cf. Miller, ibid.

34. Hegel, *Vorlesungen über die Philosophie der Religion* II, *Werke*, Volume 17, 133.

35. Sophocles, *Antigone*, in *Three Theban Plays*, trans. Robert Fagles (New York: Penguin Books, 1984), 85/ln. 585.

36. Although numerous commentators have provided excellent insights into the Hellenic background of Hegel's treatment of the family here, see, for example, H. S. Harris, *Hegel's Ladder* II, 175 ff.

37. Hegel, *Phänomenologie*, 332. Cf. Miller, § 452.

38. Ibid., 322–333. Cf. Miller, § 452–53.

39. In fact, Hegel's broader presentation suggests that consciousness's struggle to come to terms with the fact that its universal principles are nonetheless always its own pervades not only its experience of ethical life, but also its closely related, earlier experiences of the 'actualization of rational self-consciousness through itself,' and 'individuality, which is in and for itself real.'

40. See Schmidt, *Germans and Other Greeks*, 95, 98.

41. For a provocative and original treatment of Hegel's view of the difference of the sexes, see Derrida, *Glas*, trans. John P. Leavey, Jr. (Lincoln: University of Nebraska Press, 1986), 108 ff.

42. Seyla Benhabib provides a landscape of different types of feminist approaches to Hegel in "On Hegel, Women, and Irony," in *Feminist Interpretations of Hegel* ed. Patricia J. Mills (University Park: The Pennsylvania State University Press, 1998), 26–27.

43. Sophocles, *Antigone*, 105.

44. Ibid. Of course, we might wish to ask more precisely in what sense Antigone thinks that fathers and sons are replaceable.

45. H. S. Harris asserts, however, that the relationship between Polynices and Eteocles, and their demise on the battle field at each others hands, comprises a special case of the struggle for recognition. See Harris, *Hegel's Ladder II*, 180–81.

46. Hegel associates the one-sidedness of the husband/wife, parent/child relations with their emotional 'impurity,' writing, for example, that the husband/wife relation is "mixed" with a "natural relation and feeling," and that the parent/child relation is "emotionally affected." Hegel, *Phänomenologie* 336. Cf. Miller, 273/§ 456. I use Miller's translation in this footnote.

47. Hegel, *Phänomenologie*, 336. Cf. Miller, 274/§ 457.

48. Ibid., 332. Cf. Miller, 270/§ 451.

49. Derrida, *Glas*, 143.

50. Hegel, *Phänomenologie*, 352. Cf. Miller, 288/§ 475.

51. See Luce Irigaray, "The Eternal Irony of the Community," in *Feminist Interpretations of G. W. F. Hegel*, ed. Patricia J. Mills (Campus Parkway: The Pennsylvania State University Press, 1996), 45–57.

52. Hegel, *Phänomenologie*, 355. Cf. Miller, 290/§ 477.

53. Hegel claims that the Roman period sees the emergence of a sense of self absent in the ethical life of the Greeks, but only in its most estranged form. The realization of this sense of self is contingent upon its development through 'self-estranged spirit.' Hegel, *Phänomenologie*, 359. Cf. Miller, 293–94/§ 483.

54. Hegel, *Phänomenologie*, 346. Cf. Miller, 282/§ 468.

55. Lore Hühn, "Die Philosophie des Tragischen. Schellings, Philosophische Briefe über Dogmatismus und Kriticismus," in *Schellingiana*, Volume 10, *Die Realität des Wissens und das wirkliche Dasein, Erkenntnis Begründung und Philosophie beim frühen Schelling*, ed. Jörg Jantzen (Stuttgart-Bad Constatt: Frommann-Holzboog, 1998), 107.

56. Hegel's emphasis upon the issue of ethical agents' ignorance here is taken up again in a new way in his discussion of tragic drama as an art form. See Chapter 4.

57. Hegel, *Phänomenologie*, 346, 347. Cf. Miller, 282/§ 468, 283/469.

58. My suggestion to distance Hegel's notion of (Greek) ontological guilt from (Christian) original sin warrants more thorough and nuanced attention than I am able to give it here. For a consideration of questions about ontological guilt and original sin in Hegel, see, for example, Richard S. Findler, "Reconciliation versus Reversal: Hegel and Nietzsche on Overcoming Ontological Guilt," in *Hegel's* Phenomenology of Spirit, *New Critical Essays* eds. Alfred Denker and Michael Vater (New York: Humanities Press, 2003). See also H. S. Harris's claim that Hegel's notion of guilt here may be seen as a special reading of original sin. See Harris, *Hegel's Ladder II*, 214.

59. See Augustine, *On the Free Choice of the Will*, Book III, Chapter 18. Augustine, *On the Free Choice of the Will*, trans. Thomas Williams (Indianapolis: Hackett Publishing Co., 1993).

60. Hegel, *Phänomenologie*, 348. Cf. Miller, 284/§ 470.

61. Hegel, *Phänomenologie*, 591. Cf. Miller, 493/§ 808.

62. Sophocles, *Antigone*, trans. Hugh Lloyd Jones, Loeb Classical Library (Cambridge: Harvard University Press, 1994), 88/ln. 927.

63. John Jones, *On Aristotle and Greek Tragedy* (Stanford: Stanford University Press, 1962), 15.

64. Martha Nussbaum, *The Fragility of Goodness, Luck and Ethics in Greek Tragedy and Philosophy* (Cambridge: Cambridge University Press, 1986), 382. Readers of *The Fragility of Goodness* will know that Nussbaum is highly critical of Hegel's interpretation of Sophocles' *Antigone*. While I would submit that Nussbaum's work on Hegel, perhaps because her focus is primarily on Greek philosophy and tragedy, and is somewhat cursory, there can be no question that her work as a whole is quite excellent. Her interpretation of the Greek notion of ἁμαρτία, in particular, is extremely insightful.

65. Chalres Guignon and Derk Pereboom explain, for example, that

> In attempting to understand our predicament in the modern age existentialists have formulated an insightful new way of thinking about human existence. In contrast to much of the philosophical tradition, which has sought to understand a human as a thing or an

object of a particular sort (whether a mind or a body or some combination of the two), existentialists have characterized human existence as involving a profound tension or conflict, an ongoing struggle between opposing elements.

Though such a conception of human existence has roots in St. Augustine, Montainge, Pascal, and even in Plato, the primary source of the modern existentialist version of this picture is G. W. F. Hegel. (Charles Guignon and Derk Pereboom, "Introduction," in *Existentialism, Basic Writings*, Indianapolis: Hackett Publishing Company, 1995, xvii.)

66. See, for example, Pierre Verstraeten, "Hegel and Sartre," in *Cambridge Companion to Sartre*, ed. Christiana Howells (Cambridge: Cambridge University Press, 1992), 353.

67. Jean Paul Sartre, "Existentialism is a Humanism," in *Existentialism from Dostoyevsky to Sartre*, ed. Walter Kaufman, revised and expanded edition (New York: Meridian Publishing Company, 1989), 351.

68. Ibid., 353.

69. Ibid., 354 ff.

70. Ibid., 354.

71. Ibid., 355.

72. It is interesting to note that this latter difference between Sartre's example and Hegel's use of the Antigone parallels a distinction Hegel makes between the depiction of tragic conflict in modern and ancient drama. In modern drama, he claims, the tendency is for tragic conflict to focus on the internal life of the subject, whereas in ancient drama it centers on the ethical substance of a people. See Hegel, *Vorlesungen Über die Ästhetik* III, *Werke*, Volume 15, 555 ff.

Chapter 4. Tragic Wisdom

1. In his retrospective "Attempt at Self-Criticism," Nietzsche himself suggests that his exposure of the problem of Socratism, or, as he recasts it in the "Attempt," "*the problem of science*" comprises one of the greatest discoveries of the *Birth of Tragedy*. See Nietzsche, "Versuch einer Selbstkritik," 13, in *Kritische Studienausgabe*, Volume 1. In this footnote, I have used Kaufmann's translation. See Nietzsche, *Birth of Tragedy*, in *Birth of Tragedy and the Case of Wagner*, trans. Walter Kaufmann (New York: Vintage Books, 1967), 18.

2. Nietzsche, *Geburt der Tragödie*, 115. Cf. Kaufmann, 109.

3. Nietzsche, "Versuch einer Selbstkritik," 13. I use Kaufmann's translation here. See Kaufmann, 19.

4. Nietzsche, *Geburt der Tragodie*, 119. Cf. Kaufmann, 113.

5. Ibid., 97. Cf. Kaufmann, 93.

6. Gilles Deleuze, *Nietzsche and Philosophy*, trans. Hugh Tomlinson (New York: Columbia University Press, 1983), 156 ff. Stephen Houlgate offers an excellent survey of important scholarship on the relation between Nietzsche and Hegel in *Hegel, Nietzsche,*

and the Criticism of Metaphysics (New York: Cambridge University Press, 1986). See Chapter 1, "The Hegel–Nietzsche debate," p. 1 ff.

7. Hegel, *Phänomenologie*, 492. Cf. Miller, 407/§ 407.

8. Stephen Houlgate, for example, holds such a view. Interestingly, Houlgate believes that the superiority of the critical force of Hegel's thought over Nietzsche's becomes especially evident through a comparison of their respective views on tragedy. See Houlgate, *Hegel, Nietzsche, and the Critique of Metaphysics*, Chapter 8, "Hegel and Nietzsche on Tragedy," p. 182 ff.

9. Taylor, *Hegel*, 466.

10. In fact, as Merold Westphal discusses, Gadamer asserts that his thought, not just his conception of art, stands in a "tension filled proximity" to Hegel. Gadamer, "Reason in the Age of Science," cited in Merold Westphal "Hegel and Gadamer," in *Hermeneutics and Modern Philosophy*, ed. Brice R. Wachterhauser, (Albany: State University of New York Press, 1986).

11. Heidegger observes, for example, that "one cannot circumvent [ausweichen] the verdict Hegel gives [simply] by notcing that in the time since Hegel lectured on aesthetics for the last time in the winter of 1828/29 at the University of Berlin, we have seen many new works of art and directions within art emerge. This possibility he would never have wanted to deny." Heidegger, *Ursprung des Kunstwerks*, 68.

12. Kojève, in fact, claims that Hegel's view of wisdom incorporates three difference senses of wisdom. See Kojève, "Philosophy and Wisdom," in *Introduction to the Reading of Hegel*, 75 ff.

13. In my discussion, I associate Hegel's notion of speculative philosophy with the attainment of wisdom, whereas Kojève, I would suggest, opposes to Hegelian wisdom the notion of philosophy in a more general sense. See Kojève, "Philosophy and Wisdom," in *Introduction to the Reading of Hegel*, 75. Cf. Ibid., 86 ff.

14. Indeed, the difficulties posed by the intractably expansive and diverse body of scholarship on Hegel poses a general problem for Hegel studies. For one thing, the vastness of the literature might be seen to make it overly cumbersome and even counter-productive to attempt to refer to all sources on a topic in the course of one's efforts to develop an approach to Hegel. For another, the vastness, as well as extreme variety, of literature might be seen to make it difficult genuinely to master. In regard of this latter idea, one might consider K. R. Dove's assertion, in which he expresses his own agreement with John McCumber in a review of *The Company of Words*, "that no one today could be in control of the entire literature on Hegel." K. R. Dove, Review of John McCumber, *The Company of Words*, in *Journal of the History of Philosophy* 32, no. 4 (1994): 681.

15. Taylor, *Hegel*, 465.

16. Ibid. In a recent article, Burbridge argues that whereas the Hegel of the *Encyclopedia* approaches absolute spirit as a form of spirit knowing itself, the Hegel of the *Phenomenology* introduces the notion of absolute spirit as "a mutual recognition in which the acting, existing spirit sees the pure knowing of itself in its counterpart, and the pure knowing acknowledges the existence of its own principles in the actual deeds of the other." Burbridge, "Hegel's Absolutes," 32. My suggestion would simply be that these two approaches are not only

compatible, but that much of Hegel's discussion of absolute spirit in the *Phenomenology* is oriented by concerns about spirit that knows itself. Of philosophical "absolute knowledge," Hegel states, for example, that it comprises "the spirit that knows itself in the figure of spirit." Hegel, *Phänomenologie*, 582. Cf. Miller 485/§ 798. I use Miller's translation here. Of the highest forms of the religion of art in Greece, further, he states that in it, spirit aims at "pure knowledge of itself." Hegel, *Phänomenologie*, 513. Cf. Miller 425/§ 701.

17. Pinkard, *Hegel's Phenomenology*, 221.

18. Ibid.

19. Taminiaux, "Speculation and Judgment," in *Poetics, Speculation, and Judgment*, 1.

20. Ibid.

21. Ibid., 2. Cf. Ibid., 5. If to translate is always also to interpret, then it might be that Taminiaux's construal of θεωρία sounds almost as German, and, perhaps in particular, as Heideggerian, as it does Greek. But of course, this consonance itself might not come as a surprise, given that the German figures that inform the horizon of Taminiaux's research, such as Heidegger and Hegel, remained in important respects close to the classical Greek heritages of philosophy, religion, and art. It should be noted, too, that Taminiaux himself recognizes the interpretive difficulty in translation, tarrying on the idea, for example, that modern uses of the word 'speculation' (and also 'judgment') may have no exact equivalent in Greek. See ibid., 9.

22. Taylor, *Hegel*, 466.

23. See Robert Wicks, "Hegel's Aesthetics: An Overview," in *Cambridge Companion to Hegel*, 352.

24. Hegel, *Phänomenologie*, 400 ff. Cf. Miller, 329/§ 541 ff.

25. Hegel associates the attainment of absolute knowledge with the concept at a number of junctures. See, for example, Hegel, *Phänomenologie*, 582. Cf. Miller, 485/§ 798. Miller translates '*Begriff*' as 'Notion.'

26. Hegel associates religion and representation (*Vorstellung*) in his discussion of the spiritual art of the Greeks at Hegel, *Phänomenologie*, 531. Cf. Miller, 440/§ 729. Hegel characterizes religion more generally as representation (*Vorstellung*) at, for example, *Phänomenologie*, 580. Cf. Miller, 484/§ 796. Miller translates '*Vorstellung*' as 'picture-thinking,' which, though it helps to evoke a number of the word's connotations, does not pick up on the opposition and relation Hegel wishes to indicate by his use of the linguistically and semantically related *Darstellung* and *Vorstellung*. Wicks discusses Hegel's view that religion and art remain bound to sensation at "Hegel's Aesthetics: An Overview," 351. For a discussion of the problem of presentation (*Darstellung*) in the period that leads up to Hegel, see, Philip Barnard and Cheryl Lester, "Translator's Introduction: The Presentation of Romantic Literature," in Philippe Lacoue-Labarthe and Jean-Luc Nancy, *The Literary Absolute*, viii ff.

27. In the case of the revealed religion, the inheritance of the story of Christ; in the case of the Greek religion of art, the traditional myths that inform its heritages of art.

28. In more recent trends of Hegel studies, some scholars contend that it would be a mistake to over-inflate Hegel's association of scientific knowledge with the absolute, and

Burbridge, for example, goes so far as to argue that Hegel's use of the adjective 'absolute' is ironic, and must be understood to indicate that all knowledge claims are relative (Burbridge, "Hegel's Absolutes," 27). Certainly, Hegel's extensive criticisms of romantic irony might cast some doubt on this approach to his notion of the absolute. Still, even this view might imply a transhistorical perspective, if the absolute knowledge of the relative validity of other claims is itself understood to be unconditioned.

29. David Papineau cites the issue of induction as central to debates in the epistemology of science about the issue of justification in science. See Papineau, "Science, Problems in the Philosophy Of," in *The Oxford Companion to Philosophy*, ed. Ted Honderich (New York: Oxford University Press, 1995), 809.

30. Burbridge, "Hegel's Absolutes," 29. Cf. Hegel, *Phänomenologie*, 582. Cf. Miller, 485/§ 797.

31. Hegel, *Vorlesung Über die Ästhetik* I, *Werke*, Band 13, 142.

32. Hegel, ibid., 25.

33. Günter Figal, *Sinn des Verstehens, Beiträge zur Hermeneutik* (Stuttgart: Reclam, 1996), 48.

34. Heidegger addresses Hegel's claims about the pastness of art, for example, in his celebrated "Postscript" to *Ursprung des Kunstwerks*, in *Gesamtausgabe*, Band 5, *Holzwege* (Frankfurt am Main: Vittrio Klostermann, 2003), 68 ff. Gadamer takes up Hegel's claim in a number of writings; see, for example, "Ende der Kunst? Von Hegel's Lehre vom Vergangenheitscharacter der Kunst bis zur Anti-Kunst von Heute," in *Werke*, Volume 8. One of Derrida's interpretive engagements with Hegel's notion of art in general is found in "Parergon," in Jacques Derrida, *The Truth in Painting*, trans. Geoffrey Bennington and Ian McLeod (Chicago: University of Chicago Press, 1987), 19 ff. Giorgio Agamben's *The Man Without Content*, trans. Georgia Albert (Stanford: Stanford University Press, 1999) also serves in no small part to address Hegel's thesis on the pastness of art.

35. Gadamer develops these views in some of his later essays. He discusses historical consciousness, for example, in "Wort und Bild – »so wahr, so seined« " in *Gesammelte Werke*, Volume 8, 377. He considers the deterioration of traditional Christian and humanist cultural forms, for example, in Hans-Georg Gadamer, "Ende Der Kunst? Von Hegels Lehre vom Vergangenheitscharackter der Kunst bis zur Anti-Kunst von Heute," in *Werke*, Band 8, see especially pp. 207–11.

36. Gadamer, "Wort und Bild – »so wahr, so seined«," 377.

37. The Grünewald alterpiece is housed in the Musée d' Unterlinden, Colmar, France.

38. I have tried to choose an example that remains in the vicinity of Gadamer's concern about Hegel. Gadamer, in an allusion to Hegel's claim that we no longer bend our knee in the face of religious art, refers, for example, to "images of the crucified" and of the "Madonna." "Wort und Bild, »so wahr, so seind«," 378.

39. Andreas Grossmann, "Hegel, Heidegger, and the Question of Art Today," *Research in Phenomenology* 20 (1990): 199 ff.

40. Hegel, *Vorlesungen über die Ästhetik* I, in *Werke*, Volume 13, 16.

41. Robert Wicks writes, "When Hegel presented his lectures on aesthetics in the 1820s, he probably believed that his system of beauty and the fine arts was the most up-to-date and comprehensive of its time. And perhaps he was right." After all, Wicks reminds us, his aesthetic theory is "expressed in a decade of classroom lectures amounting to over 1000 pages." Robert Wicks, "Hegel's Aesthetics: An Overview," in *Cambridge Companion to Hegel*, 348–49, respectively.

42. One wonders if Hegel's brevity might have been at least in part due to the circumstances under which he wrote the final sections of the *Phenomenology*. As H. S. Harris points out, "We ought, I suppose, to be happy to have chapters VII and VIII in any shape at all," on account of the impending deadline for the manuscript's completion, as well as the looming battle of Jena. H. S. Harris, *Hegel's Ladder I*, 9.

43. Hegel asserts a critique of romanticism in general in the "Preface" to the *Phenomenology*. See Hegel, *Phänomenologie*, 15. Cf. Miller, 4/§ 6. Some of Hegel's reservations about romantic approaches to art come out, for example, in comments made about the Schlegels (thought also Solger and Tieck) in the *Lectures on Aesthetics*. See Hegel, *Vorlesungen über die Ästhetik* I, 92, 96 ff.

44. Hegel, *Vorlesungen Über die Ästhetik* I, 366. To capture the sense of Hegel's statement I have decided in my translation of this passage to diverge slightly from the letter of the German, which reads, "Das Genie ist die *allgemeine* Fähigkeit zur wahren Produktion des Kustwerks sowie die Energie der Ausbildung und Betätigung derselben."

45. Ibid., 369.

46. Kant, *Kritik der Urteilskraft*, in *Werke*, Volume 10 (Frankfurt am Main: Suhrkamp, third edition 1997), 255, 241–42, respectively (AKA A 199/B 200, A 179/B 181, respectively).

47. Hegel, *Phänomenologie*, 515. Cf. Miller, 426/§ 703.

48. Hegel, *Phänomenologie*, 512 ff. Cf. Miller, 424/§ 699 ff.

49. Robert Wicks, "Hegel's Aesthetics: An Overview," 353.

50. Hegel discusses the statue at *Phänomenologie*, 514. Cf. Miller, 426/§ 703. Cf. Wicks, "Hegel's Aesthetics: An Overview," 356. As Wicks points out, Hegel holds that architecture, though a more nascent form of art than sculpture, continues only to indicate, and not embody, the image of spirit. Ibid.

51. Hegel, *Phänomenologie*, 528. Cf. Miller, 438/§ 725.

52. Hegel, *Phänomenologie*, 526, 528. Cf. Miller, 437, 438, respectively/§ 722, § 725, respectively. Miller mentions the celebration of the mysteries and the Olympic games directly in his "Analysis of the Text," 582.

53. Hegel, *Phänomenologie*, 528. Cf. Miller 438/§ 725. Harris notes in regard Hegel's discussion of the festival, that the processions of "the drama festivals were especially important. So the Art–Religion unfolds as an unbroken continuum." H. S. Harris, *Hegel's Ladder II: the Odyssey of Spirit*, 603.

54. H. S. Harris, *Hegel's Ladder II: the Odyssey of Spirit*, 603.

55. Although the overall concerns that guide his study are quite different from mine, Mark William Roche provides an illuminating discussion of some relations and tensions

between these two issues in current and Hegelian aesthetics. See Mark William Roche, "Introduction," in *Tragedy and Comedy, A Systematic Study and Critique of Hegel* (Albany: State University of New York Press, 1998).

56. Aristotle, *Poetics*, trans. I. Bywater, *Complete Works of Aristotle*, ed. Jonathan Barnes, Volume 2, 2317/1448a20.

57. Hegel associates tragedy with a higher language at *Phänomenologie*, 534. Cf. Miller, 443/§ 733.

58. Wicks, "Hegel's Aesthetics: An Overview," 351–52.

59. Hegel raises the issue of the mask in his discussion of tragic art at *Phänomenologie*, 535. Cf. Miller, 444/§ 733. See also Hegel's discussion of the mask at *Phänomenologie*, 541. Cf. Miller, 450/§ 742. For an excellent discussion of the significance of the mask in ancient Greek tragedy, see J. P. Vernant and P. Vidal-Naquet, *Myth and Tragedy in Ancient Greece*, trans. Jean Lloyd (New York: Zone Books, 1989), 189.

60. In a different, but related context, I have considered Hegel on issues of the impression created by dramatic art, the mask, and the relation of tragedy and comedy in, "Specifications: Hegel, Heidegger, and the Comedy of the End of Art," *Epoché* 8, no. 1 (Fall 2003): 107–21.

61. Taminiaux, "Poetics, Speculation, and Judgment," in *Poetics, Speculation, and Judgment*, 4.

62. A. C. Bradley, "Hegel's Theory of Tragedy," in *Oxford Lectures on Poetry* (New York: St. Martin's Press, first edition 1909, second edition 1909, fifteenth reprinting 1965), 70.

63. Hegel, *Phänomenologie*, 536. Cf. Miller, 445/§ 735. I use Miller's translation here.

64. Hegel, *Phänomenologie*, 535. Cf. Miller, 444/§ 734.

65. Schmidt, *Germans and Other Greeks*, 108.

66. Heidegger, *Ursprung des Kunstwerks*, 25 ff.

67. Garland, *The Oxford Companion to German Literature*, 909.

68. H. S. Harris, at least, has "no doubt" that Hegel read portions of Lessing's *Hamburger Dramaturgie*. H. S. Harris, *Hegel's Ladder II*, 646.

69. Hegel, *Phänomenologie*, 536. Cf. Miller, 445/§ 736.

70. Hegel's discussion centers on Attic tragedy in general, and the *Antigone* in particular. Yet, in his treatment of the interplay of knowledge and ignorance in the tragic hero, he expands his purview to consider other tragedies, and tragedies from the modern period, as well.

71. Hegel, *Phänomenologie*, 537. Cf. Miller, 446/§ 737.

72. Ibid.

73. Ibid., 537–38. Cf. Miller, 446–47/§ 737. Hegel's allusion to the Orestes story, which is perhaps less obvious than the others, is considered, if from a very different perspective than the one I take here, by H. S. Harris in *Hegel's Ladder II*, 626–27.

74. The scope and depth of Schmidt's interpretation of Aristotle's *Poetics*, and of its place in a broader lineage of German and Greek thought on tragedy, has significantly influenced my overall approach here, though it ranges well beyond the confines of my research here to treat his work in detail. See Schmidt, *Germans and Other Greeks*, 46–72.

75. At one point, Aristotle appears to rank it, for example, as only "fourth" among the elements in importance. See Aristotle, ibid., 2321/50b12.

76. Ibid., 2334/1459a4–5. Dennis Schmidt cites this passage in his discussion of Aristotle at *Germans and Other Greeks*, 63.

77. I believe this implication is seen in some of Aristotle's claims about the element of plot, and his suggestion that those plots are best that turn on heightened forms of strife, such as between family members and friends. See Aristotle, *Poetics*, 2326/1453b14 ff.

78. Ibid., 2333/1458a28.

79. See Schmidt, *Germans and Other Greeks*, 64–67.

80. J. P. Vernant and P. Vidal-Naquet, *Myth and Tragedy*, 113, cited in Schmidt, *Germans and Other Greeks*, 65.

81. Schmidt, *Germans and Other Greeks*, 66. Although my interpretation to the riddle Oedipus poses to himself diverges in some of the details from Schmidt's, my overall approach is in the main indebted to his. See Schmidt, *Germans and Other Greeks*, 66–67. I see much of the fruitfulness and originality of my approach, however, as being to develop these insights about the Oedipus story in regard to Hegel.

82. Hegel, "Entwürfe Über Liebe und Religion," in *Werke*, Band 2, 246.

83. Hegel, *Phänomenologie*, 535. Cf. Miller, 445/§ 734. Miller offers the adjectival form 'fearful' for the German substantive 'Furcht,' and 'compassion' for 'Mitleid.' In light of the sense of its Latin origin, 'compassion' might in some regards be closer to 'Mitleid' than 'pity.' However, Hegel's italicization of the words evidences that he wishes to reference Aristotle, and so I have stuck with English words that pick up the allusion while remaining true to the German. Scholars such as Gadamer have pointed out that the standard German equivalents *Furcht* and *Mitleid* are in adequate to the original Greek φόβος and 'έλεος. See Hans-Georg Gadamer, *Wahrheit und Methode*, in *Gesammelte Werke*, Volume 1, 135.

84. H. S. Harris, *Hegel's Ladder II*, 623.

85. Hegel, *Phänomenologie*, 535. Cf. Miller, 444/§ 734.

86. Ibid. In regard to the chorus of Sophocles' *Oedipus Tyrannus* and *Antigone*, H. S. Harris notes that Hegel's claim is "somewhat unjust." H. S. Harris, *Hegel's Ladder II*, 623.

87. Hegel, *Phänomenologie*, 535. Cf. Miller, 445/§ 735.

88. Ibid.. Cf. H. S. Harris, *Hegel's Ladder II*, 623.

89. Ibid.

90. Pity, for Creon? Certainly, many interpretations of Sophocles' *Antigone* would indicate that our sympathies might lie only with Antigone, and not with Creon. But Hegel's overall approach, which sees the two figures as legitimate ethical powers, suggests that spectators might feel pity for both.

91. Hegel writes that the audience feels "pity for these [living beings, principally, Antigone and Creon], which it also knows to be the same as itself." Hegel, *Phänomenologie* 535–36. Cf. Miller 445/§ 734. In this footnote, I borrow from Miller's translation.

92. Richard Jenko, "Introduction," in Aristotle, *Poetics*, trans. Richard Jenko (Indianapolis: Hackett Publishing Co., 1987), xvi. The prevalence of scholarly interest in the

psychological dimensions of catharsis swelled greatly after Jocob Bernays 1857 essay on the subject. But the heritage of the more medical approach to catharsis may be seen as much older than this. See ibid.

93. Hegel, *Phänomenologie*, 536. Cf. Miller, 445/§ 734. I use Miller's translation of 'Ruhe' as 'repose' here.

94. Ibid.

95. Ibid.

96. Ibid.

97. Hegel introduces the metaphoric of homeland, home, and indigenousness in his discussion of self-consciousness. See Hegel, *Phänomenologie*, 138. Cf. Miller, 104/§ 167.

Postscript

1. This may be especially so of analytic approaches in epistemology.

2. See Stuart Barnett's discussion of the difference between the general reception of Hegel in the postmodern era and Derrida's. Stuart Barnett, "Introduction," in *Hegel after Derrida*, ed. Stuart Barnett (New York: Routledge, 1998), 1–2.

3. Michael G. Vater, "Introduction," in *Hegel's* Phenomenology, *New Critical Essays*, eds. Alfred Denker and Michael Vater, (Amherst: Humanities Book, 2003) 8.

4. Bernard Knox, "Introduction," in Sophocles, *Three Theban Plays*, trans. Robert Fagles (New York: Penguin Classics, 1984), 257 ff.

5. Sophocles, *Oedipus at Colonus*, ln. 1705.

6. Wicks notes that Hegel's focus on only five forms (architecture, sculpture, painting, music, and poetry) now appears to be reductive. See Wicks, "Hegel's Aesthetics: An Overview," 374, fn. 5.

7. Hegel, *Vorlesungen über die Ästhetik I*, in *Werke*, Volume 13, 390 ff.

8. Wicks, "Hegel's Aesthetics, An Overview," 353–54.

9. Hegel, *Vorlesungen über die Ästhetik III*, in *Werke*, Volume 15, 551.

10. Ibid.

11. Ibid.

12. Ibid.

13. Ibid.

14. Hegel, *Vorlesungen über die Philosophie der Geschichte*, in *Werke*, Volume 16.

15. Hegel characterizes the collapse of the Greek ethical world as its *Untergang*, which Miller translates as "ruin." Hegel, *Phänomenologie*, 354. Cf. Miller, 289/§ 476.

16. John McDermott, especially his work on John Dewey, has introduced me to the notion of the precarious. Of course, although the meaning of the term applied to Hegel's interest in tragedy resonates with the sense it gains in the American context, differences abound.

17. Jacques Taminiaux, "Speculation and Difference," in *Poetics, Speculation, and Judgment*, 45.

18. See "Anmerkungen der Redaktion zu Band 1," in Hegel, *Werke* 1, 621 ff.

19. Hegel, *Über die wissenschaftlichen Behandlungsarten des Naturrechts, seine Stelle in der praktischen Philosophie und sein Verhältnis zu den positiven Rechtswissenschaften, Werke*, Volume 2, 434 ff.

20. Ibid., 480 ff.

21. Ibid., 489 ff.

22. Ibid., 495.

23. Ibid.

24. See my "A Monstrous Absolute: Schelling, Kant, and the Poetic Turn in Philosophy," in *Schelling Now* ed. Jason Wirth (Bloomington: Indiana University Press, 2004), 136–39.

25. F. J. W. Schelling, *Philosophische Briefe Über Dogmatismus und Kriticismus*, in F. W. J. Schelling, *Werke*, Volume 3, eds. Harmut Buchner, Wilhelm L. Jacobs, and Annemarie Pieper (Stuttgart: Frommann-Holzboog, 1992), 106.

26. Ibid., 107.

27. Philippe Lacoue-Labarthe and Jean-Luc Nancy, *The Literary Absolute, The Theory of Literature in German Romanticism*, trans. Philip Barnard and Cheryl Lester (Albany: State University of New York Press, 1988), 8.

28. Ibid., 40.

29. Ibid.

30. Ibid., 42.

31. Lacoue-Labarthe and Nancy provide a helpful topical index of the fragments at *The Literary Absolute*, 155–64.

32. The extent to which F. Schlegel subscribes to a genuinely fragmentary view of the fragment may be questioned. In their introduction to *Walter Benjamin and Romanticism*, for example, Beatrice Hanssen and Andrew Benjamin note that in the *Trauerspiel* text, Benjamin became disenchanted with Schlegel's notion of the fragment because it "still functioned in an idealistic framework of organic totality," citing *Athenaeum* fragment 206, "A fragment, like a miniature work of art, has to be entirely isolated from the surrounding world and be complete in itself like a porcupine." Beatrice Hanssen and Andrew Benjamin, "Introduction," in *Walter Benjamin and Romanticism* (New York: Continuum, 2002), 5.

33. See, for example, Friedrich Hölderlin, Letter "An Bohlendorf, Nürtingen, 4. Dezember," *Sämtliche Werke und Briefe*, Volume 2 (Darmstadt: Wissenschaftliche Buchgesellschaft, 1998), 912.

34. Schmidt, *Germans and Other Greeks*, 122–23.

35. Pinkard, *Hegel, The Sociality of Reason*, 137–38.

36. Hölderlin, "Sophocles," *Sämtliche Werke und Briefe*, Volume 1, 271.

Bibliography

Agamben, Giorgio. *The Man Without Content*, trans. Georgia Albert. Stanford: Stanford University Press, 1999.

Allison, Henry. *Kant's Transcendental Idealism, an Interpretation and Defense*. New Haven: Yale University Press, 1983.

Aristotle. *Poetics*, trans. I. Bywater. In *Complete Works of Aristotle*, Volume 2, ed. Jonathan Barnes. Princeton: Princeton University Press, 1984. Fourth printing 1991.

Augustine. *On the Free Choice of the Will*, trans. Thomas Williams. Indianapolis: Hackett Publishing Co., 1993.

Barnard, Philip and Cheryl Lester. "Translator's Introduction: The Presentation of Romantic Literature." Philippe Lacoue-Labarthe and Jean-Luc Nancy. *The Literary Absolute*, trans. Philip Barnard and Cheryl Lester. Albany: State University of New York Press, 1988.

Barnett, Stuart. "Introduction." In *Hegel after Derrida*, ed. Stuart Barnett. New York: Routledge, 1998.

Bataille, Georges. *L'experience intérieure*. Paris: Gallimard, 1954.

Benhabib, Seyla. "On Hegel, Woman, and Irony." In *Feminist Interpretations of G. W. F. Hegel*, ed. Patricia J. Mills. University Park: The Pennsylvania State University Press, 1996.

Bernasconi, Robert. "We Philosophers, *Barbaros mēdeis eisitō*." In *Endings, Questions of Memory in Hegel and Heidegger*, eds. Rebecca Comay and John McCumber. Evanston: Northwestern University Press, 1999.

Bradley, A. C. "Hegel's Theory of Tragedy." In *Oxford Lectures on Poetry*. New York: St. Martin's Press, 1909. Second edition 1909. Fifteenth reprinting 1965.

Burbridge, John. "Hegel's Absolutes." *Owl of Minerva* 29, no. 1 (1997).

Butler, Judith. *Subjects of Desire Hegelian Reflections in Twentieth-Century France*. New York: Columbia University Press, 1987.

———. *Antigone's Claim, Kinship Between Life and Death*. New York: Columbia University Press, 2000.

Caputo, John D. "On Not Circumventing the Quasi-Transcendental: The Case of Rorty and Derrida." In *Working Through Derrida*, ed. Gary Madison. Evanston: Northwestern University Press, 1993.

———. *Radical Hermeneutics, Repetition, Deconstruction, and the Hermeneutic Project.* Bloomington: Indiana University Press, 1987.

Carmen, Taylor. *Heidegger's Analytic, Interpretation, Discourse, and Authenticity in* Being and Time. New York: Cambridge University Press, 2003.

Dawe, R. D., ed. *Sophocles, The Classical Heritage.* New York: Garland Publishing Co., 1996.

de Boer, Karin. "Tragic Entanglements: Between Hegel and Derrida." *Bulletin of the Hegel Society of Great Britain* (2003): 47–48, 34–49.

Deleuze, Gilles. *Nietzsche and Philosophy*, trans. Hugh Tomlinson. New York: Columbia University Press, 1983.

Dennett, Daniel. *The Intentional Stance.* Cambridge: MIT Press, 1987.

Derrida, Jacques. "From Restricted to General Economy, a Hegelianism without Reserve." In *Writing and Difference*, trans. Alan Bass. Chicago: University of Chicago Press, 1978.

———. *Glas*, trans. John P. Leavey, Jr. Lincoln: University of Nebraska Press, 1986.

———. *The Truth in Painting*, trans. Geoffrey Bennington and Ian McLeod. Chicago: University of Chicago Press, 1987.

Dews, Peter. *Logics of Disintegration, Post-structuralist Thought and the Claims of Critical Theory.* New York: Verso Press, 1987.

Dostoevsky, Fyodor. *Notes from the Underground and the Grand Inquisitor*, trans. Ralph E. Matlaw. New York: Meridian Books, 1991.

Dove, K. R. Review of John McCumber, *The Company of Words*. *Journal of the History of Philosophy* 32, no. 4 (1994): 681–82.

Dudley, Will. "Freedom in and through Hegel's Philosophy." *Owl of Minerva* 39, no. 4 (Fall 2000): 683–703.

Figal, Günter. *Für eine Philosophie von Freiheit und Streit, Politik, Ästhetik, und Metaphysik.* Stuttgart: J. B. Metzler Verlag, 1994.

———. *Der Sinn des Verstehens, Beiträge zur hermeneutischen Philosophie.* Stuttgart: Reklam, 1996.

———. *For a Philosophy of Freedom and Strife*, trans. Wayne Klein. Albany: State University of New York Press, 1998.

Findler, Richard S. "Reconciliation versus Reversal: Hegel and Nietzsche on Overcoming Ontological Guilt." In *Hegel's* Phenomenology of Spirit, *New Critical Essays*, eds. Alfred, Denker and Michael, Vater. New York: Humanities Press, 2003.

Franchi, Stefano. "Telos and Terminus: Hegel and the End of Philosophy." *Idealistic Studies* 18 (1998): 35–46.

Frank, Manfred. *Philosophical Foundations of German Romanticism*, trans. Elizabeth Millán-Zaibert. Albany: State University of New York Press, 2004.

Gadamer, Hans-Georg. *Hegel's Dialectic, Five Hermeneutical Studies*, trans. Christopher P. Smith. New Haven: Yale University Press, 1976.

———. *Wahrheit und Methode.* In *Gesammelte Werke*, Volume 1. Tübingen: Mohr Siebeck, 1986.

———. "Universalität des hermeneutischen Problems." In *Gesammelte Werke*, Volume 2. Tübingen: Mohr Siebeck, 1986.

———. "Hegels Dialektik des Selbstbewusstseins." In *Gesammelte Werke*, Volume 3. Tübingen: Mohr Siebeck, 1987.

———. "Die Aktualität des Schönen, Kunst als Spiel, Symbol und Fest." In *Gesammelte Werke*, Volume 8. Tübingen: Mohr Siebeck, 1993.

———. "Wort und Bild, »so wahr, so seind«." In *Gesammelte Werke*, Volume 8. Tübingen: Mohr Siebeck, 1993.

———. "Ende Der Kunst? Von Hegels Lehre vom Vergangenheitscharakter der Kunst bis zur Anti-Kunst von heute." In *Gesammelte Werke*, Volume 8. Tübingen: Mohr Siebeck, 1993.

———. "Verstummen die Dichter?" In *Gesammelte Werke*, Volume 9. Tübingen: Mohr Siebeck, 1993.

———. "Die deutsche Philosophie zwischen den Weltkriegen." In *Gesammelte Werke*, Volume 10. Tübingen: Mohr Siebeck, 1995.

Garland, Herny and Mary, Garland eds. *The Oxford Companion to German Literature*, Second edition. New York: Oxford University Press, 1986.

George, Theodore D. "Specifications: Hegel, Heidegger, and the Comedy of the End of Art." *Epoché* 8, no. 1 (Fall 2003): 107–121.

———. "A Monstrous Absolute: Schelling, Kant, and the Poetic Turn in Philosophy." In *Schelling Now*, ed. Jason Wirth. Bloomington: Indiana University Press, 2004.

Grey, J. Glenn. *Hegel's Hellenic Ideal*. New York: King's Crown Press, 1941.

Grossmann, Andreas. "Hegel, Heidegger, and the Question of Art Today." *Research in Phenomenology* 20 (1990), 112–35.

Guignon, Charles and Derk Pereboom "Introduction." In *Existentialism, Basic Writings*. Indianapolis: Hackett Publishing Company, 1995.

Guyer, Paul. "Thought and Being: Hegel's Critique of Kant." In *Cambridge Companion to Hegel*, ed. Friedrick Beiser. New York: Cambridge University Press, 1993.

Hanssen, Beatrice and Andrew Benjamin. "Introduction." In *Walter Benjamin and Romanticism*. New York: Continuum, 2002.

Harris, Errol E. *The Spirit of Hegel*. Atlantic Highlands: Humanities Press, 1993.

Harris, H. S. *Hegel's Development: Towards the Sunlight, 1770–1801*. New York: Oxford University Press, 1972.

———. *Hegel's Ladder I: The Pilgrimage of Reason*. Indianapolis: Hackett Publishing Co., 1997.

———. *Hegel's Ladder II: The Odyssey of Spirit*. Indianapolis: Hackett Publishing Co., 1997.

———. "Hegel's Intellectual Development to 1807." In *Cambridge Companion to Hegel*. New York: Cambridge University Press, 1993.

Harvey, Paul, ed. *Oxford Guide to French Literature*. New York: Oxford University Press, 1959.

Hegel, G. W. F. *Phenomenology of Spirit*, trans. A. V. Miller. New York: Oxford University Press, 1977.

———. "Das älteste Systemprogramm des deutschen Idealismus." In *Hegel in 20 Bände*, Volume 1. Frankfurt am Main: Suhrkamp, 1986.

———. "Systemfragment." In *Hegel in 20 Bände*, Volume 1. Frankfurt am Main: Suhrkamp, 1986.

———. "Entwürfe Über Liebe und Religion." In *Hegel in 20 Bände*, Volume 2. Frankfurt am Main: Suhrkamp, 1986.

———. "Wer Denkt Abstrakt?" In *Werke in 20 Bände*, Volume 2. Frankfurt am Main: Suhrkamp, 1986.

———. *Differenz des Fichte'schen und Schelling'schen Systems der Philosophie*. In *Werke in 20 Bände*, Volume 2. Frankfurt am Main: Suhrkamp, 1986.

———. *Phänomenologie des Geistes*. In *Werke in 20 Bände*, Volume 3. Frankfurt am Main: Suhrkamp, 1986.

———. *Grundlinien der Philosophie des Rechts*. In *Werke in 20 Bände*, Volume 7. Frankfurt am Main: Suhrkamp, 1986.

———. *Enzyklopädie der philosophischen Wissenschaften I*. In *Werke in 20 Bände*, Volume 8. Frankfurt am Main: Suhrkamp, 1986.

———. *Vorlesungen über die Philosophie der Geschichte I*. In *Werke in 20 Bände*, Volume 12. Frankfurt am Main: Suhrkamp, 1986.

———. *Vorlesungen über die Ästhetik I*. In *Werke in 20 Bände*, Volume 13. Frankfurt am Main: Suhrkamp, 1986.

———. *Vorlesungen über die Ästhetik III*. In *Werke in 20 Bände*, Volume 15. Frankfurt am Main: Suhrkamp, 1986.

———. *Vorlesungen über die Philosophie der Religion I*. In *Werke in 20 Bände*, Volume 16. Frankfurt am Main: Suhrkamp, 1986.

———. *Vorlesungen über die Philosophie der Religion II*. In *Werke in 20 Bände*, Volume 17. Frankfurt am Main: Suhrkamp, 1986.

Heidegger, Martin. *Ursprung des Kunstwerks*. In *Gesamtausgabe*, Volume 5, *Holzwege*. Frankfurt am Main: Vittrio Klostermann, 2003.

Höffe, Otfried. *Immanuel Kant*, trans. Marchall Farrier. Albany: State University of New York Press, 1994.

Hoffheimer, Michael H. "Translating *Knechtschaft*." *Owl of Minerva* 32, no. 2(2001): 169–75.

Hölderlin, Friedrich. "Sophocles." In *Sämtliche Werke und Briefe*, Volume 1. Darmstadt: Wissenschaftliche Buchgesellschaft, 1998.

———. "Anmerkungen zu Ödipus." In *Sämtliche Werke und Briefe*, Volume 2. Darmstadt: Wissenschaftliche Buchgesellschaft, 1998.

———. "Sophocles." In *Sämtliche Werke und Briefe*, Volume 1. Darmstadt: Wissenschaftliche Buchgesellschaft, 1998.

———. "Uhrteil und Sein." *Sämtliche Werke*, Volume 4. Stuttgart: Friedrich Beiser, 1943–85.

Houlgate, Stephen. *Hegel, Nietzsche, and the Criticism of Metaphysics*. New York: Cambridge University Press, 1986.

Hühn, Lore. "Die Philosophie des Tragischen. Schellings, Philosophische Briefe über Dogmatismus und Kritizismus." In *Schellingiana*, Volume 10, *Die Realität des Wissens und das wirkliche Dasein, Erkenntnis Begründung und Philosophie beim frühen Schelling*, ed. Jörg Jantzen. Stuttgart-Bad Constatt: Frommann-Holzboog, 1998.

Husserl, Edmund. *Cartesian Meditations, an Introduction to Phenomenology*, trans. Dorion Cairns. Boston: Kluwer Academic Publishers. Eighth printing 1991.

Hyppolite, Jean. *Genesis and Structure of Hegel's* Phenomenology of Spirit, trans. Samuel Cherniak and John Heckman. Evanston: Northwestern University Press, 1974.

———. *Logic and Existence*, trans. Leonard Lawler. Albany: State University of New York Press, 1997.

Irigaray, Luce. "The Eternal Irony of the Community." In *Feminist Interpretations of G. W. F. Hegel*, ed. Patricia J. Mills. Campus Parkway: The Pennsylvania State University Press, 1996.

Jenko, Richard. "Introduction." In Aristotle, *Poetics*, trans. Richard Jenko. Indianapolis: Hackett Publishing Co., 1987.

Jones, John. *On Aristotle and Greek Tragedy*. Stanford: Stanford University Press, 1962.

Kant, Immanuel. *Kritik der reinen Vernunft*. In *Werkausgabe*, Volume 3. Frankfurt am Main: Suhrkamp, 1997.

———. *Kritik der Urteilskraft*. In *Werkausgabe*, Volume 10. Frankfurt am Main: Suhrkamp. Third edition 1997.

Kaufmann, Walter. *Hegel, Reinterpretation, Texts, and Commentary*. New York: Doubleday, 1965.

Kimmerle, Heinz. "On Derrida's Hegel Interpretation." In *Hegel after Derrida*, ed. Stuart Barnett. New York: Routledge Press, 1998.

Knox, Bernard. "Introduction." In Sophocles, *Three Theban Plays*, trans. Robert Fagles. New York: Penguin Classics, 1984.

Knox, T. M. "Prefatory Note." In *G. W. F. Hegel, Early Theological Writings*, trans. T. M. Knox. Philadelphia: University of Pennsylvania Press, 1971. Seventh paperback printing 1997.

Kojève, Alexandre. *Introduction to the Reading of Hegel*, ed. Allan Bloom and trans. James H. Nichols, Jr. Ithaca: Cornell University Press, 1980. Sixth printing 1996.

Kronder, Richard. "Introduction." In *G. W. F. Hegel, Early Theological Writings*, trans. T. M. Know. Philadelphia: University of Pennsylvania Press, 1971. Seventh paperback printing 1997.

Lacan, Jacques. "Antigone." In *The Ethics of Psychoanalysis*, trans. Dennis Porter. New York: W. W. Norton, 1992.

Lacoue-Labarthe, Philippe and Jean-Luc Nancy. *The Literary Absolute, the Theory of Literature in German Romanticism*, trans. Philip Barnard and Cheryl Lester. Albany: State University of New York Press, 1988.

Lacoue-Labarthe, Philippe. *Heidegger, Art, and Politics, The Fiction of the Political*, trans. Chris Turner. Cambridge: Basil Blackwell, 1990.

———. *Typography, Mimesis, Philosophy, Politics*, trans. Christopher Fynsk. Cambridge: Harvard University Press, 1989.

Lauer, Quentin, S. J. *A Reading of Hegel's* Phenomenology of Spirit. New York: Fordham University Press, 1982.

———. "H. S. Harris's *Hegel's Development: Toward the Sunlight, 1770–1801*." In *Essays in Hegelian Dialectic*. New York: Fordham University Press, 1977.

———. "Phenomenology: Hegel and Husserl." In *Essays in Hegelian Dialectic*. New York: Fordham University Press, 1977.

Lawler, Leonard. "Translator's Preface." In Jean Hyppolite, *Logic and Existence*, trans. Leonard Lawler. Albany: State University of New York Press, 1997.

Lessing, Gotthold Ephraim. *Laokoon*. In *Gesammelte Werke in Zehn Bänden*, Volume 5. Berlin: Aufbau Verlag, 1955.

Lyotard, Jean-François. *The Postmodern Condition: A Report on Knowledge*, trans. Geoff Bennington and Brian Massumi. Minneapolis: Minnesota University Press, 1979. Ninth printing 1993.

Madison, Gary. *The Hermeneutics of Postmodernity*. Bloomington: Indiana University Press, 1988.

Marx, Karl. *German Ideology*. In *Marx-Engels Reader*, ed. Robert Norton. New York: W. W. Norton, 1978.

McCumber, John. *The Company of Words, Hegel, Language, and Systematic Philosophy*. Evanston: Northwestern University Press, 1993.

Menke, Christoph. *Die Tragödie im Sittlichen, Gerechtigkeit und Freiheit nach Hegel*. Frankfurt am Main: Suhrkamp, 1996.

Nietzsche, Friedrich. *Geburt der Tragödie*. In *Kritische Studienausgabe*, Volume 1, eds. Giorgio Colli and Mazzino Montinari. Munich: Deutscher Taschenbuch Verlag; Berlin: Walter de Gruyter, 1988.

———. *Zur Genealogie der Moral*. In *Kritische Studienausgabe*, Volume 5, eds. Giorgio Colli and Mazzino Montinari. Munich: Deutscher Taschenbuch Verlag; Berlin: Walter de Gruyter, 1988.

———. *Der Fall Wagner*. In *Kritische Studienausgabe*, Volume 6, eds. Giorgio Colli and Mazzino Montinari. Munich: Deutscher Taschenbuch Verlag; Berlin: Walter de Gruyter, 1988.

———. *Birth of Tragedy*. In *Birth of Tragedy and The Case of Wagner*, trans. Walter Kaufmann. New York: Vintage Books, 1967.

Nussbaum, Martha. *Fragility of Goodness, Luck and Ethics in Greek Tragedy and Philosophy*. Cambridge: Cambridge University Press, 1986.

Papineau, David. "Science, Problems in the Philosophy Of." In *The Oxford Companion to Philosophy*. Ted Honderich. ed. New York: Oxford University Press, 1995.

Patri, Aimé. "Dialectique du Maître et de l'Esclave." *Le Contrat Social* 5, no. 4 (1961).

Pippen, Robert. *Hegel's Idealism, The Satisfactions of Self-consciousness*. Cambridge: Cambridge University Press, 1989.

Pinkard, Terry. *Hegel's* Phenomenology: *The Sociality of Reason*. Cambridge: Cambridge University Press, 1996.

Plato. *Republic,* trans. Allen Bloom. New York: Basic Books, 1991.

Roche, Mark William. *Tragedy and Comedy, A Systematic Study and Critique of Hegel*. Albany: State University of New York Press, 1998.

Russon, John. *Reading Hegel's* Phenomenology. Indianapolis: Indiana University Press, 2004.

Sartre, Jean Paul. "Existentialism is a Humanism." In *Existentialism from Dostoyevsky to Sartre*, ed. Walter Kaufmann. Revised and Expanded Version. New York: Meridian Publishing Company, 1989.

Schelling, F. W. J. "Immanuel Kant." In *Ausgewählte Schriften*, Volume 3. Frankfurt am Main: Suhrkamp, 1985. Reprinted from *Fränkischen Staats- und Gelehrten-Zeitung*, March 1804, No. 49, 50.

———. *Philosophische Briefe Über Dogmatismus und Kriticismus*. In *Werke*, Volume 3. Stuttgart: Frommann-Holzboog, 1992.

———. *System der transendentalen Idealismus*. In *Ausgewählte Schriften*, Volume 1. Frankfurt am Main: Suhrkamp, 1985. Stuttgart: Frommann-Holzboog, 1992.

Schlegel, Freidrich. *Gespräch über die Poesie*. In *Krtische Friedrich-Schlegel-Ausgabe*, Volume 2. Munich: Hans Eichner, 1967.

———. *Atheneaum Fragmente*. In *Kritische Friedrich-Schlegel-Ausgabe*, Volume 2. Munich: Hans Eichner, 1967.

Schmidt, Dennis. *Germans and Other Greeks, Tragedy and Ethical Life*. Bloomington: Indiana University Press, 2001.

Sophocles. *Antigone. Three Theban Plays*, trans. Robert Fagles. New York: Penguin Books, 1984.

———. *Antigone*, In *Antigone, The Women of Tracis, Philoctetes, Oedipus at Colonus*, trans. Hugh Lloyd Jones. Loeb Classical Library. Cambridge: Harvard University Press, 1994.

———. *Oedipus at Colonus*. In *Antigone, The Women of Tracis, Philoctetus, Oedipus at Colonus*. Trans. Hugh Lloyd Jones. Loeb Classical Library. Cambridge: Harvard University Press, 1994.

Speight, Allen. *Hegel, Literature, and the Problem of Agency*. Cambridge: Cambridge University Press, 2001.

Steinbock, Anthony. "Spirit and Generativity: The Role and Contribution of the Phenomenologist in Hegel and Husserl." In *Alterity and Facticity, New Perspectives on Husserl*, eds. Natalie Depraz and Dan Zahavi. Boston: Kluwer Academic Publishers, 1998.

Steiner, George. *Antigones*. New York: Oxford University Press, 1984.

Szondi, Peter. *Versuch Über das Tragische*. In *Schriften*, Volume 1. Frankfurt am Main: Suhrkamp. Third edition 1991.

Taminiaux, Jacques. "Poetics, Speculation, and Judgment." In *Poetics, Speculation, and Judgment, the Shadow of the Work of Art from Kant to Phenomenology*, trans. Michael Gendre. Albany: State University of New York Press, 1993.

———. "Speculation and Difference." In *Poetics, Speculation, and Judgment, the Shadow of the Work of Art from Kant to Phenomenology*, trans. Michael Gendre. Albany: State University of New York Press, 1993.

———. "Nostalgia for Greece at the Dawn of Classical Germany." In *Poetics, Speculation, and Judgment, the Shadow of the Work of Art from Kant to Phenomenology*, trans. Michael Gendre. Albany: State University of New York Press, 1993.

———. "Hegel and Hobbes." In *Dialectic and Difference, Finitude in Modern Thought*, trans. Robert Crease. Atlantic Highlands: Humanities Press, 1984.

Taylor, Charles. *Hegel*. Cambridge: Cambridge University Press, 1975.

Toews, John. "Transformations in Hegelianism, 1805–1846." In *Cambridge Companion to Hegel*, ed. Friedrick Beiser. New York: Cambridge University Press, 1993.

Taylor, Charles. "Hegel's Philosophy of Action." In *Hegel and the Philosophy of Action*, eds. Lawrence S. Stepelevich and David Lamb. Atlantic Highlands: Humanities Press, 1983.

Vater, Michael G. "Introduction" In *Hegel's* Phenomenology, *New Critical Essays*, eds. Alfred Denker and Michael Vater. Amherst: Humanities Books, 2003.

Vernant, J. P. and P. Vidal-Naquet. *Myth and Tragedy in Ancient Greece*. Cambridge: Zone Books, 1988.

Verstraeten, Pierre. "Hegel and Sartre." In *Cambridge Companion to Sartre*, ed. Christiana Howells. Cambridge: Cambridge University Press, 1992.

Welton, Donn. *The Other Husserl, the Horizons of Transcendental Phenomenology*. Bloomington: Indiana University Press, 2000.

Westphal, Kenneth. "The Basic Context and Structure of Hegel's *Philosophy of Right*." In *Cambridge Companion to Hegel*, ed. Friedrick Beiser. New York: Cambridge University Press, 1993.

Westphal, Merold. "Hegel and Gadamer." In *Hermeneutics and Modern Philosophy*, ed. Brice R. Wachterhauser. Albany: State University of New York Press, 1986.

———. *History and Truth in Hegel's* Phenomenology. New Jersey: Humanities Press International, 1990.

Wicks, Robert. "Hegel's Aesthetics: An Overview." In *Cambridge Companion to Hegel*, ed. Friedrick Beiser. New York: Cambridge University Press, 1993.

Wildt, Andreas. *Autonomie und Anerkennung, Hegels Moralitätskritik im Lichte seiner Fichte-Rezeption*. Stuttgart: Klett-Cotta, 1982.

Wirth, Jason. *The Conspiracy of Life, Meditations on Schelling and His Time*. Albany: State University of New York Press, 2003.

Wood, Allen W. *Hegel's Ethical Thought*. Cambridge: Cambridge University Press, 1990.

Zahavi, Dan. *Husserl's Phenomenology*. Stanford: Stanford University Press, 2003.

———. "Husserl's Noema and the Internalism–Externalism Debate." *Inquiry* 47 (2004): 42–66.

Index

ability (*Können*): 71
    freedom of, 52, 84
    finite, 68
absolute, the: 33, 125
    end of encounters with the tragic, 48
    demonstration of, 1
    Hegel's commitment to, 2, 3, 137n3, 133
absolute knowledge: 1, 3, 17, 21–22, 27, 30, 34, 41, 98
    attained through experience, 39, 41–42, 46
    awareness of unity of subject and world, 42, 43
    highest form of consciousness, 37, 43
    last stage in development of spirit, 101
    life of spirit and, 28, 38
    perfected through engagement with history, 103
    self-knowledge: 37, 49
absolute spirit: 98–99, 100
    interpretive subject and interpretive object, 101
    religion, art, philosophy as forms of, 101
        consciousness and, 101
        mythopoetic function in community, 101
        philosophy,
            culminates in *Wissenschaft*, 102
            supercedes religion, art, 103
        religion, art,
            reduced to secondary status, 103
            result in incomplete forms of depiction, 102
            representation (*Vorstellung*), 102
    speculation and, 101
    theoria (θεωρία) in, 110
action, rational: (*see also* agent)
    constituted by purpose, 78–79
    cultural heritage and, 79
    expression of intention, 79
    bound up with guilt, 88
    subject to finitude, 91
activity (*Tun*): 78
Aeschylus, *Orestia*: 129
    Orestes and Oracle at Delphi, 112
aesthesis: 37
aesthetic, the:
    power of, 13
    theories of, vii
aesthetic act:
    highest act of reason, 11
aesthetics: vii, 8, 11, 45, 111
agent (*das Handelnde*), rational:
    action reveals purpose, 80
    guilt and innocence, 90
    self-legislating, 76–77, 82–83, 84, 88
Agamben, Giorgio: 103
Allison, Henry: 36
ananke/ἀνάγκη (necessity): 119
Anerkennung (recognition). *See* mutual recognition.

Antigone: 19, 23, 74, 75, 83, 85, 87, 88, 91–92, 95–96, 112, 117, 122, 126, 129, 132
Aristotle: 22. *See also Poetics.*
art: 12–14, 75, 96 (*see also under* Tragic; *under* Tragic Drama)
    form of reflective life, 100
    Greek statue, 107–108
    knowledge and, 14
    spiritual art, 107
        absolute art, 107
        abstract work of art, 107
        culmination of, 109
            acquiescence to finitude, 119
            knowledge in immediate intuition, 109
        genres of, 109
            dramatic poetry, 109
                higher language, 109
                immediacy of image, 109–110
                as performance, 109
            epic poetry, 109
                divides narration and events it retells, 109
                as narration, 109
        inferior to philosophy, 109
        living work of art, 107–108
            religious and civic festivals, 107–108
artistic expression: 12
Aufhebung. *See* supercession.

Barnett, Stuart: 2
Bataille, Georges: 65–66, 68
Begriff. *See* concept.
Bildung. *See* education.
Bradley, A.C.: "Hegel's Theory of Tragedy," 110
burial. *See under* law of singularity and law of universality.
Burbridge, John: 30, 103
Butler, Judith: 6, 55

Camus, Albert: 6
Caputo, John: 40, 148–49n44
catharsis: 46, 118 (*see also under* tragic drama)
Christianity: 10, 90, 91, 95, 98, 99, 102–103, 104, 132
    Oedipus and, 124–125
    people's religion, 9–10
classicism, French: 7
concept, the (*Begriff*):
    expression of knowledge, 7, 12–15, 16
    logic of, 20
    power of, 16
    speculative unity of, 19–20, 27
consciousness:
    conception of, 39–40
        unity of subject and world in, 39, 41, 84
    conflicted commitments to universal and singular and, 87, 92
    constituent operation in self-consciousness, 54
    constitution of the world and, 41, 43, 54
    dialectical struggle, 31, 41
    ethical life and, 76–77
    experiences of, 41, 119
    for-itself and in-itself in, 40
    forms (*Gestalten*), 42
    human and divine law and, 82–84
    intentional activity in, 39–40, 42, 54
    intentional structures, 42–44
        limitations to consciousness, 43
    master, 62
    rational agent, 84
    servile, 62
    tragic reversal and, 45
    transformed by experience, 42
    ultimate condition of knowledge, 44
consumption:
    independence of object and, 56
    life of, 55–56
continental philosophy: vii, viii, ix, 2, 4, 9, 11, 14, 121
    contemporary, vii, ix, 3, 5

continental thought: vii, viii, 4
    regarding Hegel, 50, 52, 72, 136n2

Dastur, François: 6
Davidson, Donald: 136n2
de Beauvoir, Simone: 6
death: 57, 64, 122, 124
    absolute master, 23, 61, 70–71
    integral part of life, 125, 126
    kinship of freedom and, 70, 71, 72
    origin of relations between self-conscious beings, 58
deconstruction: viii, 65, 66, 72, 144n40
Deleuze, Gilles: 98
Dennett, Daniel: 39
Derrida, Jacques: viii, 23, 40, 136n2, 144n40, 51, 64, 68, 70, 103
    "From Restricted to General Economy: Toward a Hegelianism without Reserve," 51, 65–68, 72
        recognition and signification, 65–66
        sovereignty:
            and mastery, 66–72
                repressed origin of, 67
                reversal both more and less than tragic, 67
                willingly risks absolute loss, 70
Descartes, René: 16, 40
desire. *See under* self-consciousness.
despair: 30, 38, 43, 44
Dews, Peter: 54
dialectic, 98
    development of consciousness, 31
Dilthey, Wilhelm:
    Jugendgeschichte Hegels, 9
divine law. *See under* law of universality and law of singularity.
drama:
    influence on philosophy, 74
doubt: 30, 38, 43
    and despair, 30, 43
    in independent being of reality, 43–44

education (*Bildung*): 31
empiricism: 17, 22, 78–79
epistemology: 2, 30, 36, 97, 121, 135n2
erkennen. See know.
errancy (*hamartia*),
    tragic, 91–92
erred (*hamartanousi*): 91
ethical laws (*Sitten*): 77
ethical life (*Sittlichkeit*): viii, 3, 7, 19, 21, 23, 31, 73, 74, 81, 129
    consciousness' experience of, 75, 76–77
        shifts to Greek ethical world, 81
    consciousness committed to self and society, 76–77, 129
    cultural heritage, 77
    ethical substance, 77, 87, 118
    of a people, defined, 78
    stage of spiritual development, 76
existentialism: 6, 23, 29, 51, 92–96
    and rational agency, 93
experience: 21, 22, 24, 122, 125
    conception of, 29–30, 38
    education through, 30
    higher forms of, 45
    investigation, test, 43
    limit on knowledge, 37
    negative aspects of, 28–29
    path of, 38, 42, 44, 46
    phenomenon of, 28
    reason and, 22
    science of, 18
    tragedy and, 28, 29, 47, 49
    tragic dynamics of, 48, 51
    unification of, 2, 4, 15
    variety of, 15

family: 81
feminism: 6, 74
Fest, das. See festival.
festival (*das Fest*): 108
Fichte, Johann Gottlieb: 32, 34
Figal, Günter: 150n63, 157n33

finitude:
   confrontations/encounters with, 2, 15–17, 19, 20, 25, 74, 105, 115, 131
      through experience, 30, 47, 128
   guises of, 2–3, 12, 20–21, 27, 47, 121, 125, 127, 128
      understood as rhetorical flourishes, 29
   human, viii, 3, 21, 64, 70, 88, 90, 95–96, 128
   in artistic production, 107
   of knowledge, 44
   of vulnerability, 92
   riddle as token of, in tragic drama, 114
   tragic character of, 3, 68, 70, 115
for-itself, the: 40
forgiveness: 75, 98
formalism: 22
Foti, Veronique: 6
Foucault, Michel: 136n2
fragment: 131–132
freedom: 3, 7, 21, 49, 50
   attained through education, 52
   chosen above life, 57
   finitude and, 23, 51, 52
   from dependence on nature, 62
   mastery and, 51
   of ability, 52
   presence of death as condition of, 70
   tragic aspects of, 22
   universal, 13, 49
French classicism: 7
French Revolution: 9, 10, 13

Gadamer, Hans-Georg: vii, viii–ix, 31, 68, 99, 103, 104, 111
   and Hegel's dialectic of self-consciousness, 51–52, 57
Galileo: 16
gefehlt. *See* erred.
German idealism. *See* idealism, German.
German nation-state. *See* modern nation-state.
German philosophy: vii, 6, 8, 13, 32, 94
German romanticism. *See* romanticism, German.
Goethe, J. W.: 6, 7
Greek ethical world (*die sittliche Welt*): 80
   collapses from collision of human and divine law, 88
   and *Antigone*, 81, 126
   stage in development of consciousness, 86–87
Greek tragedy. *See* tragic drama, Greek.
Grossman, Andreas: 104
guilt (*Schuld*): 23, 76, 88 (*see also* hamartia)
   and rational agent's actions, 75, 91–92
   result of incompatibility of human and divine law, 89
   results from structure of action, 90
      inevitable and unavoidable, 90
Guyer, Paul: 36

Hamann, J. G.: 31
hamartia / ἁμαρτία (waywardness, errancy): 23, 75, 91–92
hamartanousi / ἁμαρτάνουσί (erred): 91
Handelnde, das. *See* agent.
Harris, H. S.:
   Hegel's Development, 9
   Hegel's Ladder II: the Odyssey of Spirit, 108, 116
Haym, Rudolph:
   Hegel and his Time, 9
Hegel, G. W. F.:
   aesthetic philosophy, 11
   commentators on, 2, 136n2, 8–9, 19–20, 29
   final philosopher,
      definition of, 47–48
      versus tragic hero, 47
   works,
      Differenzschrift, ix
      Lectures on Aesthetics, 8, 14, 45, 105, 106, 111, 122, 123–125

Lectures on the History of Philosophy, 141n51
Natural Law Essay, 8
"Oldest System-Programme of German Idealism," 11
On the Scientific Treatment of Natural Law, Its Place in Practical Philosophy, and its Relation to the Sciences of Positive Law, 128
Philosophy of Right, 129
Vorlesungen über die Geschichte der Philosophie, 135n2
hegemonic:
    presuppositions in philosophical inquiry, 4–5, 6, 12
    text interpretation, ix
Heidegger, Martin:
    vii, 136n2, 11, 12, 14, 15, 40, 94, 103, 111, 127
    Being and Time, 93
    Dasein, 71, 93
    Introduction to Metaphysics, 6
Hellenic ideal: 10–11, 76. See also under speculative philosophy.
hermeneutical view of art: 99
hermeneutics:
    philosophical, viii, ix, 51
Herr. See master.
historical experience: 21, 27, 50, 105
historical spirit: 3
history: 7, 19, 27, 38
    philosophical inquiry and, 6, 15–19, 27, 31, 103
    of philosophy, ix, 98
Hobbes, Thomas: 16, 58–59
Hölderlin, Friedrich: vii, 4, 6, 9, 11, 25, 32, 34, 128, 132
    The Death of Empedocles, 132
    "Sophocles," 133
Hühn, Lore: 88–89
human law. See under law of universality and law of singularity.
Husserl, Edmund:
    epoché,
        conception of, 40

        criticisms of, 40–41
    phenomenology, 22, 39–40
        as foundational science, 39
        study of consciousness, 39, 41
Hyppolite, Jean: 19, 29
    Genesis and Structure of Hegel's Phenomenology of Spirit, 57, 142n5
    Logic and Existence, 142n5

idealism:
    German, viii, 11, 13, 14, 32, 33, 34, 35, 102, 103–104
    transcendental, 36, 37
identity: 2, 78
    abstract, 2
    infinite, 96
in-itself, the: 40
independence (*Selbstständigkeit*): 49, 126
    defined, 54
    mutual recognition as condition of, 53
    originates in servitude, 50–51, 58, 126
    potential for, 51
innocence:
    nonaction, 88
intellect (*Verstand*): 32
intuition: 37
Irigaray, Luce: 6

Jena, University of: 6, 8, 11, 12, 128

Kant, Immanuel: vii, 6, 32–38
    Critique of Judgment, 106, 116, 128
    Critique of Pure Reason, 32–38, 78
    deduction of the unity of apperception, 32, 50, 60
    Hegel's response to, 136n2, 9–10, 22
    absolute knowledge, 29–30, 32
    reason, 35–36, 128
    reason,
        basis of critique, 36
        dialectic in, 35, 130
        highest cognitive faculty, 33
        ideal of pure, 35

Kant, Immanuel: (*contd*)
    limitations of, 34–35, 37, 129
    purpose of, 33–34
    practical, 9
    theoretical, 9
    transcendental illusion and, 6, 32–33
    unity of subject and world, 34–36, 129
    regulative nature of, 35
Knecht. *See* servant.
know (*erkennen*): 37
knowledge: 2, 27, 37
    representational theories of, 17
Knox, T.M.: 9
Kojève, Alexandre: 55, 146n8, 59–60, 100
Können. *See* ability.

labor: 60, 62–63, 66, 70–71, 126
Lacan, Jacques: 6
Lacoue-Labarthe, Phillippe: 4, 6, 11, 77, 131
language: 18
    philosophy of, 2, 135n2
Lauer, Quentin: 144n36
law of singularity and law of universality,
    agency suffused by, 89
    defined, 81
    divine law as singular, 83–84, 86
    "eternal irony," 87
    human law as universal, 82–83, 84
    human law versus divine law regarding burial, 82–87
        reveals Hegel's blindness to gender issues, 85
    mutual repulsion of, 82
    leads to guilt, 89
Lessing, Gotthold: 111
liberalism: 13
life, 8–15, 143n11, 128
life of spirit. *See* spirit, life of.
lordship and bondage. *See* mastery and servitude.
love, 56–57, 116, 128
love-bond (Nietzsche): 5–6, 14, 15

Lukács, Gyorgy:
    Young Hegel, Studies in the Relations Between Dialectics and Economics, 9
Lyotard, Jean-François: 137n9

Marcuse, Herbert:
    Hegel's Ontology of Life, 9
Marx, Karl: 52, 61, 63
    German Ideology, 53
Marxism: 50, 64
master (*Herr*):
    and life of consumption, 61–62
    and servant, 22, 52, 60
    consciousness, 62
    maintains threat of death, 60, 126
    recognized, the, 59
    tragic fate of, 51, 63–64, 126
mastery:
    freedom and, 51
    self-certainty and, 61
    servitude and, 49, 50–51, 58–59
        arises from servant's failure to choose freedom, 69
        dependence in, 62
        established by relation to the thing, 60
        nonreciprocal recognition, 59
        origin of spirit's quest for independence, 59, 61, 126
        reversal in, 60–62
        yields genuine conditions of self-consciousness, 60
    defined, 52–53
mastery and servitude
    conceptions of, 52–53
    reversal in, 51
        Gadamer's response to, 51–52
        Nietzschean response to, 51
mathematical formulation:
    expression of knowledge, 7, 12, 16–17
mathematics: 18
mathesis universalis: 16–18
matter: 34
Menke, Christoph:
    Die Tragödie im Sittlichen, 74
metaphysics: vii, 121

mind:
    philosophy of, 22, 39
modern nation-state: 10
modernity:
    philosophy and, 16, 17, 18, 21–22, 32, 50, 103, 105, 115, 123
museum:
    emergence of, 104
mutual recognition (*Anerkennung*): 22
    condition of independence, 53, 57, 69
    duel, 57–58
    emerges by mediation of a third term, 65
        rise of signs, 65–66
    life and death struggle, 57
    self-certainty achieved through, 55, 56
myth: 78

Nagel, Thomas: 39
Nancy, Jean-Luc: 6, 77, 131
nature: 7, 18, 72, 106
negation:
    attain self-certainty through, 55
    death as, 57
    dynamic of desire, 55
    self conscious,
        practical activity of agent, 54–55
Nietzsche, Friedrich: vii, 2, 7, 12, 14, 15, 51, 52, 64, 67, 68, 127
    Birth of Tragedy, 5, 6, 97
        arguments against Socratism, 5, 97–99, 115
    Genealogy of Morals, 51, 64, 65, 72
    historical consciousness, 104
    human freedom, 51
    reactive will, 2
    sovereign,
        tragedy of, 23
        unrestricted, 51, 64, 68
Nohl, Herman:
    Hegel's Early Theological Writings, 9
Nussbaum, Martha:
    Fragility of Goodness, 19–20

Oedipus at Colonus, 25, 122, 123–125, 127
    highest stage of Greek tragedy, 123

Oedipus Tyrannus, 25, 112, 122, 130, 132
    Oedipus and Sphinx, 114, 130
    riddle in, 112
ontology: vii, 36, 55
original sin: 23
    doctrine of, 75, 90–91
        versus Greek guilt, 91

people's religion (*Volksreligion*): 10
phenomenology,
    science of logic and, 39
    standpoint of observer in, 41
    study of consciousness, 39
philosophia (φῐλοσοφία): 27
philosophy and tragedy. *See* tragedy and philosophy.
phrenology: 16
Pinkard, Terry: 76, 79, 101
Pippen, Robert: 49, 146n3
Plato: 7, 110
    Republic, 109
        criticisms of poetry, 7
Platonism: 7, 14, 15, 128
poetic, the:
    art, 7, 8, 13, 14, 15
    devices, 7, 8
    use in philosophical inquiry, 7, 11–12
poetics: 11, 12, 116
Poetics: 1, 30, 45, 74, 75, 111, 113, 116
    analytic of tragic poetry in, 45
        elements of tragic art, 46
    catharsis, 46, 118
    fear and pity, 46
        experienced in tragic drama, 116
    definition of tragedy, 46
    poetic practice, 46
        epic versus dramatic poetry, 109
    reversal,
        definition of, 46
        riddle as metaphor, 113–114
poetry: 7, 18
polis: 10, 76, 77, 78
political philosophy: vii, 7, 13
politics: 7, 11

post-Kantian era: vii, viii, 4, 5, 6, 14, 78
  interest in tragedy during, 6, 37
postmodern era: 2, 5, 50, 74
postmodernism: 4
praxis: 46, 76
psychoanalysis: 74
  French, 6

rationalism: 17
reason (*Vernunft*): 33, 34
  tragic, 131
  absolute knowledge, 38
  experience and, 22, 37
  knowledge and, 37
  purpose of, 38
recognition. *See* mutual recognition.
religion (*see also* Christianity; people's religion; *under* absolute spirit): 10, 75, 96
  form of reflective life, 100
    of art (Greek), 100, 107
      dialectical progression, 107, 108
      spiritual art as highest phase of, 107
    popular, 10
      Christianity as, 9
    Greek, 99, 102–103, 108–109
    of tragic art, 100, 107
    natural, 98–99
res cogitans. *See* thinking thing.
reversal: 22–23, 30, 44
  tragedy and, 45
  Aristotelian, 46
  concept of, 45
  mastery and servitude, in, 50–51, 61–63
  speculative, 46
  tragic, 45, 67
Ricoeur, Paul: 137n3
Rome, epoch of: 88
romanticism: 106
  German, viii, 6, 32, 33, 34, 35, 105–106, 123, 131
Rorty, Richard: 4
Rosenkranz, Karl:
  Life of Hegel, 9

Ruhe. *See* empty repose.
Russon, John: 148n34, 148n35

Sartre, Jean-Paul: 6, 93–96
  abandonment, 94–95
  and Hegel on rational agency and errancy, 94
  anguish, 93–94
  "Existentialism is a Humanism," 93–95
    agent chooses essence in action, 93
    existence precedes essence, 93
  influenced by Hegel, 93
Schelling, F.W.J.: vii, 2, 6, 9, 11, 25, 32, 34, 128, 130, 131
  Philosophical Letters on Dogmatism and Criticism, 13, 129
  System of Transcendental Idealism, 7
Schiller, Friedrich:
  An Die Freude, 91
  On the Aesthetic Education of Man in a Series of Letters, 111
Schlegel, Friedrich: 7, 11, 25, 32, 128, 131
  Athenaeum Fragments, 131
  Critical Fragments, 131
  Ideas, 131
Schmidt, Dennis: 6, 20, 46, 77, 84, 113, 114
Schnitzler, Arthur:
  Lieutenant Gustl, 58
Schopenhauer, Arthur: 6
Schuld. *See* guilt.
science:
  complete (*Wissenschaft*), 18, 27, 38–39, 102
  philosophy of, 2, 135n2
Searle, John: 39
Selbstständigkeit. *See* independence.
self-abnegation: 56
self-consciousness, 22, 50
  desire, 55–56
    inhibited, 63
  dialectic of, 51–52, 77
  in practical relations with objects, 55
  independence of, 50, 52, 54
  mastery and servitude and, 60
  negation of independent objects and, 54, 55

proto-, 60
self-certainty of, 54, 65
structure and dynamics of, 54, 57, 60
servant (*Knecht*):
   and master. *See* master and servant.
   archetype of, 53
   freedom and, 52, 69
   labor, 60, 62–63, 66, 70–71, 126
   of two masters, 52
   recognizing, the, 59
   reversal in life of, 68–69
   servile consciousness and, 62, 126
   values life over freedom, 59, 69
servitude:
   and mastery. *See* mastery and servitude.
   defined, 52–53
   finite freedom in, 70–71
   independence in, 51
   tragic aspects of, 23, 53, 68–69, 126
   success in, 53, 62–63
Shakespeare, William: 1, 112
   Hamlet, 112
      riddle in, 112
   Macbeth, 112
      riddle in, 112
sittliche Welt, die. *See* Greek ethical world.
Sitten. *See* ethical laws.
Sittlichkeit. *See* ethical life.
slave (*Sklave*): 52
social philosophy: vii, 53
Socrates: 7, 12
Socratic impulse: 5, 97
Sophocles: 1, 93, 114, 119, 133
speculative aesthetics: 45
speculative philosophy:
   absolute self-knowledge and, 37, 98
   Christianity and, 10
   claims of, 2, 5, 16
   finitude embraced in, 2, 4
   form of reflective life, 100
   genuine science, 102–103
      theoria and, 110
   Hellenic ideal and, 10–11
   independence of self-consciousness and, 53, 58
   ontological determination of transcendental idealism, 36
   purpose of, 1, 2, 3, 12, 27
   superior to art, 109
   tragedy and, 1, 3, 11, 14, 99, 118, 122
   wisdom and, 100
speculative self-knowledge:
   absolute knowledge as, 30–32, 37, 47, 98
   attained through experience, 31, 37, 49
   certainty and, 43
   limitation and, 31
   memory and, 32, 48
   tragic aspects of, 48
speculative unity:
   achievement of, 3
   artistic expression as model for, 8, 11–12, 18–19
   end of philosophy, 5, 16
   in history, 3
   of the concept, 13, 15, 19–20, 27
   use of tragedy in, 4, 8, 11, 12–13, 18–20, 128, 131
spirit:
   ix, 4, 15–16, 18, 21, 52, 69
   development of, 3, 15–16
   history of, 21, 38, 74, 88, 125
   independence and, 59
   life of, 1, 3, 15, 28, 29, 45, 63
      birth of symbolic in, 65
      dynamics of mastery and servitude in, 61
   philosophy of, 11
   tragedies of, 47, 99, 107, 122, 125, 127, 133
   tragic art and, 3, 21, 110
   wounds of, 98
spiritual transformation: 28
Steinbock, Anthony: 145n45
subject:
   and world, 34–37, 41–42
   defined, 34, 53
   spirit, 53
subjugation: 50, 61

supercession (*Aufhebung*): 43
Szondi, Peter: 11
    Versuch Über das Tragische, 19–20

Taminiaux, Jacques: 11, 12, 101, 110
Taylor, Charles: 78, 80, 100
theoria/θεωρία (theory): 101–102
thing, the,
    complex phenomenon, 61, 65–66
    defined, 60
    mediating third term, 65
thinking thing (*res cogitans*): 40
tragedy:
    basic figure of, 89
    consciousness and, 45
    human finitude and, 3, 28, 127
    in reversal, 45
    philosophy and, vii, viii, 1, 4–8, 15, 128, 132
    resources of, vii, 3, 6, 14, 18, 19–20, 28, 73, 128, 133
    speculative philosophy and, 1, 3–4, 5, 13, 18, 27, 129
    spirit and, 3, 29, 51
    theoretical works on, 27, 46
tragic:
    the, vii, 11, 12, 14
        integral part of human condition, 48
    art, vii,
        as vessel of sorrows of the spirit, 109
    poetry, 11–13, 15, 18, 45
tragic drama: vii, 1, 3, 7, 130
    acting subjects in, 111
        confront world as reality to be negated, 111
    and knowledge, 14
    Greek, vii, 1, 5, 6, 8, 11, 13, 19, 97
    highest expression of knowledge, 7, 11–12
    pre-Socratic, 5
    religion, 100
    spiritual art, 107–108
    versus philosophy, 7, 14, 15

work of art, 99
    production, 105–107
        genius versus expert, 106
        world of spirit in, 106
        imbued with finitude, 107
    reception, 107–108, 111–112, 114–116
    significance determined by disclosed tragic knowledge, 99
    chorus in, 111–112
        confronts dramatic action as truth to be known, 111
        conjunction of knowledge and ignorance in hero presented to, 112
        fear and pity, 24, 116
        leads spectators to ethical understanding, 116
            guided by "earnestness of the concept," 116
    hero of, 112
        conjunction of knowledge and ignorance in, 112
            riddle in, 112–113
    receivers of, 111
        affective response to, 24, 117–118
            negative, 118
            positive, 118
        conjunction of knowledge and ignorance in hero presented to, 112
            tragic wisdom received through, 115
        shared sense of separateness in, 116
        tragic insight of, 117
    represents self and world for individual reflection, 99
    riddle in, 113–115
        expressive medium, 113
        finitude in, 115
        metaphor, 113
        Oedipus, 115

speculative impulse in, 99
   governs the encounter with, 118
   insight into finitude from, 105, 111, 115, 127
  speculative standpoint toward, 116
   fear and pity and lesson of tragedy, 116
    positive turn in acceptance of negative insights, 118, 127
    "empty repose," 118
transcendental idealism. *See* idealism, transcendental.
Tübinger Stift: 8, 9, 12, 13, 128, 129
Tun. See activity.

Vernunft. See reason.

Wagnerian opera: 5
Welton, Donn: 40
Werk. See work.

Western philosophy: 4, 5, 95–96, 98
Westphal, Merold: 29
wisdom: 24
  philosophical, 115
   purely conceptual, 115
  speculative philosophy as pursuit of, 100
  tragic, 115–119
   allows for acceptance of finitude, 115
   imbued with sensation, 115
    communicable, 115
   transformation of self through reflection on finitude, 119
Wissenschaft. See science, complete.
Wittgenstein, Ludwig: 136n2
Wood, Allen: 53
work (*Werk*): 78
world:
  and subject. *See* subject and world.
  defined (Kant), 34

www.ingramcontent.com/pod-product-compliance
Lightning Source LLC
Chambersburg PA
CBHW021758230426
43669CB00006B/121